A Poetics of the Press
Interviews with Poets, Printers, & Publishers

Edited, compiled, and introduced by Kyle Schlesinger

Cuneiform Press & Ugly Duckling Presse

A Poetics of the Press

Copyright © Cuneiform Press & Ugly Duckling Presse, 2021

Introduction copyright © Kyle Schlesinger, 2021

Interviews copyright © Charles Alexander, Inge Bruggeman, Steven Clay, Aaron Cohick, Johanna Drucker, Philip Gallo, Jonathan Greene, Lyn Hejinian, Alastair Johnston, Mary Laird, Annabel Lee, Alan Loney, Anna Moschovakis, Scott Pierce, Tom Raworth, Keith & Rosmarie Waldrop, Matvei Yankelevich

ISBN 978-1-937027-74-2

First Edition, First Printing, 2021

Edition of 1,000

Cuneiform Press

cuneiformpress.com

Ugly Duckling Presse

The Old American Can Factory

232 Third Street #E-303

Brooklyn, NY 11215

uglyducklingpresse.org

Distributed in the USA by SPD/Small Press Distribution

Distributed in the UK by Inpress Books

Cover design by Don't Look Now!

Design and typesetting by Sarah Lawson, Paige Parsons, Don't Look Now!

The type is Sabon and Fort (courtesy of MCKL)

Printed and bound at McNaughton & Gunn

Covers printed offset at Prestige Printing and letterpress at Ugly Duckling Presse

The publication of this book was made possible, in part, by the New York State Council on the Arts with the support of Governor Andrew M. Cuomo and the New York State Legislature. This project is supported by the Robert Rauschenberg Foundation.

Table of Contents

Introduction   viii
by Kyle Schlesinger

Interviews

Keith & Rosmarie Waldrop   14
Burning Deck Press

Tom Raworth   24
Matrix Press & Goliard Press

Lyn Hejinian   44
Tuumba Press

Alan Loney   68
Electio Editions

Mary Laird   96
Quelquefois Press & The Perishable Press Limited

Jonathan Greene   108
Gnomon Press

Alastair Johnston   130
Poltroon Press

Johanna Drucker   168
Druckwerk

Philip Gallo   184
The Hermetic Press

Steven Clay   206
Granary Books

Charles Alexander   228
Chax Press

Annabel Lee   248
Vehicle Editions

Inge Bruggeman   272
INK-A! Press

**Anna Moschovakis
& Matvei Yankelevich**   290
Ugly Duckling Presse

Aaron Cohick   310
NewLights Press

Scott Pierce   322
Effing Press

Glossary   345
Notes on printing terms, printers,
publishers, producers, and printshops

For Tom Raworth

Introduction
by Kyle Schlesinger

A Poetics of the Press is a collection of sixteen interviews conducted with publishers from the US, England, Germany, and Australia spanning four generations. These publishers are also poets and letterpress printers with a unique relationship to language as a visual and material form of art.

Like many books, *A Poetics of the Press* did not begin as a book, but as a series of insatiable questions I wanted to ask of poets, publishers, and printers about the art of the book and their personal approaches to publishing. In 2008, I had the opportunity to conduct the first interview in this book with Steven Clay, the only publisher in this book who is not a poet or printer, at the Research Group for Artist Publishers' (RGAP) annual Small Publishers' Fair in London. At that time, I was researching the relationship between poetry, typography, and visual art in books printed by hand in America between the end of the Second World War and the end of the Vietnam War. At that time I realized that there was a dearth of publications on the subject, and that Clay's Granary Books had published much of the literature I found most compelling, so I asked him if we could record an interview about that subject. I learned so much about Granary's history and Clay's philosophy of publishing, I pursued more interviews to explore a wider field that would take me closer to the present.

There are hundreds of well-researched books about the history of letterpress printing, however, there are very few books about letterpress after it became commercially obsolete around 1945, particularly books and journals of poetry, which is part of why this book seemed necessary. I have compiled a glossary in the backmatter that may be useful for readers who are not familiar with the history and lexicon of printing.

I started printing letterpress in the late '90s, inspired by a teacher who had attended Black Mountain College. It was a moment when the internet was fairly new to everyday people, a moment when the relationship between old media and new media seemed particularly interesting. In my doctoral research leading up to this book, I relied heavily on archival materials such as literary correspondence, printers' proofs, manuscripts, and ephemera. Through forensic-typographic investigations in various archives, I learned more about why contemporary poetry looks the way that it does. I pondered the relationship between form and content. Where do poetry books come from? How are they made, distributed, edited, written, censored, unrealized, destroyed, recovered, and in some cases, reprinted, anthologized, and canonized? I wanted to take books apart with my hands and put them back together again in order to understand how they were made, a way of knowing by doing, to unravel biblio-histories and mysteries. After all, every book has a story, a story that goes beyond the sequence of words it contains, a story including history, design, materials, love, art, people, thoughts, and experiences. *A Poetics of the Press* is a collection of firsthand accounts of the material aspects of literary history akin to Robert Dana's *Against the Grain: Interviews with Maverick American Publishers* (Univeristy of Iowa Press, 1986).

Poetic discourse often focuses on what poetry "does" and "means," but taking a cue from Jerome McGann's *Black Riders: The Visible Language of Modernism*, these interviews address the question of how poetry comes into being and *why*—the ontology of the book. Opening a book of poems, clearing a field. What do you see? What's actually there? What does this way of seeing have to do with the making of meaning? With art? Technology? Literacy? Commerce? Compassion?

A Poetics of the Press takes us back to the root of the word "poetry": "to make, create, compose," or "to pile up, build, make." The letterpress printers and poets in this collection working with letterforms forged in hot metal understand that poetry is a material and immaterial thing. What is the difference between publishing an ebook and printing the same book on a letterpress? What is the difference as a reader, writer, publisher? What is it about this obsolete technology that continues to allure readers, writers, and publishers?

The interviews are arranged chronologically by the date of the publisher's first publication, rather than by the order in which they were conducted to give readers a sense of the arc and evolution of poetry, art, typography, and technology in book form. There were printers and poets I wanted to interview as far from my current home in the US as Alan Loney in Melbourne, Australia. By necessity, some interviews were conducted on the computer, while most were recorded in person and transcribed.

Acknowledgments

Some of these interviews first appeared in the following journals: "An Interview with Aaron Cohick," *The Journal of Artists' Books* 33, Spring 2013; "50+ Years of Burning Deck Press: An Interview with Keith & Rosmarie Waldrop," *Golden Handcuffs Review* Vol. 1 No. 16, 2013; "An Interview with Philip Gallo," *The Journal of Artists' Books* 33, Spring 2013; "Talking Tuumba: An Interview with Lyn Hejinian," *Mimeo Mimeo* 5, Fall 2011; "An Interview with Tom Raworth," *Mimeo Mimeo* 4, Spring 2010; "An Interview with Ugly Duckling Presse: Conducted by Kyle Schlesinger," *The Poetry Project Newsletter* 218, February/March 2009; "Alan Loney: An Interview Conducted by Kyle Schlesinger," *Mimeo Mimeo* 2, 2008; "Alastair Johnston: An Interview Conducted by Kyle Schlesinger," *Mimeo Mimeo* 1, 2008; "Remembering the Light: An Interview with Mary Laird," *The Ampersand,* 24.3, Summer 2007; "New Paradigms from the Outset: An Interview with Steve Clay," *The Ampersand* 24.2, Winter 2007.

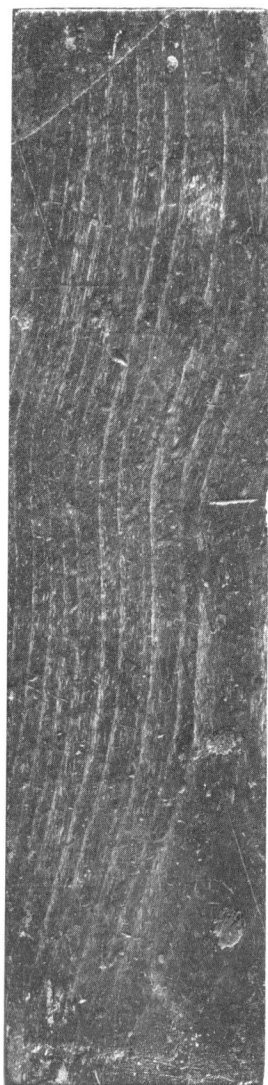

Interviews

Keith & Rosmarie Waldrop
Burning Deck Press

Burning Deck Press specializes in the publication of experimental poetry and prose, as well as two series of translation: *Serie d'ecriture* dedicated to contemporary French poetry and *Dichten=* dedicated to contemporary German writing. Burning Deck was founded by the writers and translators Keith Waldrop (born in Emporia, Kansas in 1932) and Rosmarie Waldrop (born in Kitzingen, Germany in 1935) in 1961. Although the Waldrops initially promoted *Burning Deck Magazine* as a "quinterly," in Michigan, after four issues the periodical was transformed into a series of pamphlets set by hand and printed letterpress. The transformation continued until Burning Deck became a publisher of books of poetry and short fiction.

The magazine published poets from different styles and schools. The main split in poets of that time was said to be the one between the "academics" and the "beats," but Burning Deck ignored that split to the point where authors sometimes complained of being published in the company of others so different from themselves.

By 1985, the economics of publishing had changed and it became financially more feasible to print books on offset presses and use the letterpress for smaller chapbooks. The Waldrops continued to design and print books that are made to last (using smyth-sewn, acid-free paper) but tried to keep the price affordable.

Burning Deck's archives are housed at Brown University, where Keith taught for many years. Burning Deck has published hundreds of books, including titles by Paul Auster, Robert Coover, Robert Creeley, Jean Daive, Caroline Dubois, Barbara Guest, Lyn Hejinian, Monika Rinck, Cole Swenson, as well as several books of the Waldrops' own poems. Keith is also a collage artist, and has made striking cover art for many of their books. Burning Deck Press closed in 2017, leaving 247 books in its wake.

Jackson Mac Low, *4 Trains* (Burning Deck Press, 1974)

KS: Burning Deck has been publishing continuously for more than half a century. Reflecting on the early years of the press in *A Century in Two Decades*, you said that there was a sharp editorial division between the journals and anthologies publishing "beat" and "academic" poets, and that you disregarded that common tendency, preferring to publish the poetry you found interesting rather than siding with any particular camp. I know that the terms have changed with the times (poets of my generation don't identify as "beats" or "academics"), but do you think that a similar division still exists in poetry today?

RW: Well, the distinction wasn't quite that sharp then, either. With "beat" were lumped "Black Mountain," "New York School," "San Francisco Renaissance"—all the poets published in Donald Allen's *New American Poetry*. But yes, the terms have changed to the vaguer "avant-garde" and "traditional" (or less neural adjectives!), but the division still exists.

KS: As a kid growing up outside Providence, Burning Deck did much to inform my sense of what contemporary poetry could be. Your books were in every shop and I bought them whatever I could because I thought you had such terrific taste. I thought, "If the Waldrops think it's worth publishing, it must be worth reading." Who were the particular editors or publishers that made an impression on you as young poets?

RW: Once I came to this country it was New Directions, probably taking the lead from Keith. Before that, in Germany, I seem to remember that I just gobbled up whatever I could lay my hands on in the one decent bookstore in town.

KW: I was early aware of and impressed by the publications of New Directions. Also in the early '60s there were many small presses just starting—we were not the only one, though we outlasted many of them. Most were West Coast or East Coast, but there were a number in the Midwest.

KS: Printing from moveable type began in Germany. Every time I'm there I marvel at the design of things large and small—even the theater tickets are masterfully designed. Growing up, did you have a strong appreciation for the book as a form of art Rosmarie?

RW: No, I was more interested in the contents. It was only when I went to France that I realized how well made most German books were! But I was aware of printing from an early age. The apartment I grew up in was above a printshop, and the yard I played in was full of used lithographic stones with four-color wine labels on them.

KS: You have published many students who have graduated from Brown University. Is there a relationship between Burning Deck and the University? Has Brown provided support for the Press?

RW: It's true we published many Brown graduates. I just did a rough count because you made me curious, and there are about thirty of them out of about 135 American authors, so not quite a quarter—though counting the French and German authors it becomes more like one-seventh.

We find manuscripts in all sorts of ways, and Keith's contact with Brown students is just one of them. However, we never published them while they were students. We always let a few years pass after their leaving Brown.

There has been no financial relationship between Brown University and Burning Deck. When we first came to Providence Keith could get student proctors for Burning Deck, but after a couple of years the deans realized Burning Deck had really nothing to do with Brown and canceled that. However, Brown University has bought the Burning Deck Archive, which has helped finance the Press.

KS: Someone told me that you have a Heidelberg. I thought it was a Chandler & Price? Could you tell me about your equipment? Do you still use the letterpress?

KW: We started out with an 8″ x 10″ Chandler & Price that we got secondhand in 1960 when all the printers were disposing of platen presses. It was motor driven, but handfed. Later we traded it for a Chandler & Price somewhat larger, with a 10″ x 12″ bed. Finally, when we wanted to print full-length books (which meant approximately sixty-four pages), we added a secondhand Heidelberg with a 10″ x 15″ bed and automatic feed. This must have been in 1974. But in 1985, when we had just printed five books and drove the sheets to our bindery in New Hampshire we found that they, like all the other binderies, had automated, and could no longer bind our small two-up sheets. From then on binding our books would be handwork and forbiddingly expensive. So we came into the computer age and now make files on the computer to be printed offset.

KS: Keith, your collages have appeared on the covers of many Burning Deck books, as well as in collaborations such as *Bomb* with Clark Coolidge. Is there a relationship between your poems and your collages? Do ideas generated in one medium ever feed directly into the other? What about process?

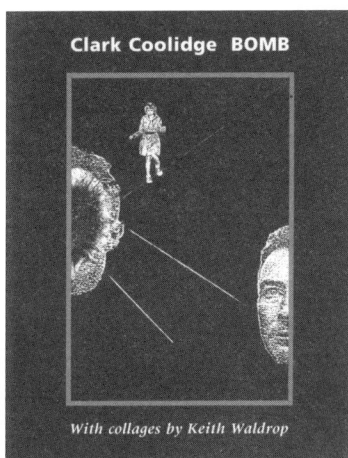

Clark Coolidge BOMB

With collages by Keith Waldrop

KW: It is not so much that there is a relation as that the process is basically the same. I, like any writer, might come up with a word not expected in the immediate context, but more usually I find the words I use in other texts. Whether visual or verbal, collage is for me a way to explore, not necessarily the thing I am tearing up, but the thing I am contriving to build out of torn pieces. To the extent that there is a purpose to what I do, its end is the "enjoyment of a composition"—a concern, as Whitehead notes, common to aesthetics and logic.

KS: In spite of the fact that the majority of the poets you publish are experimental, typographically speaking, Burning Deck books observe rather traditional rules of legibility. There are some exceptions, such as *Camp Printing*, that to my mind comes closer to an artists book or visual poetry. How would you describe this relationship?

RW: Yes, our typography tends to be classical. We have been interested in presenting texts rather than in playing with or experimenting with the printing process. The more experimental the text, the more clearly I want to define the space of the page. For instance, in Peter Inman's book *per se*, words scatter in a free, multidirectional movement. I was not satisfied with the layout until I put a line at the top to establish a sense of the page that the words can move against.

Camp Printing is an exception. While printing a chapbook by James Camp I accidentally overprinted a page and liked the result. Then I began playing, making "printing errors." The final pages go beyond the printing process: I cut pages in strips and made collages.

KW: My playing with the press mostly took place at the wash-up stage: I would place paper directly on the ink plate during the stages of cleaning and create a kind of monoprint this way.

KS: Could you elaborate?

KW: Sometimes I'd simply put paper on the ink plate while the ink was already thinned by the cleaning fluid. At times some letters showed up dimly. Another technique I added involved painting a bit on the ink plate during the process.

RW: In *Camp Printing*, I mostly overprinted the same sheet of paper more and more times, moving the paper sideways or tilting it. And, following Keith, I'd like to show you an example.

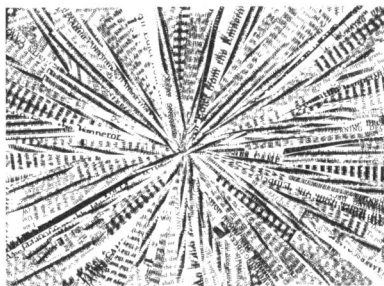

KS: You've both published in many little magazines and many major anthologies. You've also published chapbooks with fledging independent presses, major collections with presses like Random House, university presses, and in extravagant handmade editions. Looking back at all of these books and all of the editors, translators, publishers and artists involved, could you discuss some of your experiences?

RW: One of my first chapbooks was *Spring Is a Season and Nothing Else*, from Walter Hamady's new Perishable Press. It is a beautiful booklet, handset and handprinted on handmade paper in an edition of 110 copies. As I remember, Walter had ninety standing orders from collections of fine printing, he kept ten copies, and I got ten. It was actually frustrating: I had a book—a beautiful book for which I was grateful—and yet I didn't have one. The collectors of fine printing were not likely reading the text, and I could just give the chapbook to a few friends.

Keith had the same experience with *Songs from the Decline of the West.* It was a factor in our decision for Burning Deck not to aim at books that would be kept on closed shelves.

My first full book with Random House, *The Aggressive Ways of the Casual Stranger,* was a lucky fluke. Nan Talese had asked Eleanor Bender, editor of the small magazine *Open Places,* for suggestions. Eleanor, who had published my work often, knew I had a manuscript ready and sent it. Random House didn't want my second book, though, which was actually published by Eleanor Bender as an Open Places Book.

Both Keith and I published in many very small magazines because we followed the rule that if somebody asks for work we'll send it. Nowadays this doesn't work so well anymore because we both write as—or more—slowly than earlier, but get asked much more often.

KS: I believe you and Keith have both published a number of books of your own poems with Burning Deck—what motivated you to self-publish?

KW: Nobody else was doing it!

RW: That's why those books were mostly early, in the 1970s and '80s. Our collaborations are a different story: they were usually written and printed as a New Year's greeting for friends.

KS: Among all of your accomplishments as publishers, you've also translated many of the books yourselves, and introduced me, along with thousands of other readers in the States, to writers in Europe we might not have known otherwise. Could you tell me how this aspect of Burning Deck started, how it's developed over the years?

KW: I always felt I had to translate French or German poems if I really wanted to be able to read and understand them.

RW: When I came to the United States it soon became difficult for me to write in German. It felt artificial. So I thought if I couldn't be a writer, I surely could be a translator and at first translated American poems into German, then started to translate both French and German texts into English. The space between languages seems my natural place. I keep going back there and enjoy the work—even though I often tear my hair at its impossibilities!

Burning Deck's involvement started with Paul Green of *Spectacular Diseases* magazine asking me to edit a French series, *Série d'Ecriture*, for him. He published two magazine issues and three single-author issues featuring Alain Veinstein, Emmanuel Hocquard, and Joseph Guglielmi. However, his production quality was so low that I always felt I had to apologize to the authors. From number six on we agreed Burning Deck would publish *Série d'Ecriture*, but *Spectacular Diseases* would be the European distributor. The German series, *Dichten=*, began shortly after.

KS: Looking back at all the books you've published over the years, which do you return to most often?

KW: *Pegasus Descending: A Book of the Best Bad Verse*, edited by James Camp, X.J. Kennedy, and Keith Waldrop; Barbara Guest's *The Countess From Minneapolis*; Mei-mei Berssenbrugge's *The Heat Bird*; Michael Gizzi's *New Depths of Deadpan,* and Ray Ragosta's *Varieties of Religious Experience*.

RW: *The Heat Bird* by Mei-mei Berssenbrugge, Emmanuel Hocquard's *A Test of Solitude*, Friederike Mayröcker's *Heiligenanstalt*, and Elizabeth Willis' *Turneresque*.

KS: What's next?

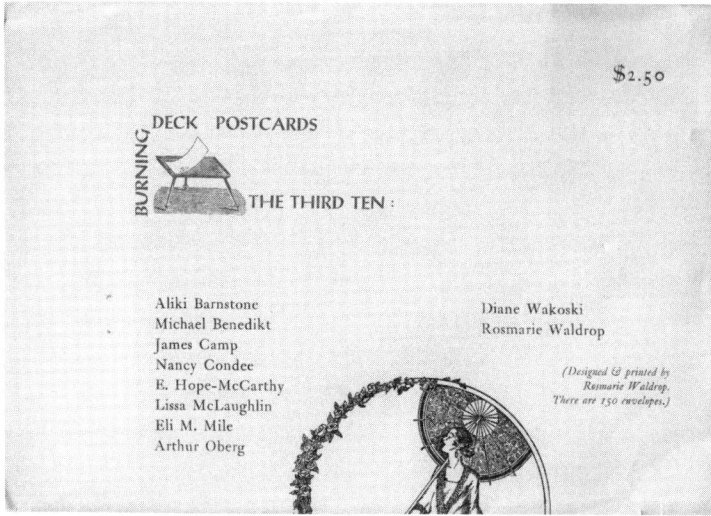

$2.50

BURNING DECK POSTCARDS

THE THIRD TEN :

Aliki Barnstone
Michael Benedikt
James Camp
Nancy Condee
E. Hope-McCarthy
Lissa McLaughlin
Eli M. Mile
Arthur Oberg

Diane Wakoski
Rosmarie Waldrop

*(Designed & printed by
Rosmarie Waldrop.
There are 150 envelopes.)*

RW: All the 2012 books are coming up in the fall this year. There are two books by American poets: Peter Inman's *per se* and Sarah Riggs' *Autobiography of Envelopes*. We'll also publish a very whimsical Austrian, Elfriede Czurda. I did the translation, and her book is entitled *Almost 1 Book / Almost 1 Life*. And in *Série d'Ecriture*, we have Sébastien Smirou's *My Lorenzo*, translated by Andrew Zawacki.

The most exciting project for next year is the entire tetralogy of Claude Royet-Journoud with the collective title *Quatre corps simples* (English translation not quite decided yet; "simple bodies" doesn't seem right. Maybe: *Four Elementary Bodies*). It contains the four books *Reversal*, *The Notion of Obstacle*, *Objects Contain the Infinite*, and *Natures Indivisible*, and will be about four-hundred pages.

[2012]

Tom Raworth
Matrix Press & Goliard Press
[with Michael Cross and Stephen Fredman]

Born in Bexleyheath, England in 1938, Tom Raworth was an English-Irish poet, publisher, editor, and teacher who published over forty books of poetry and prose during his life. His work has been translated and published in many countries. Raworth was a key figure in the British Poetry Revival. In 1959, Raworth taught himself how to set type and to print, and between 1961 and 1964, produced three issues of the magazine *Outburst*, bringing the work of prominent American poets Robert Creeley, Edward Dorn, Denise Levertov (who moved to the US in 1948), Fielding Dawson, and Charles Olson to the UK for the first time. He also published a series of small books under the Matrix Press imprint, including work by Piero Heliczer, Anselm Hollo, David Ball, and Edward Dorn.

In 1965, while working as an operator at the international telephone exchange, Raworth and Barry Hall set up Goliard Press, which published, amongst others, Charles Olson's first British collection. These ventures into publishing made an important contribution to a new found British interest in the New American Poetry movement of the 1960s.

He was considered "a particularly transatlantic writer, living in the US for several years in the '70s." * Furthermore, Raworth's connection to American poetry through his work as an editor and publisher, established his American reputation in the U.S., often considered unequal to any other British poet of that time period. Raworth died on February 8, 2017 of complications from cancer at the age of 78.

---

*Ian Drieblatt, "British Poet Tom Raworth is Dying," *Melville House*, January 30, 2017.

Tom Raworth, *A Serial Biography* (Fulcrum Press, 1969)

KS: How did you get involved in this racket?

TR: I read some things that I liked. They weren't things that were widely available in England, so I thought the way to do it was to do a magazine, and the cheapest way then was, ridiculously, to learn to set type and to print. So I got some type and taught myself how to set it and print.

KS: Did they teach it in high school?

TR: No. I taught myself from books.

KS: Do you remember which ones?

TR: The classics. Morison, Stanley Morison. There were books about book design and typography at the time, so I looked through those, but otherwise it was just trial and error. You'd have to figure out to set it backwards…

KS: …backwards and upside down.

TR: Yeah, so you taught yourself how to read backwards and upside down.

KS: Not as easy as it appears.

TR: It took a long time because I'd only do two pages at a time. I only had enough type for two pages, so I was always in the process of setting two pages, printing, redistributing, and setting them again.

KS: Did you buy the type new?

TR: Yes, you could still—Stephenson Blake, I think. That was new, but Piero Heliczer had a lot of used type. I inherited some from Piero at some point, some big letters. I think Perpetua was just the basic font, and some Gill for the titles, but those things were still easy to get because the foundries were still making type.

KS: Right. I don't know if it was the same in London, but at a certain point here everyone was throwing their letterpress equipment out on the streets.

TR: It got to be like that, yeah. That's probably how we got the press for Goliard, the bigger press, the bigger treadle press, just from somebody selling out. A little later, they did become junk, and then, like now, they became antiques and we saw wonderful fonts of wood letters broken up so you could have your initials stuck on your wall. There's a guy—do you know La Alameda Press down in Albuquerque? He's got a little press and did a broadside of Joanne Kyger's. He's a really nice printer—still finds things on eBay. Perhaps the most difficult thing to get now is type cases because people just use them to put little ornaments in and hang them on the wall.

KS: Knick-knacks! And the stuff on eBay has become expensive because printers have to compete with knick-knack culture.

TR: But there was a great period when everything was going over to offset. Asa Benveniste's press was before that time; basically it was a proofing press, a big proofing press.

KS: But Asa started printing before offset was…

TR: It was around, but letterpress wasn't peculiar and arty, particularly in those days, it was just another way of printing. It was just about to be equal but it took a while. He had a silkscreen shop as well. He had a good printshop for everything, so he could do commercial work at times. It wasn't just the publishing. I was looking at one of those films of Bob Creeley's yesterday and there's one where he's sitting underneath three big, framed Kitaj prints (*A Sight*, 1967). Those were printed at Asa's; that was a job where Creeley sent us the poem for us to raise some money. Kitaj did the design and Asa printed it because he had a fine silkscreen press. So that's how that came about.

KS: Those were lovely, huge...

TR: I've got a set somewhere still. In fact, I think there are still some sets out in Maine, Pen [Penelope Creeley*] said, somewhere. Perhaps rotting in an outhouse in Maine.

KS: And where did Asa...

TR: Where did he learn to print? I don't know exactly. He was in publishing, first of all. I think he worked for Thames & Hudson—art books—at one point in London and he got bored with it. That's how I remember the story, and then he just wanted to do things for himself. I think Pip Benveniste had some money, so they were able to get a proper printshop, and the equipment to deal with it.

KS: And he edited *Zero* before Trigram started?

TR: Yeah. That was in Paris as I remember. I saw one copy of *Zero* magazine a long time ago. I didn't even see copies at that time. It seems to have pretty much vanished by the time we became friends.

---

*Penelope Highton met Robert Creeley in 1976. They married in 1977, traveled extensively and had two children. They settled in Buffalo, where Penelope worked as a volunteer on neighborhood housing and health association boards.

KS: So when you started, did you have a press at your house?

TR: I had a very small press. In fact, one of the first things I did was on a little 5″ x 4″ press, and that was the platen size.

KS: A little Kelsey tabletop or something like that?

TR: They were called Adana; they were for people to be hobbyists and print their own visiting cards and things like that, so it was that size. I did a couple of small things like that. Then I got sort of a late wedding present of about one hundred British pounds from Val's [Valarie Raworth*] father and found a treadle press that was probably about 11″ x 8″ so you could do two pages pretty much, and I did things on that. And then I had to put that somewhere because it was too big to be in the two rooms we were living in with children. I had a friend who had a printer for a brother down in North Soho and we put it there. We used to go down after work and print the pages with whatever color ink was left on the press because there was no time, so that's why the magazine was printed with different color pages. Took too much time to clean the press just to do it, so we just put the type in to do it quickly.

KS: And which magazine was this?

TR: This is *Outburst*; there's some copies sitting right over there.

KS: And you were working on *Outburst* before you started publishing books?

TR: Yeah. I did a few really small things at that time. Let's see, I did a small book of Ed Dorn's, you know that one poem, *From Gloucester Out*, a little book of Anselm Hollo's called *History*, some things by David Ball, just two poems with illustrations,

---

*Val married Tom Raworth in 1959.

but that was before Goliard, that was Matrix—which expanded when I met Barry Hall and we realized we could work together without much problem.

KS: Those must have been pretty early publications for Ed and Anselm.

TR: It was about 1960 or '61, pretty much; maybe '61 or '62. *Hands Up!* (Totem Press/Corinth Books, 1964) was out of Ed's and maybe one other thing, but there wasn't much around. Just added to it.

MC: This is kind of related—how did you find people? What was the communication system like?

TR: There were some people I read that I liked. I was thinking about that because I came to Bob through Ed. Ed and I corresponded in December 1960, and the first letter from Bob was January of '61, so I'm sure Ed gave me Bob's address and then Bob gave me various other people to get in touch with. There were people I read but didn't have addresses for then. That's how Fielding Dawson came into it and so on, eventually Charles Olson. And Allen Ginsberg, I was in touch with. I can't remember how I got in touch with people, but there they were, and they all were happy to be published. And then it becomes too much doing a magazine, as you may also know. You begin to wonder if your taste is gone: *Can it all be as bad as this?*

MC: The audience of *Outburst*—how many copies would you produce?

TR: I figure, probably, of *Outburst*... for the books we used to produce about 750, and there were probably fewer of the magazine at the time. Some shops would take them; in London there was a shop called Better Books that would take things like that. There are many more now than would take things then.

KS: That's where you got the news?

TR: I think word-of-mouth, people telling other people. It was impressive to me that the 750 books we did for Goliard would go, and I think it's still about the same market, 750 people buy books of poetry in the world. I don't think it's gotten much larger.

KS: It just grows organically, I think. Person A introduces you to Person B, and you tell them about Person C.

TR: Oh yeah, exactly. The same way you do if you have a group of friends and you tell each other what you like, what films you like, what you've read, and it just spreads out from there.

KS: Same with music.

TR: It's all marketing. [checks price of *Outburst*] That was cheap enough then. Let's see, it was two shillings and sixpence—that'd be, what? About forty or fifty cents? Still seems reasonable to me.

MC: In terms of funding it, were you jobbing?

TR: No, I was working, full-time regular work.

KS: What did you do?

TR: At that time I was working in the telephone exchange I guess, most of the time, and for Goliard. Before that and when I was doing *Outburst* I was working for a manufacturing pharmacist in London, stealing Methedrine, which enabled you to do two pages a night. But that was

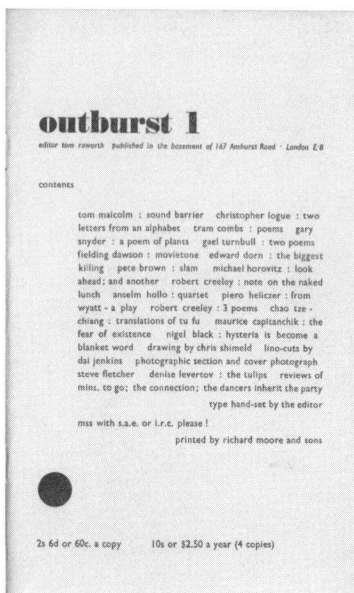

outburst 1

editor tom raworth   published in the basement of 167 Amhurst Road · London E.8

contents

tom malcolm : sound barrier   christopher logue : two letters from an alphabet   tram combs : poems   gary snyder : a poem of plants   gael turnbull : two poems   fielding dawson : movietone   edward dorn : the biggest killing   pete brown : slam   michael horovitz : look ahead; and another   robert creeley : note on the naked lunch   anselm hollo : quartet   piero heliczer : from wyatt - a play   robert creeley : 3 poems   chao tze - chiang : translations of tu fu   maurice capitanchik : the fear of existence   nigel black : hysteria is become a blanket word   drawing by chris shimeld   lino-cuts by dai jenkins   photographic section and cover photograph steve fletcher   denise levertov : the tulips   reviews of mins. to go; the connection; the dancers inherit the party type hand-set by the editor

mss with s.a.e. or i.r.c. please !

printed by richard moore and sons

2s 6d or 60c. a copy   10s or $2.50 a year (4 copies)

Outburst 1 (London, 1961). Tom Raworth, editor.

it, you know, just sit on the carpet, on the mat, and set two pages and occasionally kick over the type, which is very irritating. The other thing is you get to wonder why some people write very long lines when you're setting it by hand, and that's how I probably got to like Bob's work. I mean, I liked reading it, but I did appreciate the fact that you could set it then just slide in spacers all the way to the end.

KS: Really, when you look at all the people who were doing hand-printing, Creeley had so many books, beautiful handset books.

TR: It's a good theory! Who is this Allen Ginsberg?! [gestures as if he is frantically setting very long lines of type in a compositor's stick] I'm trying to remember, I thought there was something by Amiri [Baraka] in one of these or maybe we just corresponded. [leafs through *Outburst 2*] Ah, here it is, that's right. Ah, that's the thing I remembered: "As if drunkenness / was something / with a back door." I was trying to think of that yesterday.

MC: This might be a bit outside your area, but the Morden Tower series… I know this was going on up in the North, but how involved were you?

TR: It's the first place I ever read actually, for Tom [Pickard] up there. Way back before any books of my own were published.

MC: He was quite young.

TR: Seventeen or eighteen?

MC: Were there publications coming out of that series?

TR: He did a little thing—what was it called? *King Ida's Watch Chain* if I remember; it was almost loose leaf.

KS: Who else read in that series?

TR: Ginsberg read up there the first time he came over in the '60s. It was actually only a tower in a Roman wall that was quite ruined. Inside, there were a few chairs you could sit in. It was small, it was friendly. Newcastle was an interesting city—as cities go, I like it. All ports are interesting. It's still going. Tom's ex-wife Connie [Pickard] still does readings there. She did an anniversary thing a few years ago and I went up, and Bill Griffiths was there, and a lot of people came down. Tom [Leonard] and Eck [Finlay] came down from Scotland. So that's probably the longest running thing I can think of, and that started in the early '60s, so a good 40 years it's been going pretty much without a break in the same place.

KS: And that was your very first reading?

TR: Yeah, in fact I remember being driven up there by Stuart Montgomery of Fulcrum so exhausted that we ended up swerving off the highway and bouncing across a field—you see we didn't quite make the turn. It was too expensive in those days to get a train to Newcastle. There always was that.

KS: So you started with *Outburst* and Matrix, then Goliard and then kind of stepped away?

TR: Yes, the Cape deal came through, and Barry was quite happy to do it and they did good books. I think they became Cape Goliard books. Cape actually kept to do the things that we agreed to do, but gradually they got more into producing books, rather than just doing books quickly, which was how I liked to do them.

KS: Can you break that down for me?

TR: How I remember it was Nathaniel Tarn—who had done that interesting Cape Editions series, those little tiny books that I thought were really good, a lot of European things, Barthes and so on for the first time in English—was asked by Tom Maschler about small presses. The interest then, to go back to what we were talking about in the beginning, was how were these people who wrote things that weren't really poetry, how were they gradually selling 750 copies when he can't sell 200 copies of the things that he was doing? So Nathaniel Tarn knew the books and took various small press books to Tom Maschler who liked the ones that we were doing, and so there was an approach from that that sort of developed.

KS: Matrix or Goliard?

TR: We're talking about Goliard. Matrix was just the few things that I did, this and that, just about three small books and I was getting bored and tired of doing it when I met Barry and we got along and we put the presses together. My press went there and we got the other press from people who were selling stuff off, a bigger treadle press. So, that was Goliard.

KS: And you physically moved your press over to his place?

TR: Oh, yeah.

KS: And where was that?

TR: It was an old stable in back of Finchley Road. There were cobbles on the floor and the loft was actually still full of shit. We had to level it out with bits of wood under the presses. But it was dry down there, so that was good. We were there all the time, and it remained there when it became Cape Goliard, except they put money into it and cleaned the place up and did work. But that's what happened, and then I didn't feel like doing that. I didn't want to work as part of a big company. I'd have to do things like have the cover of a book a year before it came out so that a marketing person could go around and try to sell it. It just seemed… not what I saw as interesting. But, as I say, they were honorable and kept to the agreements with the books that we were going to do and they did some quite good books from then on—Olson's *Maximus*, the great big one.

KS: How did that relationship begin?

TR: Asa had done a book of Nathaniel Tarn's. It's round about the same time, so he was moving in similar circles, and he came round, then they arranged a meeting and we went to Bedford Square to Cape and there was the accounts manager and Tom Maschler, who was the fashionable publisher at that time at Jonathan Cape. And you know, it was just boring to me, finally, how it was developing out. They were going to be available to put some money in, and you could never really get clear whether they thought they were going to get editorial control as well, and I didn't want to be doing books by people I wasn't interested in. So then I left and at almost the same time Donald Davie wrote to me and asked if I wanted to go to Essex. Just about that time, my first book came out, which he liked, so we moved out. Barry went on with another guy named Chris Breyer, an American, who I saw some years ago in San Francisco. He's still around. They were there for some years. I can't think when, precisely, but Barry got bored, he did eventually, and as I remember it left the rollers inked just across the type as being printed, locked the door and went to Africa. Asa told me he went by—that was some months afterwards—and looked through the window and things were still there. Cape hadn't even bothered to go in and clean up or anything. The machines were still in there.

KS: Sounds like he wigged out.

TR: Yeah, he just got bored of it all. He went to Africa, then he went over here, to New Mexico, down to Santa Fe for a bit, and finally to Kenya.

KS: And how did you and Asa come to meet one another?

TR: Asa... I met Barry and his then-wife through Jonathan Williams at a reading Jonathan was giving in London. And Barry had been on some sort of artist's grant for a year because he was an engraver, a process engraver, of course he was also a painter, so he got himself something in San Francisco for a year. They'd been living there. So he met Jonathan, and I had been corresponding with Jonathan because I liked the Jargon books and so on. So that brought us together and we met at this reading and got on, so then we started seeing one another and Asa about the same time. I just remember going and meeting Asa at his house and I can't even remember how that came about, but it was exactly the same period so it seems quite possible that Barry had met Asa before somewhere, or that Jonathan had come in contact. I can't be more specific than that—it all just blends into a moment... I've known these people all my life.

And so then, we all got on, and Stuart Montgomery sort of appeared a bit afterward, and [his press] Fulcrum, which I always thought was a solid, middle-of-the-road press—you know, he really wanted to be a publishing house in a sense, and we were happy just doing odd little books.

KS: Fulcrum published your *A Serial Biography*, right?

TR: Yeah, yeah.

MC: And an edition of *Briggflatts* [Basil Bunting] as well?

TR: The big edition of *Briggflatts*, yeah, we printed that on Asa's press. Yeah, set the type and you had those sort of uncials, those red and black initial letters, one of which is upside down because we didn't have the right letter, so I think it's a "u" that becomes an "n" or something like that. But that was how it worked, seemed to be a combination of presses. There didn't seem to be some particular sense of competition. What was available, who had space to do something: *Do you want to do this? Would you like to do this? And do you like this?* And then there was another edition, I mean that was like the luxury edition I suppose. Well, they did a lot of books—they're all somewhere I suppose, stacked up. I'm sure they have copies here. Everything resurfaces. [examining a copy of *Common Sense*] Three dollars? That was supposed to be $1.49. I guess there were seventy-six copies of this? Because it was 1976.

KS: How was *Common Sense* conceived?

TR: I'd written those little poems and we said, "Well, how should we do it?" I was writing them in—do you remember those rainbow notebooks they used to have that didn't have a cover exactly like that but the paper was like that? So with Holbrook Teter and Michael Myers, we sat down and decided to do it like that, and did a good job doing it, I think. The cuts were from some newspaper just dumping all of its stuff, and we found a whole batch of those zincs.

KS: Zincs?

TR: Yeah. One of them's Bela Lugosi, *maybe*, but the others, who knows who the others are? Just people.

KS: When I look at this it reminds me a bit of Simon Cutts' Coracle Press, even Williams' Jargon, insofar as they make a lot of small, ephemeral, everyday objects. Do you know if Teter and Myers knew Cutts or Williams?

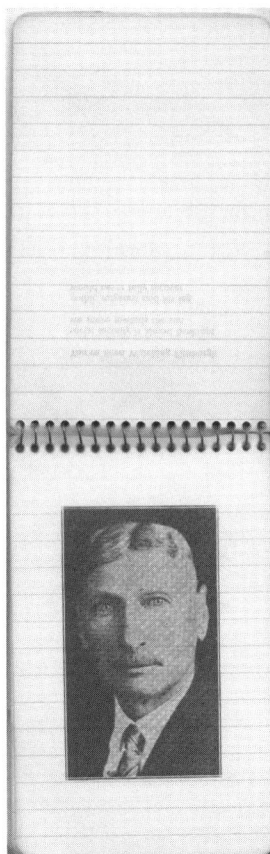

Tom Raworth, *Common Sense* (Zephyrus Image, 1976)

TR: No. Can't say with certainty. It's quite possible. Michael came out of Wisconsin, and out of Hamady there. That was his printing house. Clifford Burke I remember, and Five Trees, those presses, and the Auerhahn stuff had been going for a long time, and Graham Mackintosh was legendary. The ephemeral…

Clifford was a sort of perfectionist printer, you know? He didn't see, exactly, why Holbrook and Michael would do these things, just to put them on mailboxes and throw away. He was a serious printer in that sense, but I didn't know him too well. I knew him to say *hello* and to talk to, and actually he was only a few blocks away from where Zephyrus Image was at that time. That was about the point when Eileen Callahan and others were doing Five Trees at Clifford's as well.

KS: I think Alastair wrote that Teter and Myers met one another at Burke's open studio at Cranium. Burke seems like a generous guy. He's still printing things, but it's mostly, well, positive social and environmental messages, elegantly displayed. Not the heyday of poetry there once was. Have you seen this? [passes a copy of the *Daily World Bean Special* (Zephyrus Image) to Michael]

TR: Those were the days.

KS: This one, I've tried to read it. [passes a copy of *Bean News* 4 to Tom] I don't understand it.

TR: Ah, *Bean News*. Yeah, that's it… here's the back of a dollar food coupon.

MC: Tom, are you working on anything now?

TR: In the sense that I'm always working on something, you know, there's never anything I'm working on but what goes through my mind.

MC: Well, a collection?

TR: No, there's just odd things that I do. I think there are a few things that people want to do in that sense, they want to do a book but I have to write more books. I do more collage than writing a lot of times. But it's always been like that, long periods where I don't do anything, then it's more interesting to write again. Something takes my interest.

KS: So you sometimes do more of one than the other?

TR: Yeah, I'm not a regular writer in that sense. I tend to write when it needs to be written and that's the only thing that I can do. I mean I just add bits to things now and then. I have one long thing going on now that I'll add to until it's finished, I guess.

KS: What is that?

TR: It's a piece called "Caller" that's been in *Echo*... what is it called?

KS: *Ecopoetics*?

TR: Yeah. Exactly. There was a bit in that. And that sort of still goes on, even though it may be a comic book at one point. The comic book ends, but the thing actually still goes on in the text after. It was a way of distorting the photographs I was taking at the time. I was just curious to see if each line worked in a balloon.

KS: That reminds me, how did you and Frances Butler work on *Logbook* (Poltroon Press, 1976)?

TR: We didn't work together. She and Alastair [Johnston] did the design for that, completely, and that was her work. It wasn't a collaboration in any sense. They had the text and that is how they wanted to do it. Yeah, the hardcover one was pleasant as I remember. It was bigger, slightly bigger, and in cloth, cloth of that texture and the same pattern that is on the softbound. Couple of pink rubber stamps. Poltroon did good books I always thought. I like Alastair's printing.

KS: And how did you and Alastair make this one? [passes *Muted Hawks* (Poltroon, 1995) to TR]

TR: That again, he had the text and said he wanted to do something, wanted to illustrate something. He was into that for a while, so I gave him the text and he produced that. I think he wanted to raise some money. It's a nice job, I always liked it. He's done a number of little books of poetry that were of interest to me at the time when they came out, especially the one that was printed diagonally on the page if I remember. I don't think he's publishing much poetry these days.

KS: Do you know why? I never asked him.

TR: I think that was enough. There were a couple of little books of poems but most of Morden Tower prose. In his case maybe a few little books of poems were all right. But no, I don't know. He obviously thought of himself as a poet, but primarily a printer, or a writer on printing and typography. That big book, what's the name of it?

KS: *Alphabets to Order* (Oak Knoll, 2000)?

TR: That's really an interesting book. It's really interesting that nobody else wanted to do those bibliographies of those presses.

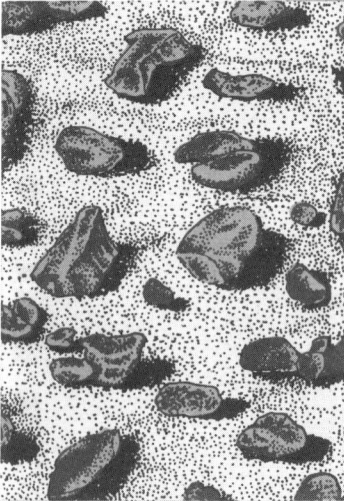

Logbook (Poltroon Press, 1976)

KS: The gravity of the social history that Alastair brings into the Zephyrus Image one is exceptional. There's a bit of that in the Auerhahn, and maybe even a little less in White Rabbit.

TR: No, I thought it was a really good thing that he did, and it's one of the few books that I got a few copies to give to people who wouldn't otherwise stumble on it.

KS: Fantastic poet, I mean a lot of these poet-printers get ideas for books and just fill in the blanks with language.

TR: Yeah, anything will do, as long as it looks...

KS: Alastair kind of describes his writing like that, but I think he underestimates his poetry. Sort of like Asa and Piero, Alastair is a poet that people my age don't really know.

TR: It's been good to see them survive, Piero in particular, to have that book from Granary, *A Purchase in the White Botanica* (2001). I came across a whole load of his manuscripts the other day, and I don't have the Granary book, so I had to go out for a moment to compare, to see if there's anything there that wasn't in the Granary book. There's a batch of stuff he had left with me years and years ago. Second carbons, they used to be a bad thing; they're slightly smeared. I'll compare them at some point and see if there's anything to extract.

KS: It seems like they did a nice job.

TR: Yeah, it was good. [picks up Piero Heliczer's *The Soap Opera* (Trigram Press, 1967) and thumbs through] Oh, this is a nice book. Yes, there again it's elaborate but it all works—it's actually quite simple, isn't it? 1967.

KS: And this one, was it Pip's son? [referring to Paul Vaughn's illustrations in *The Soap Opera*]

TR: Yeah, Paul Vaughan is Pip's son.

KS: From another marriage or affair...

TR: Right. Yeah, Paul lives in Morocco with his wife.

KS: I'd like to see Piero's films.

TR: Yeah, there's never been a DVD as far as I know, but they are listed on, what was it, The Film-Makers' Cooperative website? And there's that guy in Czechoslovakia that did the Piero website. He was trying to track some stuff down. He was all right. He wrote to me and out of that I put him in touch with Pip and a few other people. That came about, I guess, through an interest in Angus and the early days of The Velvet Underground and then he drifted into Piero because of Angus MacLise.

KS: There's a few albums of them jamming together that have been released recently. Angus reads his poetry, you know, from *Year*.

TR: I wonder where those films are. He certainly made seven or eight of them over the years.

KS: Some were stolen I believe. I read that he was living on a boat of some sort.

TR: Yeah, and I understand that the boat was mysteriously sunk. He mentioned that at some point when I saw him, but I didn't know things had been lost like that. I thought there were copies still over here somewhere in New York.

KS: Some of them survived through Warhol's friend—the photographer?

TR: Gerard Malanga?

KS: Thanks. Yeah. At one point he apparently urged Piero to leave some stuff at his place, and he did, which is good since I heard that he used to borrow money from people and wasn't always good about paying them back.

TR: Oh, definitely.

KS: I guess that's why someone stole his duffel bags, which contained a number of films.

TR: I saw Gerard in March, actually, when I read at Bard. He turned up and I hadn't seen him since he was a glowing youth. He's living in Brooklyn; I thought he was still living in Great Barrington, Massachusetts, but he's got an address in Brooklyn. I was interested to see him after all those years. And he did well by Piero because he was involved in that *Little Caesar* thing years ago.

Piero's wife at the time is still around, in London. Pip's still around. A lot of people are just about on their last legs, but you could get in touch, before it does vanish, firsthand knowledge at least.* And things do turn up, as I say; I had forgotten completely about this big batch of Piero's until I was going through some box.

MC: I think the library is closing now.

[2005]

....

*Pip Benveniste died in late August, 2010.

Lyn Hejinian
Tuumba Press
[with Michael Cross]

American poet, essayist, translator, and publisher of Tuumba Press, Lyn Hejinian was born in California in 1941. The press and her writing are central to the formation of Language poetry. *My Life*, originally published by Burning Deck in 1980, is a seminal work associated with the movement, as is her book of essays, *The Language of Inquiry*. There is an aesthetic relationship between the chapbooks published by Burning Deck and Tuumba that suggests a lineage. Tuumba Press published fifty chapbooks printed letterpress between 1976 and 1984, including works by Clark Coolidge, Kathleen Fraser, Rae Armantrout, Kit Robinson, Ron Silliman, and Hejinian herself. The press issued a series of poetry postcards as well as Robert Grenier's large-format poster *Cambridge M'ass*. Long after Hejinian quit printing, she revived the imprint in the late 1990s to produce trade paperbacks. In 1995, Hejinian and Travis Ortiz began commissioning books of poetry under the Atelos imprint, with the goal of publishing 50 books that are "involved in some way with crossing traditional genre boundaries, including, for example, those that would separate theory from practice, poetry from prose, essay from drama, the visual image from the verbal, the literary from the non-literary, and so forth."

TUUMBA 29

WITTGENSTEIN'S DOOR

Curtis Faville

Curtis Faville, *Wittgenstein's Door* (Tuumba, 1980)

KS: When I was a kid growing up in Providence, all of the used bookstores had Burning Deck books. I joke with Keith and Rosmarie Waldrop that Burning Deck was my first "curriculum" because I didn't really know how to begin navigating the world of contemporary poetry. I didn't know what letterpress was when I bought a gorgeous book by Rae Armantrout that was completely unlike anything I had ever read before. I latched on, and from then on out I would read anything with a Burning Deck pressmark because I had trust in Keith and Rosmarie's editing. How did you conceive of your role as a publisher when you established Tuumba?

LH: I thought I should start printing books with a work of my own; that way if I ruined it I wouldn't have the embarrassment of going to someone I respected to say, "I destroyed your work, it's a horror!" I was living north of the Bay Area, outside of San Francisco, and was depending largely on print to get news of what was going on. *Sparrow*, from John Martin's Black Sparrow Press, was produced largely as promo for forthcoming books or for books that he had already published that needed a little boost. I loved the format, and even though it was a publicity piece, it had a sense of a newsgram, a sense of immediacy, and it was beautifully produced but unashamed of its staples. So there was something un-precious about the production values. The other press that interested me aesthetically, both in terms of book arts—although I don't think I had that term in my lexicon at that time—and in terms of the poetry was Burning Deck. The Waldrops have inspired untold numbers of people who publish books. So I liked that sort of breaking-news quality of the chapbook; I liked the size, and I thought it was something I could do because it wasn't technically overwhelming. I understood how to staple things, but I didn't understand how to perfect-bind, etc. So I decided to start Tuumba.

I began with what I now consider a completely erroneous misconception, which was that you introduce new writing, or new writers, by piggybacking them on the reputation and work of better-established figures. I learned that you don't need those better-established figures because when enough new writing is collected, it speaks for itself and suddenly announces something's happening. You don't need credibility—borrowed credibility—to make that happen. So the first series is a bit eclectic, and then I sort of figured out what I was doing. By the time the second series began, I had been in touch with the writers whose chapbooks would later be published by Tuumba, and, likewise, these were the writers who were publishing works of mine—largely the group known as Language poets.

MC: Were you living on a farm?

LH: I was living on a piece of ranch land—it wasn't really useful for farming. Larry [Ochs] and I had little kids and we wanted to get out of the city. It was sort of a back-to-the-land, hippie thing of the time. We talked about moving to Norway—it was a fantasy life. I already owned part of the land that we lived on with my brother and sister; it was a commune-like thing, although we never really became a commune. Everybody had their own cabins and the others only spent a few weeks up there in the summer. It was pretty funky.

I can't remember at what juncture I got in touch with Rosmarie Waldrop. I think she had written to me, just prior to my starting Tuumba or just after, asking me for a manuscript. I really can't remember the exact sequence of events, but she and Maureen Owen, who did Telephone Books, and Barbara Barracks, who did *Big Deal,* and I were in correspondence but had never met. So I asked them naïve questions that helped get Tuumba started. There was a printing establishment in the nearest town, which was Willits, called Willits Printing, run by a former sheep farmer and his wife. I didn't know the difference between offset and letterpress printing, and they had both. The printer, Jim Chase, suggested letterpress—not for any aesthetic reason, but because that equipment was "useless." And he had a big, old Linotype machine, so he would type and these lead slabs would come out. I wanted to learn all of this but was pretty much forbidden to go near it. I was told it was men's work.

KS: Linotype?

LH: All of it. I looked over Jim Chase's shoulder for the production of the first couple of the books, and then asked if I could be hired just once or twice a week as an apprentice. He said "no," but they sold stationary at the front of the shop and I could run that and do general light janitorial tasks. So I did that and slowly worked my way back to the machines. He let me do a few hands-on things by the end of my period of employment and then Larry and I and the children moved to the Bay Area. The first ten Tuumba chapbooks were produced in Willits. When we moved back to the Bay Area, I bought a little Chandler & Price and a lot of type. I met Johanna Drucker and Kathy Walkup, who was teaching at California College of Arts and Crafts, as it was then called—now it's just CCA. They were hugely helpful in teaching me how to handset type and use a Chandler & Price and so forth. Tuumba gave me an excuse to correspond with poets whose work I found interesting, and in retrospect I think it was the smartest career move I could have made because I was suddenly of interest for something more than just my own writing; I was of use and becoming a participant in a community.

KS: Speaking of Jim's stance towards women in the printshop, 1976, the year that you started Tuumba, was same year that the Grolier Club in

New York and the Caxton Club in Chicago—perhaps the most prestigious clubs for bibliophiles in the United States—began to allow women to become members. Women's Studio Workshop and The Center for Book Arts NYC were established about two years earlier with the desire to make the art of the book available to everyone. Was Tuumba, in any sense, a feminist initiative?

LH: Not that I'm consciously aware of. Only in the sense that this was a craft-like undertaking, and that I knew how to do other crafts and enjoyed them. I found them relaxing. I was amused rather than offended by Jim's exclusionary gesture. I thought it was eccentric, and that it wouldn't be true in the larger world. I later learned that the Printers' Union excluded women, but I didn't know that at the time. Becoming a printer-publisher was really just an extension of my being a poet. My generation of women keeps moving as the horizon moves, and we're partly responsible for moving it, but partly it was just on the move by its own kind of collective force. In my world of poetry in the '70s, sexism was not a particularly oppressive factor. There was a lot of room for the women and the women were getting a lot of respect—people would stop and listen. For me, there were a lot of internalized sexist prohibitions to get over, like willing to be the one speaking and interrupting, and that took some work, some consciousness-raising, conversations with other women, but the press wasn't a deliberate feminist gesture.

Don't you feel that part of the intense pleasure of making these books is the pleasure of craftspersonship? These days I do a lot of the typesetting for the Atelos books in Quark, and even that—which is much less beautiful than letterpress—is still fun. When I have a free evening, I think, "Oh great, I'm going to get that Word document into Quark, try out some different fonts, print it out, hold it up...." It's all really incredibly satisfying in a way that is much less painful than trying to write.

Second only to teaching in a classroom setting, making books with others is my favorite form of parallel play. You talk, but you're not bored if the conversation drifts away from areas that are of pressing interest to you because you have other things to do. It's very convivial, collegial—it's fun.

KS: Working alone is fun, too. Sometimes I'll be in the workshop from nine in the morning to nine at night and it feels like the day has passed in an instant. Writing, music, whatever sustains or reorients your attention...

LH: And *you* didn't exist, right? And in a sense you're making the work all over again, by suggesting stanza breaks, selecting fonts, etc. You're kind of working the text into its next manifestation.

KS: I've always thought of typographers as translators. Many of the same rules and considerations apply—we actually attempt to translate, or at least find connections between, Walter Benjamin's essay "Art in the Age of Mechanical Reproduction" and the visual construction of meaning in the typography classes I teach in Buffalo.

LH: Apparently, at least on one occasion when he taught at Naropa, Ted Berrigan would have his students choose either a poet or a poem and he would ask them to type the work—just go home and type up a poem. Make it your own, and in some weird, material, physical way, allowing your own body to reproduce someone else's work is very interesting.

KS: One consideration that we don't have to contend with so much anymore is translating the spatial relationships of the monospaced, typewritten manuscript into print. I spend a lot of time comparing printers' proofs to manuscripts, and I enjoy figuring out how poems transform into books by getting into the correspondence between publishers, poets and typesetters. Let's take Bob Grenier's *Oakland* (1980), for example.

LH: I had to go buy type for that book. I think that's Stymie, which I ended up loving, because he wanted something as close to a typewriter as possible. The first dozen chapbooks were Linotype and the thirty-eight that followed were handset. You can actually see, here and there, the Linotype lines. Well, the slugs, and once in a while it works out so you can see the impression. The prose was trickier to set than the poems, but I was obsessed.

KS: And you had young children at this time?

LH: Yes. They would come and sit with their homework. My son would have been eleven in 1977 and my daughter nine. So they would come after dinner and I'd be setting type, and they would sit and we'd talk. The room where I had the press and the type was adjacent to the kitchen, so I'm sure the lead wandered.

KS: In *Printing Poetry*, Clifford Burke has romantic memories of the kitchen smelling like typewash, but I can't say that I share in his nostalgia.

LH: I would do it differently now, but then, of course I didn't know. Apparently alcoholism is a common ailment among printers. I don't know if it's something in the lead or a chemical in the ink or cleaning up or something, but there's a chemical that hastens the effect of alcohol, so a little goes a long way. This could be a myth, but I've been told that this is the case.

KS: You mentioned that you thought to use the names of the "better known" authors to draw attention to emerging writers. I was born the year you started Tuumba; it's hard for me to tell which authors were better known than others at the time you published their work. There are so many early and first books here by poets who are now widely read—could you elaborate on who was doing what when you commissioned their work?

LH: I had read some of Susan Howe's work in Maureen Owens' *Telephone* (1970–1983), and our correspondence began right away. She had two children, I had two children, and we had various parallels in our private life circumstances. We had both

TUUMBA 33

STATE LOUNGE

ALAN BERNHEIMER

$ 2.00

Subscription: $9 series
Individual copy: $2
TUUMBA PRESS
2639 Russell Street
Berkeley, California 94705

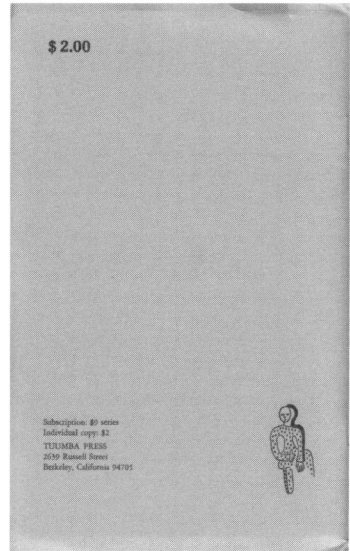

divorced, remarried happily, stuff like that. We maintained a passionate correspondence for years and met only a few times during that exchange. She was living in Connecticut, but was coming into New York all the time and had a poetry radio show on WBAI that I appeared on. Later, I had a poetry show with Kit Robinson on the Pacifica station at Berkeley, but I was less talented on the radio than Susan. Ours was live and she would tape them. We would sit with Kit at one side, then the poet, then me, so I could look at the page and see what our guest was reading. The closer the poet got to the end of the poem, the more panic I could feel coming over me as I realized I had not understood the poem, didn't even know how to ask about it, and the reading was about to end! Kit was just as bad—well, a little better, but not *good*. I tried smoking dope, I tried drinking booze, I tried coffee, and nothing would ever facilitate the sense that I could just flow into the poem.

Back to your question about what I guess one might call the "career status" of the poets—Jeremy Lipp's *Sections from Defiled by Water* (1976) turned out to be his only published book; he became a screenwriter in Hollywood. Ken Irby was at the time well

STATE LOUNGE

state of vector

Silkworms eat mulberry leaves. The berries soak the air's pavement.

the path is on

Olive wood makes the best charcoal for art.

folded fog warnings

Dark furry mold grew inside the channels of the harmonica. Snuff made from moss growing on a churchyard skull was thought a cure for headaches.

first river crossing

Alcohol aside, absinthe was five times the concentration of Pernod, plus wormwood. Its traditional proof stood at 136. Some attribute the power of the dry martini to a similar combination of high proof alcohol and the minute amount of wormwood (German: *Wermut*) contained in the vermouth.

racing the weather

Jets chalk their path across the sky. Chalk is pure levigated whiting.

torn and sew

On account of bilateral symmetry we learn to tell left from right, punctuating the fearless landscape.

shake up the sedimentary record

Donald Turnupseed, a 23-year-old college student whose Ford James Dean's Porsche Spyder ran into.

wishes of the damned

We cover our eyes with a camera, half hours with a microscope.

pale gram straw

The humidity element of a hydrograph consists of a sheaf of blond human hairs.

small bore

A state of things is a constellation of objects. Fish lack sense of relative.

interest in interest

Americans shoot their favorite presidents in the head.

cushion rail

Movies were silent then, but not still, diminishing gelatin.

living atmosphere

Mrs. Valentino had things to do at Poiret. I notice my head tailor to bend as we round the corner.

known within certain circles. He had been a graduate student at Harvard when I was an undergraduate there—a very good friend and a source of inspiration. He knew Charles Olson and Robert Creeley and invited me on a number of occasions to go visit Olson, which is something I did not do. I had the sense that Ken was someone who was in touch with people. He gave me a copy of Creeley's *For Love* for my twenty-first birthday, so that was my coming-of-age volume. Dick Higgins, whose *Cat Alley* I published in 1976, was very well known as a Fluxus avant-gardist. I had not met him in person at that time, but when I did meet him later I found him to be a very sweet guy.

Ultimately, I think I didn't publish any unsolicited manuscripts. Somewhere early in the process, I came up with the idea of organizing the Tuumba chapbooks into series and soliciting subscriptions. There were ten volumes in the first series, and after that there were six—six chapbooks per year, one every other month. In advance, I would solicit the works for the given series, and once I had them in place I made up a flyer and mailed it to likely (and probably unlikely) suspects. I think the cost of a subscription was ten dollars. By soliciting work and knowing well in advance what

Tuumba was going to publish, I avoided the awkwardness and anxiety of having to deal with submissions. Maureen Owen once told me that, when she was publishing *Telephone*, she would find four sacks of unsolicited manuscripts awaiting her every week at the post office. I knew I couldn't deal with that.

KS: Did you ever ask anyone for work who said no?

LH: Did anyone turn me down? No. Oh! Isaac Asimov.

KS: I knew it!

LH: I knew he would, which is why I wrote to him. My son was a big Isaac Asimov, sci-fi fan. He said, "Mom, you're publishing books, won't you please publish one by Isaac Asimov?" So I wrote to him, and enclosed copies of whatever I had in print—my book and Sukey Howe's probably. He wrote back a really sweet letter saying that he didn't have anything currently that seemed to fit with my *interests* and gave his regards to my son, who he was sure was a *splendid* young man. A totally kind response.

Except for Clayton Eshelman and Kathleen Fraser, no one else had a widely established reputation. Kathleen was a real presence in the Bay Area. She was teaching at San Francisco State and had already had a few books published. But I published first books by a lot of people: Rae Armantrout, Peter Inman, Jean Day, Carla Harryman—there must be others. There was a sense of community that grew out of the press scene in the Bay Area. There was Barrett Watten's *This* magazine and This Press, Geoffrey Young's The Figures, Ron Silliman had *Tottles* magazine for a while, there was Bob Perelman's *Hills* magazine, Carla Harryman's *QU*, etc. Virtually everybody was running a talk series, had a magazine, had a press, had a radio show or ran a reading series. So everyone was contributing a part of what was making this thing happen. You should note, lest you feel you're not doing your part for your generation, that the economic situation at that time was so much easier to live in and inhabit. We were all doing just fine on part-time jobs and the grant situation was fantastic. As a matter of fact, in Noe Valley, which is a very desirable section of San Francisco, you could rent a four bedroom, two-bathroom house for three-hundred dollars. Most homes in that neighborhood sell for over a million dollars today. And National Endowment for the Arts grants, which I didn't apply for my first year, were incredible. The National Endowment for the Arts was established in 1965 and the first Bush Administration sort of pulled the plug on it. It still exists, but in a very modified way. Between around 1978 and the early 1980s, I applied for NEA editors grants and did get a few, but the sums were relatively small. The fact is that it wasn't very expensive to publish the chapbooks. The Chandler & Price cost me only $250, and the only other real costs were for paper, type, and postage, and those were entirely manageable. Each issue cost me around three-hundred dollars to produce, if I remember correctly. Producing the volumes took time, of course—something that almost no one has anymore but which seemed ample enough back when I was publishing Tuumba. Apart from me, none of the poets I was hanging around with had children, and none of us were in the position of having to sell our time completely away. And only Carla Harryman was in graduate school. Bob Perelman and Barrett Watten went back later. Carla was getting a Master of Fine Arts in Interdisciplinary Art at San Francisco State, and I'm sure that was demanding, but she is a genius and somehow she seemed to have time. I never had the feeling that she was oppressed by her studies; it was more that she was energized by them. And generally the university didn't seem to figure in to the things we cared about—it was all happening outside the academy.

MC: Can you say something about the number fifty? I know there were fifty Tuumba books and that Atelos will publish fifty. Is that a coincidence?

LH: No, it's no accident. I figured if fifty could be enough of one thing it could be enough of another. Barrett Watten took me to task for setting it up that way and I think he's right. His argument was and is that it casts all of this work into the mold of "the body of work" as opposed to an ongoing activity, that it makes it more product-like or emphasizes its product-like facet rather than saying that this is material in action. And my decision to staple the chapbooks together was intended to undermine the commodity value of them. Staples are functional, and also somewhat damaging—they rust and eventually cause stains. As I said, I wanted to emphasize the immediacy rather than preciousness or permanence of the texts. The works are not here to be pretty, they are here to be read. They'll all end up in other volumes, hopefully. Atelos, which I began with Travis Ortiz in 1998, was just kind of overwhelming to take on, the thought of starting another series, and I thought I wouldn't panic if I knew it was finite. I knew there would be a point where I could say "done" and stop.

KS: What do you think of projects like Craig Dworkin's *Eclipse*, that is, the idea of putting out-of-print editions up online?

LH: I think it's a great project but I'm not in love with the online world. I don't like it aesthetically and I don't like it better than books. I think it's a myth that it's longer lasting or that it's a better archive. That said, it's a great resource, and without it this stuff basically disappears. And Craig is absolutely ethical about it, and committed, and I have absolutely no argument with his views of why he's doing it or how he's doing it. He's putting up some stuff of mine, so I'm readily, enthusiastically, saying, "Yes please."

KS: So you're working on a project at home and you can either go to *Eclipse* or search your stacks for the hard copy—which do you choose?

LH: I would immediately go to the shelf. It wouldn't even occur to me to look it up online. But that's me. It's not a considered choice, it just wouldn't occur to me to check the machine when I know it's on the shelf.

KS: Although you printed your books on a letterpress, I think of Tuumba as part of the mimeograph revolution that Steve Clay and Rodney Phillips masterfully documented and curated for an exhibition at the New York Public Library. That is to say, there's a sumptuous utilitarian quality to these books devoid of the austerity of most private press editions that make use of the same technology. Were you ever interested in publishing deluxe editions? And how do you feel about seeing your own writing in extravagant, limited editions?

LH: I didn't think I was a good enough printer to do something like that, not even close. It was a utilitarian craft for me, not an art form the way it is for Charles Alexander, Johanna Drucker, Janet Rodney, or Emily McVarish. These are *great* printers. So, no. I did wrestle with agreeing to have these very expensive books of my work published by other people. *The Traveler and the Hill and the Hill* (Granary Books, 1998), which I did with Emilie Clarke, sells for $4,500. So that takes the work out of a world where it is immediately accessible and puts it into another category, which is the category of the visual art world. I actually don't mind having a little bit of experience in the world of visual arts. There are only sixty-five copies of that book, and every monoprint in every copy was done by hand. It took Emilie two years of nonstop production. I helped a *little* bit, by putting registration marks in the corners of the sheets of Rives BFK paper and shared in the inhaling of toxins and chemicals out of camaraderie, so I actually don't have a quibble with the presence of books in the fine arts world.

On the other hand, the thousandth edition of *The Psalm of Psalms* or *Moby-Dick*—you know, these grand productions where no one really goes to the book for the content—are another story. There are shows about fine printing and not a single thing in the show has been written in the last hundred years. I met Andrew

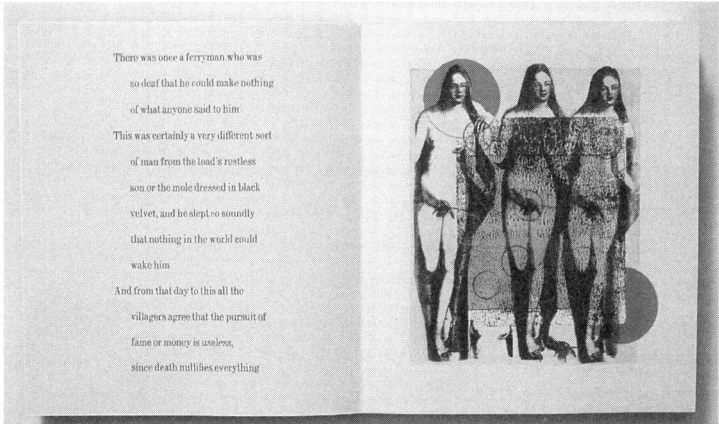

There was once a ferryman who was
so deaf that he could make nothing
of what anyone said to him
This was certainly a very different sort
of man from the toad's restless
son or the mole dressed in black
velvet, and he slept so soundly
that nothing in the world could
wake him
And from that day to this all the
villagers agree that the pursuit of
fame or money is useless,
since death nullifies everything

Lyn Hejinian, *The Traveler and the Hill and the Hill* (Granary Books, 1998), images by Emilie Clark

Hoyem once but we're not really friends. I'm much more friendly with Alastair Johnston at Poltroon, largely because we're both friends of Tom Raworth's and we live in the same neighborhood.

The *Individuals* (Chax Press, 1988) project started because I was stuck and wasn't getting any writing done. I complained, whined, to Kit Robinson about it and he told me he was writing ten lines every morning. So I said, "If I did that, could I mail them to you?" So really I was just leaning on him for support. He had a job in the high-tech world that involved a long commute, and I think I was teaching at New College, which did not involve nearly as many out-of-home hours, so I wrote way more than he did ultimately. So my contribution to the project became *The Cell* (Sun & Moon Press, 1992), and Kit's was scattered through various of his books. More than anyone I can think of, Kit has used the workplace as a source of material for literary composition. He established a non-separation, and there could have been a risk, but he never disguised his poetic identity at his workplace, and his colleagues like that. For *Individuals*, Charles Alexander came up with a design and figured out a way for our poems to play off each other to create new configurations, mixing and matching.

KS: Did Charles arrive at this design after the manuscript was complete?

LH: Yes. And Charles invited Kit and me to Tucson to give a reading together. I don't remember if that was before or after he published *Individuals*, but presumably it was after. Charles' vision was as much a part of the book as the writing that Kit and I did. He published another collaboration that I was involved with—the book *Chartings* (Chax Press, 2000), that Ray DiPalma and I wrote. We'd initially sent the *Chartings* manuscript to Joel Kuszai's Meow Press. Or, rather, I did.

KS: It would have been different!

LH: Yes. It would have been very different! Ray rejected the Meow Press idea. He said that he didn't want to be published by a press that had so little self-respect that it called itself "Meow." I had already been in touch with Joel and had to withdraw the manuscript. About that time Ray got in touch with Charles Alexander and Chax did this incredibly beautiful job and I'm completely happy, but I feel somewhere I owe Joel a manuscript. Though I don't know if he is still publishing books, I certainly wouldn't expect him to produce a book that was so laborious to print and expensive to buy.

KS: Steve Clay has put portions of most of the high-end books up at the Granary website. I've talked to him about this issue before, and I think he feels very strongly that he doesn't want to deny anyone access to a text, but on the other hand he sells books that are works of art.

LH: Yes, he's clear on just that issue. He's such an ethical person.

KS: For reasons I don't entirely understand, some people feel offended by books that cost more than twenty dollars, as if all books should be priced relative to the disposable paperback economy. It's fast food: cheap, consistent, and totally limited. The book arts are forms of art and should be priced accordingly. This may in part account for why most book artists are sheepish when it comes to asking a fair price for their work. Architects and painters don't have these hang-ups because their work has a clearer cultural value. Could you talk a little bit about where you see Tuumba going now that you've made the transition from letterpress pamphlets to perfect-bound books produced on an offset press from layouts you've designed on the computer?

LH: Tuumba is really for special projects now, like Anne Tardos' book *Uxudo* (1999), which Tuumba published in conjunction with Leslie Scalapino's O Books. Anne had finished this book and had not found a publisher for it. Leslie Scalapino and I really liked the book for its interdisciplinary, mixed-media, polylingual qualities, so I decided to start Tuumba back up again. Leslie and I published that book together by splitting the cost. Anne did the typesetting, which was well beyond our capacity.

The next Tuumba project was Jack Collom's *Red Car Goes By* (2001). Clark Coolidge, Reed Bye, Merrill Gilfillan, Larry Fagin, and I were the editors, and we read through everything that Jack had written—he is an unbelievably prolific writer. And we published it for his seventieth birthday, a selected poems in lieu of a festschrift. And this I also pre-sold; I sent out a flyer inviting people to order a copy in advance and make donations, so I actually had the money for this book before it went to press. I did the typesetting, and prior to that I had to scan the entire manuscript, as the works were produced on a typewriter rather than a computer. It cost a lot of time, of course, but no more money than the advanced sales and the donations provided.

The third new Tuumba project was a book by Leslie Scalapino (*Orchard Jetstream*, 2001) writing as Dee Goda—a detective novel. She and I trade detective novels, we both enjoy reading them, so I thought it was great that she wrote her own. She and I wrote a book together called *Sight* (Edge Books, 1999), and we went away for a weekend to do revisions before it was published. That was where she told me she was working on a detective novel. Then she told me in *complete* seriousness that she was worried about the pseudonym Dee Goda because it can be read as a Japanese name. What if she went on television, like the Oprah show, and people realized that she's not Japanese? Then she told me the plot! There are three detectives, one of whom is named Grace Abe and some of the time her body is inhabited by the ghost of a Marine, and there's projectile vomiting going on, largely by young girls, and well, that's just in the first couple of pages. The idea of this being a bestseller, and the pseudonym being a danger… I mean, it's highly improbable, and I love it. Anyway, that was the next Tuumba project.

Katy Lederer's Spectacular Books published my book *The Beginner* (2001) in a small edition, I think just two-hundred copies, and it sold out, and Simone Fattal's Post-Apollo Press had published *Happily* (2000). I was thinking of *Happily*, *The Beginner*, and *Slowly* (2002) as a kind of trilogy. I wanted them all in print, so I republished *The Beginner* myself. A press in England was going to do *Slowly*, but they sent it back with a long excuse—I can't remember what it was, but they didn't do it. So I did that one too.

So the only other Tuumba book that is in the works now is an interview-correspondence between Bernadette Mayer and Bill Berkson that took place be-tween 1977 and 1985 [*What's Your Idea of a Good Time*, 2006]. This book is *really* good. There's so much inter-est in the history of New York School and Language School, I think it's a book that will ac-tually get some attention. They talk about all kinds of stuff: sex, love, gossip, the Poetry Project, and so forth. A lot of it is them quizzing each other about what they're writing,

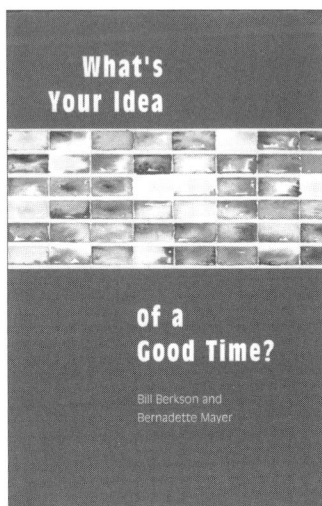

What's
Your Idea

of a
Good Time?

Bill Berkson and
Bernadette Mayer

reading and what they're thinking about writing. I think it's going to be a useful and inspiring book for some kinds of writers and scholars.

One issue that we haven't brought up relates to the choice of authors or works I have wanted to publish. A critically important, as well as participatory and creative, aspect of the work of an editor or publisher involves his or her role in bringing new artistic works into existence, as well as into the world. Editors and publishers contribute enormously to the shaping and substance of the literary reality of their times. This is true with respect to whole communities of publications, as well as to individual works. Geoff Young, of The Figures, solicited a work from me, and *Writing is an Aid to Memory* (1978) is the result of that. I knew that I could write anything and he would publish it. So it's really this incredible opportunity, especially for younger writers. All the Atelos books come from open commissions. I try to pay attention to who's writing and who's doing interesting things. I know that a lot of people have unpublished manuscripts sitting in a drawer, and I know that there is a tremendous need to publish those, and I regret that I don't do that sometimes, but that's just not what I do. Bruce Andrews and Clark Coolidge, for example, have stacks of manuscripts that should be published.

KS: I assumed that they could send their work anywhere and someone would snatch it up.

LH: You haven't asked me how many of my books I've paid for. Leslie Scalapino and I paid for *Sight*. I paid for *Oxota: A Short Russian Novel* (1991). *Sunflower* (2000), the little collaboration I did with Jack Collom, we paid for together. There just aren't that many people out there willing to lose money at this.

KS: I think that the turn towards artists books compounded by the DIY, *Whole Earth Catalog* culture of the '60s began to change poets' ideas about the values associated with self-publishing. It no longer meant that your writing isn't worth reading, or that you've been chumped by a vanity press.

LH: In Marxian terms—but in utterly practical terms, too— self-publishing is, or can be, about taking control of the means of production. Aesthetic control, economic control, distribution control to some extent. To the best of my knowledge, self-publishing was excluded from the literature program at the National Endowment for the Arts, and I think that prohibition was justified. But... Gertrude Stein, Virginia Woolf, and Anaïs Nin all self-published. So did Dickens, Coleridge, Shelley...

KS: Pound, Whitman, Yeats...

LH: It's not an un-noble situation to put oneself in. But book publishing is getting expensive, and it is that, rather than pride, that will discourage people from self-publishing. I would never have felt able to start the Atelos publishing project without start-up funds from John Zorn's Hips Road Foundation. He was extraordinarily generous. Now it's kind of paying for itself, but it will never recover that initial investment. Once one has a few books in publication, their sales can generate money necessary to pay for the next ones, but the funds needed for the first few books will never get recovered. Publishing first books by writers, as Tuumba often did, and publishing work written in response to an invitation, as Atelos does, adds to the risks—aesthetic, as well as financial—but those are risks worth taking. So far Atelos hasn't come out with a bomb. There will probably be one, but that will be okay—maybe I'll write it myself!

KS: I'm going to ask a gossipy question. What were the best and the worst experiences you've had working with someone on a book? I mean, have you ever just had a ball, or conversely, encountered someone who's just awful? If it's too gossipy a question, we can just move on.

LH: There are some grouchy people in the Tuumba and Atelos series, but nobody pops into my mind as difficult. There are typos I regret, but people have even been tolerant about those. Small press publishing at the level I've been involved with is a highly social activity. In the early days, publishing Tuumba allowed me to get to know poets whose work excited me. It established the credibility of my enthusiasm—better than saying, "I love your work" is saying, "I want to publish your work." And designing and typesetting the various books has helped me to understand technical, structural aspects of it that I might otherwise have overlooked. An editor-publisher has an occasion to be a very practical reader of a text. And proposing to publish somebody's work was a way to initiate a possible friendship. Especially when I was communicating with poets who didn't live nearby—people outside the range of other social interactions. I'm thinking here especially of Susan Howe and Clark Coolidge. I had been somewhat in awe of Clark's writing and status as a poet. Tuumba gave me a reason to be in touch with him, and subsequently—through the poetry—we have become good friends. Tuumba published *Research* (1982)—along with *The Crystal Text* (1986), one of his very great works—and Atelos published his delightful and disturbing *Alien Tatters* (2000). Maybe working on these texts gave me close enough experience of some of his work to read it in ways he doesn't. I think Clark is one of the most philosophically sophisticated, thoughtful, and groundbreaking of us all. He says little *about* his writing, but it's really *in* his writing that I see him working on and working out a number of important questions that poetry faces, or that humans face. *What is a sentence? What is death?* I think Clark is a profound metaphysical thinker, but he denies it. He feels his work to be much more about rhythm and music; he has said that his great regret is that he did poetry instead of becoming a great drummer. Poetry is a type of drumming with words, for him, of course, and you can see that in *Polaroid* (Adventures in Poetry/Big Sky, 1975) or *The Maintains* (This Press, 1974). He has a characteristic after-beat to his phrasing, or what one might term after-phrase.

MC: I've always wondered about setting Larry Eigner's texts. Was he very staunch about keeping the lines where they were?

LH: No. *Flat and Round* (1980) had been published before, and it got lost or destroyed, but I had his marked-up, corrected copy, so I knew how he wanted things to line up. In my experience, it was the initial letter of a line, or when there's a gap in a line between phrase "A" and phrase "B," the initial letter of phrase "B" might have to line up with something above or below it. Bob Grenier knows better than I how much or how little Eigner was concerned with vertical alignments in his work. In my experience of working with Eigner's poetry (and Barrett Watten, who published a number of Eigner's works, either in *This* magazine or as books from This press, has said much the same thing), what was important were the placement of the beginnings of lines or of discrete phrases in a line—this was sufficient to establish what one might call the landscape or thought form of a poem. Eigner worked with a typewriter, and hence with a non-proportional typeface: every letter, from "i" to "m," is carried on the same size key. Insisting that the fonts in which his work appears in books should conform to non-proportional spacing seems at risk of fetishizing something that wasn't particularly important.

KS: That reminds me of the Vito Acconci book that Craig Dworkin edited recently (*Language to Cover a Page*, MIT Press, 2006) I think that he must have transcribed all of it and set it in some sort of digital typewriter font, while Ugly Duckling's collected *0-9* (2006), edited by Acconci and Bernadette Mayer, is basically a facsimile meticulously cleansed in Photoshop.

LH: Well, there's Courier, but actually Courier is foxy, because it looks like its non-proportional, it looks like a typescript, but when you work with it on the computer you realize that the letters are just not lining up. Curtis Faville has figured out a way to override the proportioning in Quark with that typeface. I didn't ask him how he did it—I don't want to know! But that's what's being used for the big forthcoming Stanford University Press edition of Eigner's *Complete Poems* (2010). By the time Tuumba was bringing out the reprint of *Flat and Round*, Eigner had moved to Berkeley, so I was able to discuss the typesetting of the book with him in person. He could be hard to understand, because of his disability, but as long as I knew the context I could understand him very well. And I had another occasion to think closely about the structure—the literal situating—of an Eigner text. The Berkeley Art Museum at the University of California, Berkeley was closed for a period for an earthquake retrofit, and a curator, Lawrence Rinder, wanted to use the outside façade of the building as something like an alternative exhibition space. He came up with the idea of putting up a poem, and asked me if I could suggest something appropriate. I suggested "Again dawn," a short, four-line poem of Eigner's. We went to Eigner's house to discuss the idea with him—he was entirely in favor of it, and so the work proceeded. Eigner was very specific about how the first letters of the line should line up with what was above, but otherwise, he had nothing to say. He was rapturously happy with the result. The poem was exhibited on the Berkeley Art Museum façade from June 15 to October 15, 1993.

I went sometime after his death to look at his manuscripts in the Green Library, Stanford. It was all in typescripts, and there was one page where in pencil he had laboriously noted where everything is supposed to line up. And then at the bottom he had typed, "I don't know, it's all an experiment anyway, and people will do what they want to do." So you get a sense, but you don't have to be a curmudgeon about it. I mean, I feel that way about my own work when it gets published. If I care enough about the particulars of the poem's presentation, I have to do it myself. Which brings us back to the theme of self-publishing.

KS: What Bay Area presses are most important to you?

LH: The Grabhorn Press, but only contingently. My grandfather had a winery as a hobby. Grabhorn designed and printed the labels for his bottles of wine. That might have been my first exposure to fine press printing—the labels for Hillcrest Vineyards. But you are asking about literary presses. I realize now, in retrospect, that it was always the writing that I was paying attention to, not to the presses making it available. That must be why your question immediately prompted me to think of Grabhorn—rather than The Figures, This, Hills, or even Poltroon. Somewhere on the landscape, too, was a comic book printer-publisher—I think his name was Don Donahue. He had done a lot of R. Crumb's comic books. I sought him out around 1969 or 1970—before I had any thought of becoming a publisher myself. I had a manuscript called *The GRRReat Adventure,* and I wanted to publish it as a comic book. I was attracted to an underground, rather than literary arts, aesthetic. I was reading a lot of the political "dirty" comic books—featuring ludicrous motorcyclists with huge penises, rebellious drooling females, precocious brats. The stuff embodied the "quick and dirty"—it literalized what the marketing of "the news" depends on. It presented some version of the underside of rebellion. And I liked the juxtaposition of word and image—or, especially, incongruous texts, even sometimes a high art vocabulary, accompanied by grungy images.

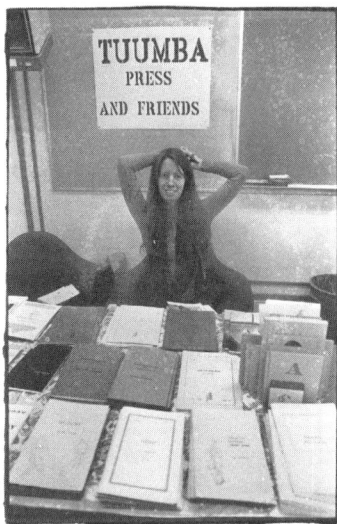

[2005]

67

Alan Loney
Electio Editions

Born in Lower Hutt, New Zealand in 1940, Alan Loney is a poet, essayist, handpress printer, and translator. The oldest of eight siblings, Loney dropped out of school at fifteen to explore music and bohemian life, eventually settling in Christchurch in 1974, where he founded Hawk Press and began publishing young poets from New Zealand, including his own book, *Dear Mondrian*, which was co-winner of the New Zealand Book Awards for Poetry in 1976. That year he also met the American poet Robert Creeley, and printed his book *Hello*, a poetic account of his time in New Zealand. Hawk Press closed in 1983, and in 1987 Loney started Black Light Press in Wellington.

In spite of his lack of formal education, Loney was a Literary Fellow at the University of Auckland in 1992. In 1994, he became the co-director of the Holloway Press at the University, where he served until 1998. The author of many collections of poems, collaborations with visual artists (many published in deluxe limited-editions), he won the Poetry prize in the 2016 Victorian Premier's Literary Awards for *Crankhandle* (Cordite, 2015), and the Janet Frame Literary Trust Award for a life's achievement in poetry in 2011.

Following his retirement from printing at Electio Editions (2004–2015), he published *Verso,* a magazine for the Book as a Work of Art (2015–2018). His latest book is *In Search of the Book as a Work Art* (Opifex Books, Australia, 2019). He lives with his partner Miriam Morris in Melbourne, Australia.

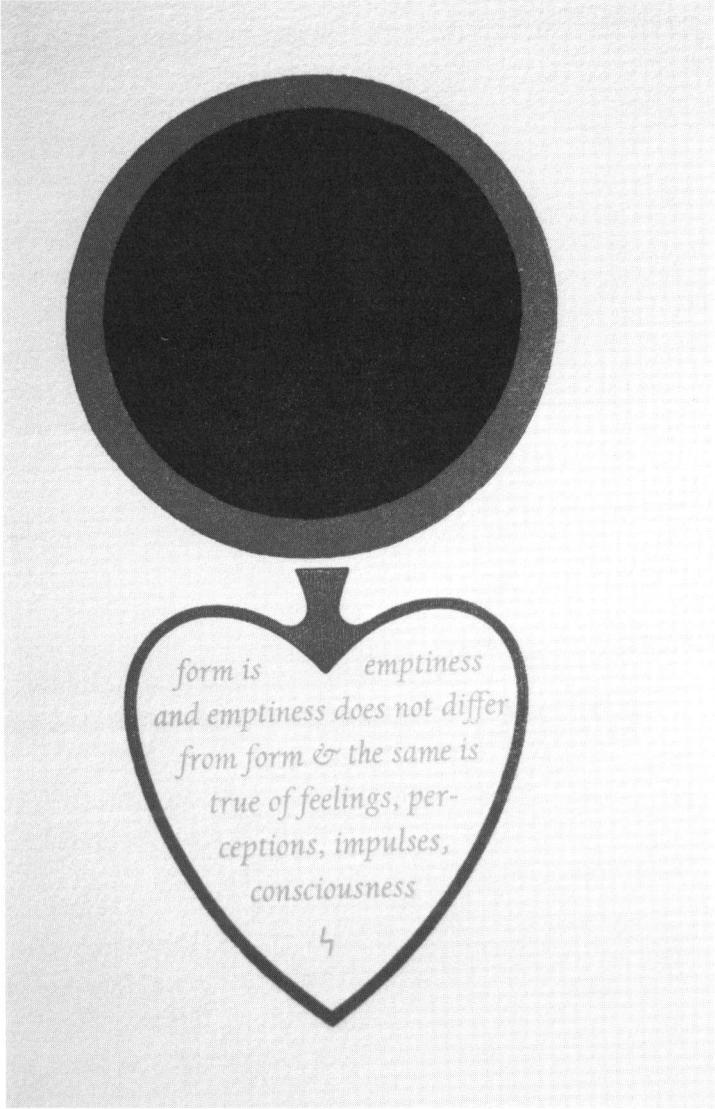

form is emptiness
and emptiness does not differ
from form & the same is
true of feelings, per-
ceptions, impulses,
consciousness

Alan Loney, *Heart sutra* (Electio Editions, 2009), illustration by Alan Loney

KS: Alan, you're a remarkable writer and printer. I knew you as a writer first because Bob Creeley urged me to read your work. I often think of printing and writing as harmonized, sometimes wonderfully dissonant histories. You've articulated some of your thoughts on the relationship between poetry and typography, writer and the written word, idea and object beautifully elsewhere, but I don't know very much about your personal history. Pardon the proverbial chicken or the egg question, but which came first—the desire to print or the desire to write books? It isn't unusual for aspiring poets to publish or print their own first poems—did you?

AL: Kyle, let me begin by saying thank you for this opportunity, and for honoring me in such company as your interview proposes. Normally I tend to shudder at the prospect of "personal history," but it's clear your question is more about "history" than "personal," so I am reassured enough to proceed. I like your pairing of "harmonized" and "dissonant." It points to the simplicity that writing and printing are, within those of us who do both (as well as the social structures of writing and publishing at large), twin histories with the generic similarities and the individual differences of "things-in-themselves" that characterize all of what Buddhists wonderfully refer to as "the ten thousand things"—all the things, including ourselves, of the universe.

In my case, an egg did precede a chicken. I began writing in 1962 or '63, with the example of my dear friend George South plus Babette Deutsch's book *Poetry Handbook*, and for the next seven years I wrote heaps of sestinas, villanelles, ballads and ballades, sonnets and so on, almost none of which I showed anyone. All I have left from those years now are a few unpublished short lyrics. They are dated 1963 to 1965. In late 1970 I encountered Charles Olson's *Maximus Poems,* and that changed everything in terms of how I then began to think of the line of poetry. Soon after, I met Trevor Reeves when he set up his Caveman Press in Dunedin, New Zealand, and he printed the first fruit of my new writing, *The Bare Remembrance,* in 1971. Our arrangement was that I'd set the type—he showed me how—and he'd work the Chandler & Price treadle platen press. So, while I didn't publish or print my first book, I did set the type for it and began to think from "the line of poetry" to "the line of type." It was that experience that first suggested to me that I too might learn to print, and four years later I set up Hawk Press in Taylors Mistake, Christchurch, New Zealand, with an Arab treadle platen press and a tray of Eric Gill's twelve-point Perpetua type.

KS: Perpetua? A splendid font for poetry, but why Perpetua?

AL: I'd seen part of its story in Stanley Morison's *Tally of Types,* one of the first books I acquired, along with Lewis Allen's *Printing with the Handpress*, towards figuring out what printing was about and what models might be available for me to learn from. It was the thirty-point size of Perpetua, capitals and lower case, in a small showing in that book that clinched it for me. I quickly moved up from twelve point to fourteen point, but a mild dissatisfaction with the italic led me to adopt Centaur as the primary text type for the books. My idea was always to have a single text type and a good group of display types on which I could ring the changes in the design from one book to the next. On the other hand, Perpetua and Centaur were the only contemporary (this is 1975) types able to be supplied by the one trade Monotype setter left in Christchurch, where I began printing.

KS: Could you discuss your thinking about the relationship between poetic and typographic forms when you were writing and printing in Christchurch?

AL: In the beginning I was more interested in the accurate rendering of texts, that typography follow the lines and spaces of the poems to be set. Based on my newfound sense of the formal possibilities of poems, and my earlier experience as a proofreader on newspapers ("follow copy, even if it flies out the window"), the first few years of the press were very much involved in a notion of fidelity to the text in typesetting. After all, the lines I was printing were not mine for the most part, and I wanted to be as accurate in my own practices as I wanted other editors and publishers to be accurate about my lines. At that time, and for some time later, I found it all but impossible to get my work accurately printed in New Zealand magazines, and apart from the occasional recidivistic stumble here and there I eventually abandoned the effort and stopped sending material to magazines altogether. But it was some time later, when I'd set up Black Light Press in the late 1980s, that I began to get a sense that setting type might act as an extension of the writing process itself. Stanley Morison had described typography as "the disposition of words on the page," and I started to think of poetry also as "the disposition of words on the page"—though, as I think about it, my printing of the last book from Hawk Press, *Squeezing the Bones*, when I was making large typographic prints of small poems, was a hint of things to come. Olson's work remained crucial throughout this time. Questions of where one's lines end and begin were to me questions about a new way of understanding the craft of poetry alongside my struggles to get a decent grip on the craft of printing.

KS: I think that as one comes to live with one's words, words live lives of their own. They evolve from, say, the handwritten notebook, to typescript, to printer's proofs, etc., and in each permutation find a form that resembles the former, but is in no way identical. Could you discuss how form acts on content, and vice versa, when you edit your own writing? Would you, for example, rewrite a sentence to avoid an orphan or widow if there wasn't a convenient typographic solution?

AL: Sure. Increasingly over the years I have allowed the form, shape of the book to become a factor in rewriting, both in books I am typesetting and in books typeset by others. Occasionally, I have altered my text to accommodate the discovery that I have no more of a particular letter in the type-case, that literally I don't have enough type to set the next word or line of the original text. But these sorts of accommodations are almost incidental to the way in which a total physical form of a book can shape the writing before the writing begins, rather than adjust to it after the writing has been done. William Everson has famously highlighted the problem in his edition of [Robinson] Jeffers' poems with their very long lines, which needed a long landscaped-shaped book to accommodate them. Such long lines are a real problem for conventional publishing procedures. Yet it was in 1976 in my first meetings with Bob Creeley that we discussed how the lines of his poems became longer when the small, narrow pieces of paper he typically wrote on were no longer available to him. And that, to begin with, he found writing on the larger sheets quite difficult to come to grips with. In this case the writing itself alters "when it alteration finds" [quoting Shakespeare's "Sonnet 116"]. When I printed the New Zealand section of Bob's longer work *Hello* (Hawk Press, 1976), I gave my printed book the same physical dimensions as the notebook in which he was writing.

Another aspect of this enters when one takes the double-page spread as the basic unit of the opened book and not simply the page. And these days I am acutely aware of how the two pages make up the single visual impact of

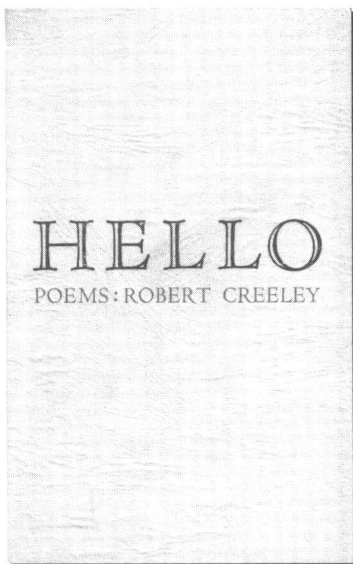

HELLO
POEMS: ROBERT CREELEY

the double spread—both in the writing and in typesetting. Even if what's to show on one such page is a visual image I can rethink either the text (in terms of what words are "there"), or the shape of the text, or the position or place on the page the text might occupy. I guess one way of thinking about it is that writing is a process that can continue right up to the point of printing. On the other hand one might say this isn't new—writers who turn reading proofs into acts of rewriting are legion, but actually most of them are not necessarily responding to the physicality of their book. For me, the fluidity of the relations between actual book and text are my daily portion. I still believe utterly in notions of open form, and if I didn't I couldn't do the work I do. The form of the poem and the form of the book overlap, intersect, interfere, overlay each other in the pleasure of the work, and the layers or degrees of openness required for that to happen have not in my experience come easily, nor can they be taken for granted, but none of my work now takes place without them.

KS: A number of the poets and printers you've mentioned are from the United Kingdom or the United States. I confess that I'm not very familiar with contemporary poetry in New Zealand, nor do I know much about the recent history of the book there. Would you discuss the periodicals, pubs, presses, and other literary hubs in the area that were important to you as a younger, or "emerging" writer?

AL: This is an interesting question. When I think on it, I was never much of a social being. I never liked pubs, was not influenced by New Zealand writers, and I must be one of the least published in magazines of any poet of my day in New Zealand. For many others, the business of sending off poems to the magazines was a regular practice, but I started writing books early in my work—1971—and I was thirty-one years old then. Like Wystan Curnow, Roger Horrocks, and Tony Green, I was somewhat older than the new wave of writers who emerged in New Zealand in the late 1960s, and I was older than most in the beginnings of my life as a published poet. I printed my second book of poems at Hawk

Press in 1976, and Auckland University Press published my third in 1979. Not until 1992 did another book get published, and in the meantime I had stopped sending poems to magazines and simply from time to time responded to the occasional request for a poem or two. Only for a short time, 1971 to 1974, was I part of any real grouping of poets, and while there were a few magazines about—*Edge, Cave, Mate, Islands, Lipsync, Freed*—I was published only once or twice in some and never at all in others. By the time I started Hawk Press in 1975, I had become somewhat distant from any groupings, though of course there were certain people whose work I wanted to publish. One sign of this perhaps was that I rarely received unsolicited manuscripts in the mail. Usually I asked for a manuscript, and while mostly they were supplied, I don't think I ever found a real sense of "community" among poets. The friendships I now enjoy have, some of them, endured over a few rocky times—I think I didn't have a sense of humor over serious differences of opinion—and my early senses of alienation from community in general stay with me even now, though I am better I hope at handling them than I was. If it wasn't for Hawk Press and my editorship of *Parallax Magazine* (1982–1983), I would have had little if any contact with other writers prior to 1992 when I became the happy recipient of the Literary Fellowship at the University of Auckland.

KS: What changed after receiving the Fellowship?

AL: Gaining the Literary Fellowship at the University of Auckland in 1992 was critical in a social sense as much as anything else. I was given a large room on the seventh floor (the top one) of the department of English, where I went "to work" every day to read, research and write as if it were an ordinary job. I lived in Old Government House on the University grounds for most of that year, and in going thus from Wellington to Auckland I moved from a city where I had no literary friends to a city with literary friends. To be able to talk with Wystan Curnow, Roger Horrocks, Tony Green, Michele Leggott, Murray Edmond, and Elizabeth

Wilson was liberating to me. The Fellowship required nothing in particular of the Fellow—it simply gave the recipient time to write on a salary. But it was there that I spoke to a large number of literature classes, gave a talk to the Classical Association, gave a staff seminar on typography, founded the Holloway Press with Associate Professor Peter Simpson and, a couple of years later, set up the magazine *A Brief Description of the Whole World* (1995–1998). When my stint as the Fellow ran out, I applied for and got a job tutoring in the English Department, which to me was extraordinary as I have no educational qualifications of any kind. In 1995, I also convened the first Conference on the History of the Book in New Zealand, on the suggestion of the great scholar D.F. McKenzie. In terms of community participation it was no doubt the most active and stimulating period of my life. Since then, and coming to Australia, my general isolation has kicked in again, and I am no longer involved in literary politics—which is a great relief. I write and send the books to publishers, and my current printing activity is so small (editions of thirty or so copies only) that it barely ripples the surface of things.

KS: I'd like to ask about increment in your work, units of measure, parts and parts-of-parts. As one who has spent years building up words from individual letters in a composing stick, and as a writer capable of thinking in terms of points and picas as well as phonemes and syllables, I'm interested in learning more about how you think through the relationships between the parts of a book and the book as a part of something not necessarily larger than, but perhaps "other" than itself?

AL: I remember once reading someone who said that they write "one word after another" and that nothing is less lyrical than that. But for me, even the most intense, the most romantic lyrics, are written "one word after another." I see myself as a romantic poet, a lyricist, a nature poet, a philosophical poet, a language poet, and why not. Certainly there are what some have called "necessary corrections," where intellectual and cultural swings in another direction become vivid in the works of new generations. And while becoming a technician or craftsman in writing poetry has been very important for me, I still want to be moved and to allow certain modalities of depth of feeling to be exhibited in the poems. Even so, poiesis is paramount. One is a maker—one puts things together, bit by bit, discontinuously, like any child making something out of Lego. The poem is built up from multiple "whole fragments," to use the lovely notion of Ann Lauterbach. I remember with great pleasure seeing Jacques Derrida write that he had no interest or skill in narrative. He didn't like "telling stories," with its hint of lying, and my mother saying to me as a child, "You're not telling stories again are you?" I can't read narratives, don't read novels (maybe one every two or three years). So the piece-by-piece building of the poem is all I really know how to do. The questions are two: Which bit goes next and where does it go? If this is a kind of content and form in the same inkling (I always write poems by hand), then it's a good rendering of what I'm doing when I write. So notions of form and content come after the act of composition and are not considerations about how things are to be thought beforehand. For example, in a recent book, *Zephyros : the book untitled* (Electio Editions, 2007), I had written the poems, then my partner Miriam Morris did five paintings to accompany them in the book, and then I started typesetting. And for all of the poems, their shape changed in the typesetting in response to the paintings, so that composition of the poems and composition in type was, for a few minutes each day, the same "act of composition."

In setting type, the time it takes for one letter to appear after another in the composing stick is a lot longer than the time it takes for one letter to appear after another on the computer screen. In that time, anything can happen. It has something to do with slowing down, from the uninterrupted sound-flow of speech to separating words on the page to handsetting type where every letter, mark of punctuation and word-space is a separate entity. Between the conduct of those entities any worldly event can occur, even one's own and another's death, or lunch or love-making or

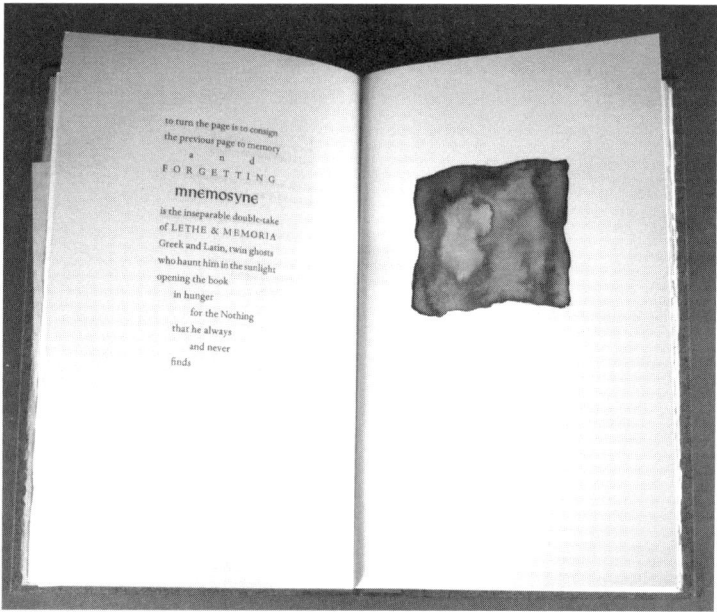

to turn the page is to consign
the previous page to memory
a   n   d
FORGETTING
mnemosyne
is the inseparable double-take
of LETHE & MEMORIA
Greek and Latin, twin ghosts
who haunt him in the sunlight
opening the book
in hunger
for the Nothing
that he always
and never
finds

Alan Loney, *Zephyros : the book untitled* (Electio Editions, 2007), ink drawings by Miriam Morris

a walk in the park. In this sense, what is a word-space? After all, the earliest Greek writing doesn't have them, yet we tend to behave as if word-spaces are the most natural thing in the world. And again, "the world" is where they exist, not in speech. It is even uncommon to hear a clear word-space when reading aloud, however slow one does it (as I do it). We'd have to stretch the notion of silence beyond sense (which never shuts down) to propose that somehow "nothing" happens in the space between written words. It is, as far as I can see, more accurate to say that, instead of "nothing" happening in word-spaces, everything happens in there. The world doesn't stop, and nor do we. And what I am doing in between words and in between letters in the typesetting process is listening—both to the word, the letter and all else one's thoughtful sensorium may experience in those moments. What the word or letter or punctuation mark does is narrow the focus down, and what the space or time between picking up letters does is open out the mind again to anything that comes. It's not all that different from how we switch back and forth from foreground to background in visual perception, a kind of existential dynamic between world and thing, or principle and exemplum, or generality and particular. It's not the terms here that are important, but the to and fro movements between them—between slotting a metallic letter into the composing stick and picking up the next piece of metal and figuring just where it should go. It suggests that experience is as discontinuous a process as is typesetting. And that our experience of greatest awareness is not of either, but of their dynamic in one's own behavior. As a poet, I have little patience with poetics that focus solely on the politics of result. Certainly one wants one's results to be contiguous with one's process, as I do, but I value more than I can say the composer Stravinsky's notion that "poetics is the art of work yet to be done." And the next letter is the piece of metal yet to be picked up from the case, including as in "the world is everything that is the case" of Wittgenstein.

To get back to the other part of your question, I always find, after the piecemeal acts of making in the book, that the finished book is somehow other than I had imagined. As if the whole is never, for me at any rate, simply the sum of the parts I have put together (and sometimes wrestled with). When the printing is done, the sheets are gathered for binding and the binding is completed, there is a sense of "the whole thing" that is not actually inferable from the parts with which one has had such intimate contact over a period of weeks or months. That the entire making process is now over seems to mean that another order of perception is then in place. I'm not talking about quality here—even a poorly manufactured book will be other than its parts in this way. And perhaps that too is a better way of talking about it, that the book as a whole may be *other* than its parts rather than *more* than its parts. For I can certainly imagine a book that might seem *less* than its parts once it is put together. That a bound book may be more than the sum of its parts is thus simply a special case of the book being other than the sum of its parts.

Once made, the place of the book is locatable in two ways. First, it is and always merely one book alongside all the others. In this location it has no special value, and I am yet vividly aware that this view is a determinedly secular one, and this is the view I take. A sacred book can never be merely one book among others, and the rituals around scripting a new copy of the Torah or of the Koran, for instance, attest to that. But I don't have that kind of history or that view of the world. So every book is merely, and absolutely merely, if one could possibly say such a thing, one book among all the others. The second location for a finished book is whatever special place any person or group reserves for it. And I guess my controversial view here is that this special place is chosen for it by the people who so regard it, and not by divine ordinance. And if it is okay for me to value the books I value, then it is okay for anyone and everyone else to value the books they value. The problem occurs when anyone thinks that others should value the books they do and to the same degree and for the same reasons.

The being of entities is not an entity, and the book of books is not a book. If the Bible is taken to be the Book, for example, then this simple rule is violated in a multicultural world. The Book, as I use the term, is neither more nor less than the name for the overall concept of "book" by which we understand any object whether or not it is a book. In this sense, every book is an equal participant in the concept of Book. No book can be any more "Book" than any other book. It is only the special value that I assign to a book that suggests any kind of inequality of one book with another. And for all of us, those "special values" can and do differ dramatically from person to person and group to group, and that is actually the normal state of affairs.

KS: Since scholars like Clive Philpot and Johanna Drucker began writing critically on "artists books" there has been an ongoing desire to define the term as a practice, as an object, and even as a discourse related to, but not the same as "book arts." Even the spelling is a point of contention, as Stefan Klima demonstrates in *Artists Books: A Critical Survey of the Literature* (Granary Books, 1998). It seems to me that an important division between "artists books" and "book arts" is the division between art and craft as well as the artist's conception of the work as an extension of a practice that involves a letterpress, handmade paper, illustrations and quality binding versus the intermediary practice that Dick Higgins and other book artists explored in the 1960s. One of the great challenges of bookmaking, and I mean this in all senses of the words "book" and "making," is the difficult negotiation of craft and concept, object and idea. This may be part of the reason I see more and more books produced by art students who have learned a lot about gluing and folding but whose work seems to fall into the "pretty but pointless" category. Do you make Artists Books? Bookworks? Fine Press Editions? Are you a Book Artist? Publisher? Typographer? Printer?

AL: Yes, I am a printer, a typographer, and I make fine press editions of which I am also the publisher. And no, I have no need to use such language as "bookwork," and I don't make artists books. Living in this part of the world means that I have never seen the works of Dick Higgins and other book artists of the 1960s, and for the most part I am thus extraordinarily ignorant about artists books other than what I read in such authors as Johanna Drucker and Stefan Klima. I have no experience for instance of any book that Drucker writes about in *The Century of Artists' Books* (Granary Books, 1995). In Australia the term "artists book" has become an institutional catch phrase for any book, made on any basis, in which an artist's work is featured, though I need to qualify that by saying that a few people here have been reading Drucker at least with some attention. It has meant that my fine press editions are almost invariably referred to as "artists books," even by people who one would have thought might have made the distinction.

Australia's special problem here is that while there have been many private presses in its history, only a handful of them had any interest in pursuing book crafts to a high level—private presses aplenty but only a handful of fine presses. There are thus many more people here making artists books than there are making fine press editions. One of the major libraries in the state of Victoria put all its purchases of my books in a special category, titled "artists books." Happily, I have managed to talk them out of that, to the point that I am to curate an exhibition of fine press books at that library in 2009, at which there will also be a lecture or two, a seminar, a printed catalog and an essay by yours truly, etc. State libraries, university libraries and major regional galleries have held book exhibitions in recent years, all under the heading of "artists books" and independent of any documentation or scholarship that distinguishes them from other kinds of book. I know this seems overgeneralized, but one major library had a show a couple of years ago of artists books where more than half the exhibits were definitely fine press books, a few were livres d'artiste, and a number of others included unconventional texts and images within an entirely conservative book structure. Of the one hundred or so books on show I think that less than ten would have coincided with Drucker's criteria, in that wonderful phrase of hers, "zone of activity," for an artists book.

This of course leads to a difficult area, an old discussion—one that not many people seem to want to have—about art and craft. It's complex, and I don't know if an interview of this nature is the place to have it, for I would want to spend a lot of time going "all round the subject," probably taking up much more than the rest of the space available. I really met this difficulty for the first time when I edited *New Zealand Crafts* magazine at the end of the '80s, and the issues are real, and I'm not at all sure I have a decent handle on the problem. Many people allude to the problem, but hardly anyone I know of spends any time being as precise about the "relations" between art and craft as Johanna Drucker has spent on the differences between artists books and other sorts of books. On the other hand, I do have a few notions about what sort of terms might be apposite for that discussion and I have seen enough to know it cannot be encompassed by simple assertions like "craft equals teachable skills and art does not."

KS: I won't exhaust you on this subject Alan, but I do find what you've said of great interest. Speaking historically, would you agree that typesetting, for example, is a craft, a trade within an industry that required little imagination, but demanded great speed and accuracy? As I see it, design has become another enterprise altogether, as Tschichold remarked on the commission that became Sabon, "Design has nothing to do with self-expression." To look at it another way, is self-expression a necessary part of a work of art?

AL: One of the great things I learned from doing one year of philosophy, which included logic, at university (in 1963, I think) was that each noun or term, in whatever way it was used by anybody, had a "scope" of usage. It had to do with what one allowed and what one excluded in one's use of the term, and what one allowed in was referred to as its "scope." One could say for instance that the scope of "typesetting" included "craft skills" but excluded "aesthetics of design." Or, one could suggest that skills and design exist on a spectrum on which they fully overlap in the middle but at the outer edges only a small amount of one is included in the other. After all, every act of typography, or typesetting, still has an appearance to which anyone looking at it will respond. Or one might say that all typesetting *is* design, it's just a question of whether it's good design or dreadful. Language, perhaps, separates things out in a seamless world in which everything is implicated in everything else.

If I may focus on the wording of your question for a moment, there is a degree of space and/or movement between "little imagination" (implying some) and "nothing to do with self-expression" (implying none at all). And while "imagination" and "self-expression" are different terms, what I am attending to here is the structure of the proposition. My own preference is to see skills and design, or craft and art, on a spectrum of inclusive meanings in which the degree of each varies in every given case, and neither is ever completely absent. The great Chinese image for this of course is the black and white Yin/Yang symbol, in which there is always a tiny spot of white in the area of the greatest concentration of black, and *vice versa*. Complete separation proffers an absolute duality that the overall philosophical position does not allow. There are many Tschicholdian absolutes in the field of design and typography, his own two contradictory ones being famous enough, but another is Beatrice Warde's "printing should be invisible," where in fact whatever is on the page is never invisible and any mode of typographical arrangement can be seen in contrast with any other mode. So, if I were to state a position on this question, I'd say that there's always at least a "little imagination" in the practice of craft skills, and there's always at least a little dollop of self-expression in design. Is self-expression a necessary part of a work of art? It seems to me that even if one's intention is to eradicate "the self" in one's art, something has to account for the simplicity of that art which does not appear without the agency of a person, and that person has a history, a culture, an education (or lack thereof), a set of experiences, a number of predilections, a cluster of possibilities etc., etc., etc. Art is always at least a function of being human, and in that sense, even if it is that sense alone, something in that art is being expressed about the person who made it, independently of their intentions, and independently of the debates we can have about what it is in any instance.

KS: Thinking of Jackson Mac Low or John Cage, have you ever used chance operations or, in another formal sense, Oulipian constraints in composition? Does indeterminacy play a significant role in your work?

AL: More Oulipian than chance, I suspect, though I have just had to look up "Oulipo" on the Web, a term unknown to me. Some years ago I realized that to break away from the sorts of things that habitually occurred to my rather dogged and obsessive nature, I should seek out writing procedures that both constrained and directed the possibilities for what words might appear on the page. The poem "dear Webern" for instance was made entirely out of phrases taken from the letters of Anton Webern, arranged in two columns on each page in such a way that they could be read both down the columns and across them. On the few occasions when I have read them at readings I have always done both, listening to the way a single phrase acquires different resonance when placed alongside other phrases. The whole poem was structured as thirteen lines down the page (twenty-six phrases) and thirteen pages (twenty-six columns), where a simple decision was taken to use twenty-six, the number of letters in the roman alphabet, as an overall limit to the length of the work. More recently, in the long poem "Mondrian's flowers" one of the pieces there is made up of one phrase from each of the fifty-two poems about flowers in New Zealand poet Ursula Bethell's first book *From a garden in the Antipodes* (1929), and another from phrases from my own writings in which the words "nothing" or "nothingness" appear, and yet another from phrases in newspaper articles about the works of Piet Mondrian.

A more complicated process was that of the poem *The erasure tapes*, (Auckland University Press, 1994) which I characterized at the time as being "an autobiography in which I refused to tell the story of my life." I had collected the erasure ribbons from my old electric typewriter (and you guessed it, there were thirteen of them), which operated by lifting the letters to be erased off the paper and onto the ribbon. Omitting verbal connectives I thus had a string of nouns and verbs which were randomly ordered on each tape. I wrote these strings of words down and took each word in the actual sequence as a kind of hook to fish around in my past, which I took as being from this moment backwards, to see if it latched on to a memory. When it did, I wrote a sentence about that memory containing the word that hooked it, and went on to the next word which would fish something up from another time and another place in my life. The number of words per page was twenty-six times the nine muses—two hundred thirty-four words (and, of course, two plus three plus four equals nine, the muses again).

So, yes, I have used such processes, though not for a while now. I have been under more recent pressure to speak "from the heart" as they say, after the death of my son. But those more radical procedures have been incredibly important to me, and just because I am not doing them now does not mean I have rejected them in any way—another one could easily pop up tomorrow and I'd be happy with that. On the other hand, while these procedures are fairly radical, I have never really thought that my content (if one may so arbitrarily separate such out for a moment) was particularly radical, even in New Zealand terms (I'm thinking here of Wystan Curnow, Tony Green, Judi Stout, Michele Leggott) and I increasingly find myself out of kilter with a great deal of contemporary writing. I'm still trying to catch up with Sappho! And Keats and George Oppen and Herakleitos and Wittgenstein and Kafka and Heidegger's *Being and Time* and Han Shan and Muso Soseki and Ursula Bethell and Mary Stanley and Gertrude Stein's wonderful *The Geographical History of America* (equal to Wittgenstein's *Tractatus*) and Jane Ellen Harrison and Joseph Joubert and Maurice Blanchot and the Buddhist *Heart sutra*, and other writers in the Zen and Taoist traditions. The list isn't complete, but this is where my attention has been directed for some years now.

Indeterminacy seems to be a tricky metaphor in poetry. I'm not sure that Keats' negative capability is the same thing. The original idea was that one cannot measure the velocity and the location of a thing at the same time. It isn't a matter of not having a sophisticated enough measuring device, it is that those two measurements can never be simultaneous *in principle*. The other side of it is in the description of a photon: in some experiments it behaves as a particle, and in other experiments it behaves as a wave, and these two results are always consistent, and the measurement of one always precludes the other. Negative capability is more I think closely aligned with the New Zealand poet Kendrick Smithyman's "Open, to experience that satisfying/feeling of what goes unexplained." At this point, I flail around in the dark, because I'm not aware one can make use of indeterminacy beforehand—one can only discover it after the fact of writing. But maybe this is in turn because I am not aware that I have ever had a kind of writing program worked out beforehand: "what I'm trying to achieve in my work is…"—I can't answer this question. Mostly, I have no idea what sort of thing I will write next. To extrapolate from Olson's, and I'm sorry I can't find the quote or its exact rendering, "we are as we find out we are," I write as I find out I write. I have always been unable (so it's maybe a fault, flaw, inadequacy of mind) to travel from description to prescription, however accurate the analysis.

KS: And yet I have the sense that procedure and indeterminacy don't play the same role in the books you've printed—or maybe that's the question. Letterpress has an intrinsic resistance to identical reproduction, and as an aspiring printer I'm constantly monitoring variants when working on an edition. A printed sheet may be over- or under-inked, a serif may chip, or the weight of the impression might change in the course of an edition. I want to preserve the handmade qualities of the printed book, while at the same time there are certain inconsistencies that I don't consider part of the art. I call these "errors," but I would also be willing to think of them as a kind of typographic indeterminacy that I find fascinating as a scholar of other people's work, discouraging when it comes to my own. Brad Freeman, for example, was one of the first artists to use the offset press, which as you know was designed for speed and to do away with variations, to improvise much in the way that many people are using the letterpress.

As works of art, contemporary fine press editions are underestimated in terms of their monetary value and I attribute that, in part, to the question of originality (and here I'm thinking of Walter Benjamin's often misunderstood essay *Art in the Age of Mechanical Reproduction*). Is the book printed by hand necessarily an original work of art? And if so, how do you define "copy" as either a noun or verb?

AL: I suppose what one does with notions like indeterminacy in poetry is let them in. If they occur in the poems, let them stand. In a sense, this is for others to elucidate, but there is so little written about my poetry (my printing gets nearly all of the documentary attention) that I often still wonder what it is that I am doing. That said, there is at least in principle plenty of evidence in the accounts of the work of others that indeterminacy is a factor in puns, resonances, echoes, multiple meanings, slippery propositions, etc., almost as a normal state of affairs in the elucidations of recent (last century) poetry—"here is nowhere near where there is," for example, from *The erasure tapes*. Derrida, in *Cinders*, begins with a notion of what he calls the "polylogue," in which a single set of words has more than one possible meaning, and in which each meaning requires a different vocal articulation for it to be heard. Both he and Blanchot, by the way, seemed to know nothing at all about the history of the physical book over the last century nor anything of the formal properties of European and American contemporary poetry over the same period.

On printing, it has often intrigued me that some folks have talked about the possibility of "a single copy." Getting pedantic for a moment, this phrase implies either that there is an "original" somewhere of which "this" is a single copy, or that there is no "original" but there are two versions of which one is a copy of the other. In both cases, there are two objects involved. If there is just one object, say, a book which does not reproduce anything outside itself, then I'm not sure we have a standard piece of nomenclature for it. I've seen "unique copy" used, but each of an edition of a thousand copies could be a "unique copy." Some of my editions contain images that do not replicate anything outside or prior to the edition, so the term "copy" can only refer to other books within the edition. Then, how exact does one want the word "copy" to be? Some printmakers, for instance, are meticulous in ensuring that each item in their editions is practically indistinguishable from all the others. If I followed that precept, I know I couldn't afford to buy the amount of paper required to permit the amount of wastage that would result. As it is, I use forty sheets to get thirty copies, and if that means one or two "imperfect" sheets get into the edition, then that's what happens. Fidelity and precision are not necessarily interchangeable terms, like the "spirit and the letter," say, of translation, or of the law. And "craft" is not necessarily interchangeable with "technical perfection"—look at traditional Chinese or Japanese tea bowls to see that "perfection" is not necessarily technical. I agree with you totally that we can look at our own work with a different sense of what's permissible from that with which we look at the work of others. But then we are not just "looking" at the work we are doing, we are doing it, and the hands and body are implicated there in ways not available to the eye alone. Craft at the least has something to do with doing something *well*, just as Plato said "Orphics used *soma* for the body, referring to *sodzesthai* to keep guard." Another way of saying it is that "body" and "craft" are not neutral terms.

If we make books in editions, however small, I wonder if there's a question to be asked about what is the work. In terms of the labor involved, the work is the whole edition. But I wonder if there has ever been a commentary by a critic on the whole of an edition. Reviews of fine books or artists books in editions are invariably based upon the experience of a single item. Printmaking has the same pattern. When someone buys a print or a book from an edition, what have they bought in terms of the whole working process of the making? Pricing also participates in this. If one sells the whole edition, then the price of the work, as a whole process of making, is the price of one copy times the edition number. At that rate, one could be well paid for one's effort, but most book and print editions do not sell out, and then one's return on one or two copies does not look or feel particularly nourishing at all. Of course the hard reality of commercial life is not interested in questions of this sort—if you only sell a handful of copies, then "welcome to the real world" is a common and ready response from the trade. But if we want to ask questions about the language in which we operate as printers or bookmakers, then perhaps our current nomenclature could do with some examination in this regard.

"Is the book printed by hand necessarily a work of art?" Well, if "art" and "craft" are relative rather than absolute categories, and the spectrum of the scope of terms I mentioned before is relevant, then the answer is "yes," even if, in a given case, the level of "art" may be poor or negligible, and even if there was no intention of art by the maker. It's less, it seems to me, of an ontological question than an operational one. It might be, in other words, perfectly legitimate to treat any handprinted book as if it were a work of art, whatever the outcome of the discussion or analysis.

KS: In your essay on Bruno Leti*, you draw some distinctions between forms of collaboration. On one hand, there are those who are directly involved in the evolution of a book (poet and painter, for example) and on the other there are those who are employed to provide a particular service (letterpress printing, screen printing, papermaking, bookbinding, etc.). I imagine that your observations on Leti's work may also lend themselves to your own. While distinctions between words and images are useful to a certain end, it is equally useful to remember that words, insofar as they are graphic, are images, from Werkman to Warde. Once a typographer puts a new face on the market, she loses control over the use and abuse of her letters. They can say anything. Thinking specifically of your collaborations with Max Gimblett, I would like to know how typefaces factor in your collaborations, which is to ask in a long-winded way, if and how you would invite the typographer into your dialogue?

AL: Looking at that essay I wish now that I had read Johanna Drucker as carefully as I did later. What I don't think I took into account there was Drucker's notion that the artists book includes a refiguring of binding processes, where Bruno's work, which I still think of as artists books, generally uses conventional fine binding processes, even if the materials used in some of them may not be so familiar. On the other hand, I am interested that some of his books are painted on the outside of the binding, so what is generally not touched or handled, the artwork, has to be

* *Bruno Leti: Survey, Artists, Books 1982–2003* (Geelong Art Gallery, 2003)

Alan Loney & Max Gimblett, *Fishwork* (The Holloway Press, 2009)

handled just to get the book open. Some of Max's sketchbooks and journals are like that too, so if you put a slipcase on them to protect that "external" marking, then either of those artists are then quite capable of splashing paint onto the slipcase, and then you'd have to protect that. You could end up with an indefinite number of protective casings that have themselves to be protected—a nice idea, but eventually you'd have to dismantle your studio in order to take it anywhere. It also raises the prospect of having a work of multiple protective coverings or bindings inside which there is no book at all, just the cases.

What you say about typefaces is interesting. Generally I have never had enough access, or enough money, to have real choices about what types I use. My present printery is also too tiny to accommodate a range of text types, so I just have one text type and a small range of display types, some of them only in one size, with which I have to do everything. It has meant that I think about typography in any book differently from the way I could if I were able to consider each book as a fresh occasion for choosing the type. Even those notions of choosing a type "appropriate" to the subject matter have not been available to me. So, while my restricted types have made me canny about what I can do with limited resources, I haven't thought about the shapes of a type in relation to the shapes of images which may appear alongside them, or the shape of the book in which they might appear. One's thought, then, restricted by one's resources.

One place where all your notes about collaboration, word and image, type and matter, etc., are writ beautifully, to my mind, is the Peter Koch *Parmenides* (Editions Koch, 2004), in which the work of poet, wood engraver, digital type designer and stone letter cutter, type designer and punch-cutter, printer, binders (two of 'em), came together in a most extraordinary way. The book about this, with essays by each of those involved, is *Carving the Elements: a Companion to the Fragments of Parmenides*. I have not seen the limited edition, but it is one for which a new type was cut in metal by Dan Carr at Golgonooza Type Foundry, based on a previous letter digitally designed by Christopher Stinehour. *Carving the Elements* is the most exciting and detailed account I have ever read about the birth of a book—not just the physicality of its making, but the thinking of those involved about the book in general and about the basis of their crafts.

KS: In *Meditatio : the printer printed : manifesto* (Cuneiform Press, 2004) you discuss the overwhelming availability of digital fonts and allude to some of the chaos the personal computer has instilled upon everyday typographic practices. The computer has certain advantages, like never being "out of sorts," but then again "limits are what any of us are inside of" according to Olson. Do you consider letterpress printing and design superior to digital composition combined with offset printing?

AL: Personally, I like the bite of metal type into handmade paper but for many people of a later generation, that bite is kind of nice but a bit old-fashioned. My own computer skills are seriously confined to Word, a word processing program, not a typesetting or typographic one, and I have never used anything like Quark or PageMaker or InDesign, yet there are programs which many commercial designers use which are capable of considerable typographic nuance and sophistication. And now of course such programs can be available to the handprinter because of the photopolymer plate, which allows one's typesetting to be done solely on the computer, exposed to the plate and printed on the handpress. And a number of fine printers are doing this, as did Inge Bruggeman at Textura Printing in Portland, Oregon, when she printed my *Mondrian's flowers* (2002)for Steve Clay at Granary Books. I'm not sure it's a question of one being superior to the other. Digital type printed offset is done on very smooth, coated papers; relief type in the hand or cylinder press is done on less smooth, even textured papers, and both processes are capable of the highest standards—maybe it's simply a matter of "horses for courses" as they say. The great value of the photopolymer plate is it keeps the availability of type going for printers for whom the resources of metal typesetting are shrinking worldwide. At that point, the question is what typesetting program is one using. If the one being used can't kern, and you can't on my Word program, then you're not getting the best out of the process. For me, the sheer cost of digital typesetting programs is prohibitive, so, if I go to photopolymer, then I have only Word to go by. But I will keep buying Dante as a text type from Winifred and Michael Bixler in New York when I need fresh supplies. As it happens I have a good quantity on hand because they set a prose text for me which I am not now going to print, and my small type pages and small poems mean the type will last a good while.

KS: I'd like to ask now about "the book to come." I'm thinking of Blanchot (loosely), your own immediate ambitions and projects as a printer and writer, or perhaps more conceptually, your thoughts on the fate and future of the Book?

AL: Immediate plans? I've now reached a stage as printer where I no longer print the texts of others. Recent events in my life have led to a questioning of what is it I am doing this for. Ideally I'd write and not print at all now, but the economics of life don't allow it. I'm on an age pension, which is quite small, and I need extra to simply live in Melbourne. But I print only my own writing, with images by a small group of artists who are close friends and whose work I love, and of course that of my partner Miriam Morris, who is a professional musician as well as a painter. Our next book together is *Music of the Spheres*, where once again, as with *Zephyros*, she will do original paintings throughout the edition. I really like William Everson's remark that "…the richest thing I can do is to write a poem, and the next is to print it."

"The book to come," of course is tricky. While I thoroughly accept the need for the recent valorization of the artists book, it does cloud the issue for someone like me whose "making book" processes are profoundly text-based, and will remain so for the rest of my printerly life. It is easy to resent some of those valorizations when they come at the expense or down-grading of the "mere" fine press book and "mere" levels of craft. I would have hoped those axes had been ground quite away by now, but they do keep popping up. My own happy involvements in collaborations with artists bookmaker Bruno Leti are continuing, and I have no sense that such work is any less than the work of my press books—it is all part and parcel of my life as a printer and poet.

On the other hand, it's getting clearer to me that, for many artists bookmakers, the word "book" is becoming more and more stretched so it's hard to see how that term stays whole when applied to both artists book and press book. I am tending to think, though I'm sure others will shoot me down, that, as the terms "paperback" and "press book" really refer to different things, so "artists book" and "press book" do likewise, and the modalities of assessment applicable to one are not fully applicable to the other. Historically, press books had an impact on the design of commercial books prior to the Second World War. This is no longer so. The technologies of first offset printing and then digital printing have become autonomous to what they were designed for, and press books now have their own very separate life, values and discourse, and likewise for commercial books. Artists books are a recent development more in art than in the book, and while I can see them having an impact on the press book they have no observable impact on the commercial book. So long as the press book is text-based, as mine are, and the artists book is art based, and my books are not even though there's art in all of them, then the modes of talk appropriate to both of them will remain very different, or so it seems to me. Perhaps the very word "book" complicates the discussion in ways that would not be so complicated if the term was not used of artists books at all—I don't know. Maybe it's simply that it's hard enough as it is to have my own work validated in the face of the current dominance of artists books in the general conversation, especially when so many press books are so much better as what they are than so many artists books are as what they are. Sour grapes? Possibly, but then working at this distance from the "centers" makes it all the harder to survive.

So how might one think of "the book to come?" The trope about the book being replaced by the computer should by now be well buried, as the whole printing and publishing industry as well as artists have utilized the computer in spreading and enlarging opportunities for the book beyond anything that was imagined when the trope was first posited. Yet, I can't see ahead, and have no idea what might emerge next outside the simplicity that the more people there are on the planet, the more of everything there is and the more chances there are for novel occasions. However much the artists book has extended the possibilities for artists, I don't believe that it has extended the notion of "book" at all, and that, however appalling this may seem to be in the face of the innovative, the ground-breaking, the boundary-crossing, the transgressive intentions or assertions of anyone, the codex remains one of the most doggedly conservative and conventional technologies of all human activity, whatever means are developed or employed to make them.

[2007]

Mary Laird
Quelquefois Press & The Perishable Press Limited

Mary Laird has published letterpress books since 1969 as Quelquefois Press and as partner in The Perishable Press Limited from 1969–1984. She received her MFA in printmaking from UW Madison and loves teaching letterpress; her ricochets include San Francisco State University, Kala Institute in Berkeley, Naropa University, and the San Francisco Center for the Book, where rumor has it, editions of forty chapbooks are cobbled together and printed in a day with six itinerant devils.

She uses a Vandercook Universal I for all the letterpress. Her latest edition of seven includes paintings on etchings, drawing, hand sewing, washes and the like, marrying her love of color and nonverbal with the word. "To paint and to print, that is the answer…" to badly paraphrase the Old Bard. Her production style is slow and ornery so she works best alone. The Bixler's Type Foundry has set many of her books for which she is most grateful. Poetry, jazz, painting, drawing, the mystics of all traditions and participating in long silent retreats all over the country lend meaning to her life and inspiration to her work; her books may be found in many collections across the country and in London. She has three grown children, and lives in Berkeley with her husband John Malork.

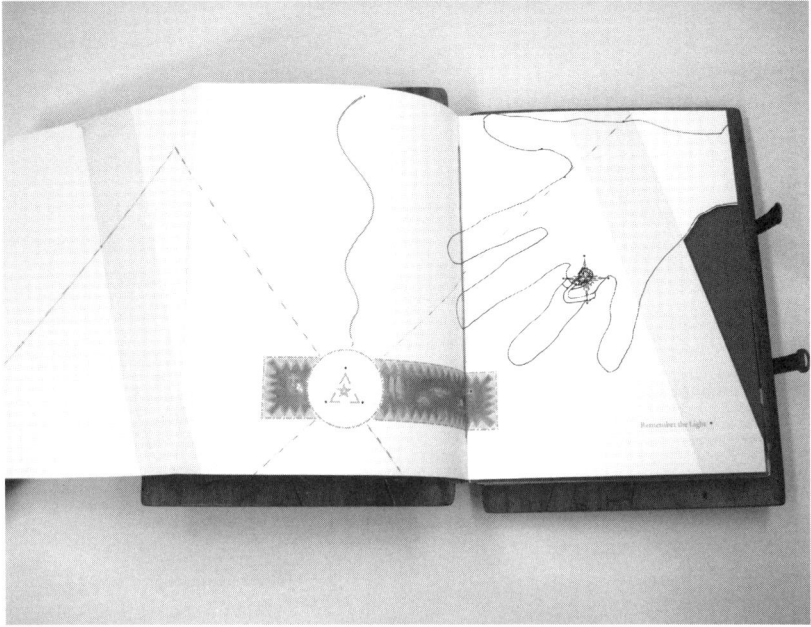

Mary Laird, *Remember the Light* (Quelquefois Press, 2005)

KS: Perhaps I could begin at the beginning, so to speak, by asking about your earliest associations and affinities for books. For example, were there books in the home where you grew up? Did you write or keep scrapbooks as a kid? Who were some of the first writers and artists that enlivened your imagination or got you thinking about books as an exploratory medium? I know, for example, that Robert Duncan and Jonathan Williams treasured their libraries from childhood, and I think that there are traces of that ongoing affinity in their mature work.

ML: When I was growing up in Wauwatosa, Wisconsin, a suburb of Milwaukee, we had a whole room upstairs dedicated as "library." In it were editions of Dickens, John Burroughs, Cervantes—complete with etchings—Jane Austen, Thackeray, and Samuel Clements, to name a few. They were all from my paternal grandfather Arthur Gordon's turn-of-the-century collection. One memorable tome on the world religions, published in 1893, featured an etching of Muhammad—which, as you know, is forbidden! Arthur Gordon was a student at Cornell in Ithaca, New York back then, having made his way from Charlottetown, Prince Edward Island, Nova Scotia. His father, the Honorable David Laird, ran a newspaper on the Island and later negotiated treaties with the First Nations People in the Northwest Territories of Canada. So, the books were my legacy—all those leather-bound, small print, gold-stamped volumes! I always admired my grandfather who taught Greek and Latin at the University in Madison and took trips to Europe and Greece.

In the attic I also set up all the antiques, which were covered with sheets, and I used to pretend I was crossing the ocean on great boats, with all the aristocracy and educated folks! We had beautiful turn-of-the-century china and clothes from Paris. It was a child's great fantasy! In junior high I had the opportunity to have the best teacher in my life—William Brueske, an art teacher who inspired me to pursue all I believed in. Period. From silverpoint to encaustics, ceramics, oil painting, puppetry, mechanical perspective, ice sculpture, silver casting. We did everything. Art history. Practicum. Everything except books. I look back and I smile.

I read a great deal as a child. I was a regular at the library. I associated reading with birds and expanse. Freedom. Escape. Totality. Expression. Vastness. Creativity. I loved Beverly Butler books, romantic and historical. I loved how she could describe everything, even though she was blind. I thought about all our human limitations and how we go beyond them in the allness, the nothingness. What is beyond eternity, I used to wonder when I was eleven. I still have no answer.

When I was almost nineteen, I met a wonderful bookmaker named Walter Hamady who set type and wrote beautiful poems and I fell in love. He was also a professor; I was his student. We got married. I learned how to make books, to make paper. I learned so many things. I grew up. We had three children. We printed ninety-three editions of books together over fifteen years. We had differences, but my interests remained: I was still seeking vastness, space… the capacity of the human soul to encompass unspeakable things, great, glorious and all-encompassing. Eventually I got divorced and went to graduate school, getting my master of fine arts in printmaking in Madison.

I moved to California in 1988. Around 1990 I bought Andrew Hoyem's proof press—one of them, at any rate. I still have it. I don't print many books, nor quickly, but I love the process, the entire process. I love the setting, printing, binding. I love the designing. I love the interaction.

KS: The first book of yours that I remember reading was *The Eggplant Skin Pants*. Was that your first, and could you tell me a little bit about how it was conceived and constructed?

ML: *Eggplant Skin Pants* came out in 1972. I spent nine months working on pen and ink drawings in my room upstairs at the farm. I wrote the poems sometime between 1967, when we met, and 1971, two years after we married. I chose the paper, Hosho, because of its transparency. The way the images came through the paper and created shadows was of interest to me. So I did the whole book, except the binding. I suppose that means the design, setting, and printing. I don't recall sewing the book, rather that we shipped it off to New York City where it was bound with the wonderful blind stamping on the cover. It was a bit of an adventure for me, as it was the first distributed book I had printed, but it was not the first one I did. *An Everyday Celebration* was my first—a chapbook with horribly cut wood engravings after our trip to Portugal on our honeymoon. If I recollect rightly, there were fewer than fifty copies of that one.

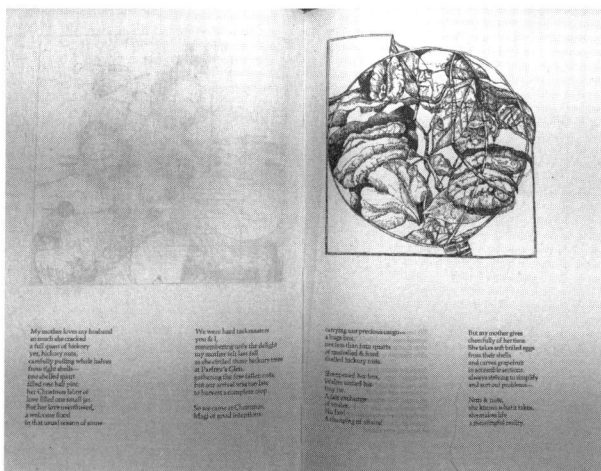

Mary Laird, *The Eggplant Skin Pants* (The Perishapble Press, 1973)

On *Eggplant* I ran into incredible difficulties with the fine lines in the drawings. We had magnesium or zinc plates made of the drawings, which filled in almost right away. Actually the line quality was quite poor on the plates; the delicacy of the drawings was lost in the process. So we had them remade and had somewhat better clarity, but far short of the drawings. Lesson number one: do not use crow quill pen point drawings (interesting, because now that would not be a problem with polymer). I had fun making the drawings, especially putting a hat on a bald eagle, and using *Gray's Anatomy* for the drawing about eating abalone. I also discovered that I did not have the capacity to become a medical illustrator!

KS: Did you identify with the artists and artisans you knew when you lived in Wisconsin? Who were they and what were they up to? Did your move to the West Coast have any direct bearing on the evolution of your work?

ML: I recall someone looking at my books and saying, "Oh, Perishable Press clone!"

It's hard to deny such a statement, since I was Perishable Press with Walter Hamady for fifteen years. So, my joint work with him for all those years was just that—joint work. We worked with poets whose writing appealed to us. We made the paper, set and printed the books, and kept most of the bindings simple. He did all the printing except on my authored books, and I did most of the other work. Division of labor. I was inspired at that time by the work of other graduates who took classes in Madison. Kathy Kuehn and Pati Scobey, to name two, are visual artists who took to the printing press with elegance and enthusiasm. I loved their styles—then and now—their integration of art, word, and page. They both have such strong artistic statements to make, their life/ spiritual force predominating. They both work with poets and artists and bring a *joie de vivre* to a craft often associated with tight precision and rigidity. Their buoyancy and creativity combined with their mad relief rolled etchings drew me up into their stratosphere. Kathy's ability to conjure up really fine, elegant and appropriate bindings for any given text continues to amaze me.

In terms of the West Coast, I had heard disparaging things about printmakers when I was in the Midwest, things like "California printmakers take perfectly good paintings and smash them through an etching press to create a monotype, mostly decorative in purpose." But when I took up a residency at Kala Institute in Berkeley, it was the earthquake, not monotypes, that influenced me most. The day I was drawing on hard ground in my apartment, at basement level in Albany, the quake of '89 swung my hanging plant to and fro, dropped a chunk of freeway onto the bridge and caused many houses in the Marina District of San Francisco to sink into the quasi quicksand of their fabricated foundations.

Tornados influenced my prints before the quake; the one in '84 wiped out the town of Barneveld, eight miles from Mt. Horeb, Wisconsin, ten days after I moved into a duplex there with my children during my divorce. We hid in the cellar and listened to what sounded like a roaring train overhead. Or the high winds of 2001, when sixty trees were ripped to toothpicks. The barn collapsed, and the outhouse and pond raft were uprooted and tossed into a field while I cowered behind a heavy sofa in a friend's bermed boathouse in the sticks of Hollandale. So for deep influence, read "Natural Disasters." I suppose it's my penchant for drama, and nothing does it better than Mother Nature. About the time of Hurricane Katrina, I had finished a painting of a former hurricane weather mass. In my book, *Remember the Light*, which I have been working on for over fifteen months, there is a signature wrapped in Mylar with a hurricane photocopied on two sides. In the etching I was working on in '89, I wrote in Tibetan (which I still remembered then), "How's the weather." So I guess I have John Muir and his escapades up pine trees in storms with his pocketful of tea and oatmeal in my Scottish gene pool psyche. I love the outdoors.

I also love contrasts of chaos and order, life and death. Symbols of sun, moon, lightning—the elements (earth, air, fire, water) all work their way into my poetry, drawing, etching, and binding. I'm deeply engaged in pursuit of the alchemical process: light, evanescence, and our temporary existence here. Lest that sound too pretentious, the age-old question, "Why are we here, what is it all about?"

Back to the West Coast! I find myself hanging out with the Sufis and Buddhists. And agnostic poets. I spend as much time as I can going on silent retreats. From that process I write down dreams. From the dreams and from observing nature I draw, paint, and write. I love to travel and used to try to learn the language of the country I would visit, but after Tibet I gave up on that one. I had studied Tibetan for ten weeks, an intensive written and spoken class for Nepal-bound students. I was only going to be in China and Tibet for three weeks. In Tibet for only nine days! Nevertheless, the trip deeply influenced my love of mountains, the inner life and my thoughts about the persistence of life amidst enormous difficulties. And now I have finally printed up the poems I wrote there, which are included, as are the etchings I did during the earthquake, in this current, tiny edition of seven books.

KS: What about travel?

ML: My trip to Jerusalem in 1999 got me started on painting icons. I was deeply moved by visiting the Monastery of St. Jean du Désert, thirty minutes from the city; here six Russian Orthodox monks repaired old icons and painted new ones. One of them had worked at the Louvre in Paris. He demonstrated grinding up rubies and lapis for color. *I have to do that*, I thought to myself. So when Vladislav Andrejev of the Prosopon School of Iconology in New York State came to San Francisco, I took the icon class four times: twice with him and twice with his son, Dimitri. I try to incorporate some of these painting techniques into my books. I was surprised and delighted to learn that the Sufis and the Orthodox

Russians share a great love of light and its manifestation. Having been raised Baptist, with a minister who later became a Unitarian, I am always happy to see how my past and present come together in nuanced ways. Nothing spectacular on the outside, but subtly revealing on the inner. So I am always grateful for revelation that occurs through the arts, nature and personalities.

Oh yes, and craft! My maternal grandfather was a cabinet maker. I thought about this while I hand planed those cherry and maple boards for covers for this latest book, and carved bas-reliefs of my hands into the inside covers; I felt the presence of my grandfather. I should also mention the wonderful artist and binder Laura Wait, in Steamboat Springs, Colorado, who kindly shared her studio with me for four days, teaching me how to plane the wood and drill the covers and to make the prototype for this edition. When I visited Sheridan, Wyoming, I came across two incredible ostrich skins, lavender and teal—colors I couldn't resist. They will serve as the outer covers for some of my drop spine boxes housing *Remember the Light*. I really enjoy the bookbinding process. Filling in the hole where the tail was, with a different tad of leather, drawing attention to it… I like that! Life has holes. How we smooth over the rough spots—that makes it worthwhile to me. Perfection is elusive. May it stay that way!

KS: Indulge me in a flashback: Some years ago I enrolled in a printing course through the continuing education program at the Rhode Island School of Design. The studios were situated between the river and the bottom of a great hill on the East Side of Providence. I would occasionally look up from my tinkering and see students working on computers through a glass partition at the far end of the studio. One day, during a break, one wandered out from behind his monitor and asked what we were doing with these "machines." I explained what letterpress was, and we started talking. I asked him what he was studying at Rhode Island School of Design—of course, typography!

Now I'm teaching typography, and students do most of their work behind the monitor on the computer. Classes in the printshop are classic field days—a break from everyday work. Could you talk about your relationship to new media and old in your work? Also, the first generation of computer-mediated children has come of age, and some of them are involved in typography and artists books. Your thoughts on the future of the book and the work of emerging printers and artists?

ML: Currently my husband, John, is taking a Dreamweaver class on building web pages. He has been taking classes four to six hours a day, five days a week for ten weeks now and there are some light bulbs exploding! But when he shows me the Dreamweaver code, my eyes cross. I live in another century. For years I sat on my high horse about giclees (Iris prints or fancy expensively-made reproductions of original artwork), probably the same high horse as polymer plates but I think we're talking apples and oranges. Polymer plates on the letterpress produce letterpress! Giclees are reproductions. Both modern, both made my teeth grate, at least at first. I really didn't want to take on the new technologies.

But let me explain with another digression. In my "Book in a Day" workshop at the Center for the Book in San Francisco, seven folks give up their time and money to make a four-up (half-title, title, text and colophon) "book" with a two-color cover and blank endsheets. We print an edition of forty copies. It's just an exercise for them to set some lines of type, lock it up, ink the rollers, run the paper through the press, fix some typos, print the forty, distribute the type and clean the press with Crisco before a final wipe of roller wash. The Crisco is the new technology, although any brand trans-fat will do. Kudos to Columbia School of Printing in Chicago where I saw it done first! Most of my students come from graphic design backgrounds. They know new technologies but they want to get their hands dirty. Usually one day with the old and somewhat abused type is enough for many of them to give up on the metal and to try the polymer plate making class. After all, they want to design their text, use fonts they love, and in many cases, use multiple colors when they print it. Plus they want the text to come out looking good; if the embossed look [rolling of eyes] is in their cross hairs they can apply pressure without worrying they are rounding the shoulders of their type, or worse, breaking off the serifs.

Marrying old and new technology in my art has been a challenge. I consciously tried to do this in *Remember the Light*, where I printed and painted on etchings. I used acrylic, watercolor, egg tempera, and Prismacolor pencils. Areas have been excised; one page has a blanket-stitched circle. I photocopied on acetate and sprayed it with Krylon. Several poems were laser printed: one on acetate with acrylic under the printing, one on commercial "column" paper. I mounted letterpress furniture type-high and printed it; the shape echoed shadows falling on the table toward sundown. The book is sewn eighth-century style, on linen cords inserted into boards. I am constructing leather boxes using ostrich, Niger goatskin, deer and elk skins. The book has brass ring and post closures on straps. And yes, I do own a digital camera. Mostly I don't know how it operates. So maybe tomorrow I will want to learn Quark or the most current computer book-design class, but I doubt it. You will have to ask others about the future of the book. My friend, Gillian Boal at the Bancroft Library, tells me libraries are turning into museums. This made me pause, but I had to ask myself when was the last time I was in a library—when I was trying to sell a book was the answer. That was a shock! I buy books at stores or online and rarely use the public library.

I think books will continue to enthrall and fulfill people. Nothing will take their place. A flat computer screen and an index of movies to watch on the TV, all those cell phones and excitements in the hurry-hurry mod... fun for a while perhaps, but not soul fulfilling. Holding that book, and daydreaming, reading in a tree or a hammock... reading at a coffee shop... these are "ah" experiences. Slow and enjoyable. Setting type is slow. Folding the paper is slow. If Slow Food has made a comeback, let's watch those headlines for Slow Books!

I think there is a wonderful abundance of emerging young artists and poets who bring, and will continue to bring, incredible vitality to the form of the book. Many of them are using the dinosaur letterpress machines. Just wait! They will surprise us all with their integrity, delight, originality, and prowess.

[2005]

Jonathan Greene
Gnomon Press

Jonathan Greene started writing in the late 1950s. His first book, *The Reckoning*, was published by Robert Kelly's Matter Press in 1966. He now has thirty-seven books to his credit, the latest the third edition of *Gists Orts Shards* (a commonplace book) and *Afloat* (poems) both published by Broadstone Press.

In 1965, he started Gnomon Press, an independent small press, with sixty-six titles published under its imprint in the fields of literature and photography.

The genesis of his interest in fine printing and typography started in December of 1961 when he met Victor and Carolyn Hammer during a trip to Kentucky. That friendship continued with Greene moving to Kentucky from San Francisco in the Fall of 1966. He worked for a number of years as a book designer and production manager for the local university press. He then continued to design books for Alfred A. Knopf, The Ecco Press, Graywolf, Copper Canyon, The Jargon Society, Duke University Press, New Directions, Anvil Press, Rizzoli, Ten Speed Press, The University Press of Kentucky, Broadstone Books, North Atlantic Books, Pressed Wafer, Green Shade, and other numerous small presses.

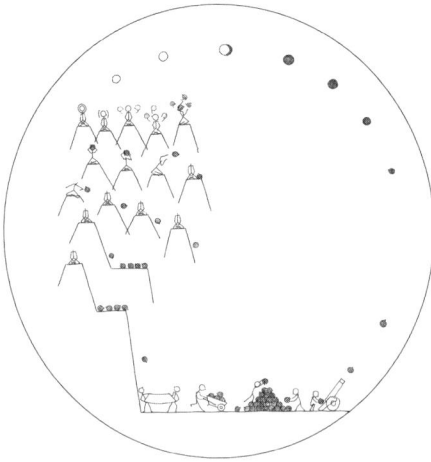

Frontispiece from Audrey Robinson, *Foibles* (Gnomon Press, 2012)

KS: Jonathan, I realize that you're especially busy these days, so I want to thank you for taking the time to discuss your work with me. I understand that you're currently working on three books. Although I'm tempted to begin this interview at the beginning, perhaps we can talk first about these projects in order to give our readers a detailed sense of what you're doing today, the considerations on your mind now with regard to book design and typography.

JG: Actually, one of those three projects shipped to the printer yesterday—always a weight off my shoulders. Looking back I see this project took a little over five months to get to the printer. A 208-page book by a Zen Master who now has a retreat center in the Kentucky mountains, quite a beautiful spot with a traditional meditation hall with an azure tile roof. The second is a book of cartoon-like graphics that I have to wrestle with, figure out how to scan and make into a viable looking print-on-demand book. The third is a book of poems by a Bulgarian poet who lives here now. This versus the Zen project is a study in contrast. The Zen Master is thankful for my design and editing work, and though he had some input as to shade of color of the dust jacket, he mostly let me just do my work. The poet started her own press two years ago and is highly opinionated and seems intrusive into my design choices: on the cover she does not like my color scheme and has suggested one that I and the publisher do not like as well, etc. This happens. Typography is "applied art," and as they say: "opinions are like assholes, everyone has one." And to further the degradation of our times: now politicians think opinions are equal to facts, religious zealots think the Bible or Koran are the source of all truth, scientific knowledge be damned.

Typography might be caught in the nets of evolutionary development where we might be in a dumbing-down phase just at the point that with OpenType fonts and InDesign and Quark we can produce really good-looking books—and we get e-books with no typographical finesse at all. Likewise, in music where CDs can now really sound wonderful, we get the onslaught of mp3 which is a dumbing down in quality.

KS: As a letterpress printer who was involved with book design before the revolution in desktop publishing, do you feel that you approach the computer differently than those who were trained on the screen?

JG: Well, I feel having been "raised" in the days of Linotype and Monotype gives me a grounded knowledge of type that those younger don't have. Strange to me that now everyone knows the word "font," which was not true earlier. And it had a different meaning when one bought foundry type "by the font" instead of "by the sort"—in the first instance the foundry had determined in handsetting you would need many more vowels than you would need the letter "x" and letters with low usage, so they would send you a font predetermined on a normal usage, and then if you needed more of particular letters you were running out of, you ordered them separately ("by the sort") in something akin to a shopping list.

I should give you some background, for my keen interests in poetry and printing were guided by the serendipity of mentoring friendships. Because I needed some "space" from an affair I was having, in the winter of 1961–62 I visited Alan Shavzin, a poet friend who took a job teaching philosophy at the University of Kentucky. During that visit I met Victor and Carolyn Hammer. They, unlike the general population, had a high regard for poets. They took me out to lunch and gave me a small essay book that they had printed, *Prometheus* by Thomas Merton. I am not sure I had ever really looked at a hand-printed book before, though later I found there was one James Joyce limited edition in my family's library. Victor was probably the last living person to cut punches of his own typefaces by hand and then sell them to the public, the whole process. I have a flyer somewhere for American Uncial that you could order directly from him.

The friendship with the Hammers continued by correspondence. I was a student at Bard and there Ted and Renée Weiss published the *Quarterly Review of Literature* which just happened to publish special issues on two poets—Hölderlin and Leopardi—that Victor was especially interested in, so I sent those to the Hammers. At one point they lent me their copy of *The Encyclopedia of Type Faces* by Jaspert, Berry, and Johnson. I studied that book diligently and tried to identify every typeface in the books I had. At the same time, during my second stint living in San Francisco (1965–66), I hung out at the rented space in a dead-end street where Graham Mackintosh did his printing and I learned much from him. In my earlier 1963 stint I had also known Andrew Hoyem and Dave Haselwood at Auerhahn Press. Andrew once took me over to see the august Grabhorn building where he was doing some work.

In the fall of 1966, I moved to Kentucky to take an editorial job at the University Press, but before I arrived they gave that position to someone else. Instead I worked at the printing department and started to do some design projects for the press. Eventually, I became their book designer and production manager. I remember how blessed I felt when I could design an ad using Bembo, a typeface I revered. The journal to publish the ad, the *Renaissance Quarterly,* was printed by Stinehour Press. Now I have Bembo on the computer but, as with a number of faces, the digital quality of that face does not quite match its excellence as a metal typeface.

KS: Did your early printing resemble Hammer's in any way? Have you ever used any of his type or fonts in your books?

JG: I have only used a Hammer face—Neue Hammer Unziale—for display in one book. I would now use a version of American Uncial instead, but back then [2001] the versions of that available were inferior.

I have this notion that Hammer's caps in a way prefigure tapered (as opposed to monotone) sans-serif faces. His friend R. Hunter Middleton designed his typeface Stellar for Ludlow in 1929 and this in its way was a pioneering effort of a tapered sans-serif design. Then came Berthold Wolpe's Albertus (1932–40). Much later Zapf designed Optima (1958), and José Mendoza y Almeida designed a somewhat similar typeface called Pascal (1960). Then I would trace this line to Matthew Carter's recent Carter Sans (2011). Carter stated that this is a "sans serif with stroke endings that show the effect of the chisel more than the pen."

I am not a great fan of sans serif in general but I have used Optima—set in metal by a Linotype—Gill Sans, Albertus, and Carter Sans for a logo. I may try and point up this early prefiguration of Hammer's type again in using his caps for display. An odd notion probably, as most would think of uncial in its original historical setting and not as anything contemporary. Its use has been mainly to suggest things medieval and Irish. Though in 1970 on the M-2 in England, in a WC at a rest stop, there was a vending machine for condoms that used American Uncial for its display, embossed in gold, and I just had to put my shillings in and buy this to show such an oddball use to Carolyn Hammer.

I did use American Uncial for a series of T-shirts for our farm and for Gnomon Press.

KS: Designing a book of poems requires typographic and poetic literacy, which makes your specialization somewhat different from others where

extensive knowledge of the subject doesn't necessarily make for a "better" design. How does being a poet inform your sense of book design?

JG: In theory, poets should have a greater "sensitivity" to words in all realms, including how they look on a page. A few excellent printers (Andrew Hoyem and Kim Merker, for example) started as poets. Along this line one can also think of poet/designers Robert Bringhurst and Asa Benveniste. Luckily I have been able to design a goodly number of my own books and have had the good fortune at times to have good printers (like Jerry Reddan of Tangram Press) print my work. Some other times I have had to bite my tongue.

Designing poetry books I have a number of rules of thumb I try to practice, but at times I'm nixed by the publisher by their own house rules. One is using single quotes instead of the more cumbersome double quotes. I haven't yet been brave enough to use single quotes as the norm in prose books as per such usage in England. Another preference is hanging quotes, but once again there have been times others have nixed my preference in this. I try not to break stanzas at page breaks, but a book I am working on right now is for a poet who does not care about breaking stanzas but wants poems to break in such a manner that if poems go beyond one recto page she would rather break mid-sentence so the poem makes no sense unless you go on to verso page and finish the poem. This is to avoid a reader thinking they have read the whole poem when they hadn't (which happened to her twice on radio shows).

Another thing I do is center a poem "visually" on longest line. If a book has poems that have both very short lines and very long lines, this works best visually. This is more labor intensive but I have a quick eye for this and don't try to be mathematically exact. Most poetry books I see don't bother with this and just set the poems flush left. The only time I set flush left is if the manuscript has poems that consistently have long lines. There was one book I recall doing that has poems of three different length lines in a fairly regular manner and I created three different indents for this (Tom Meyer's *Staves Calends Legends* that was set monotype in Della Robia).

Of course I have designed many types of books besides poetry: quite a few photography books, history books, *Bats of America*, *White Trash Cooking*, *Bhutan*, etc. Plus over a dozen recordings (LP, CD, and cassette), one of which I hear rumors about selling a million copies. It goes without saying, I have not gotten rich designing or writing poetry.

KS: I just designed a book of prose poems and the author condemned my use of hanging quotes—why do you like them?

JG: Well, I think there are all sorts of prejudices out in the world that often have not to do with the best options, but simply what people are used to, and at times these prejudices are hard to overcome. An example is the first recording you might have of a particular piece of music and how ones that come after cannot measure up to that initial take. Hanging quotes I liken to that initial prejudice of most seeing things set without hanging quotes. I like them for the way my eye sees the type alignment flush left with hanging quotes whereas without them the type indents look wrong to me.

Prose poems might be a bit more problematic than regular poetry regarding hanging quotes since it has the look of prose. The only prose poems I've worked with are my own and I don't remember them having quotes at the beginning of lines. Which suggests a possible way around the dilemma—change the measure so that the quotes do not start a line, if this is possible. I work from my own tastes and prejudices and at times these inevitably butt up against others with different typographic tropisms.

KS: Could you talk about the similarities and differences between designing a book for a client and designing a book that you've solicited?

JG: A project should hopefully inspire and suggest typefaces and treatment. I work by intuition in this, but now ideas can be tested on the computer fairly quickly by comparing different fonts for the same text, adjusting size and leading, something that in past times would require a lot of painstaking time and work. Now it's almost instant gratification. The starting ideas would be the same for a book that I was publishing and for another publisher. But things can evolve in more and less pleasant ways if a client comes with a lot of baggage as to how he or she envisions a project. I once designed a rather high profile poetry book and my name is still there as designer, but I hardly recognized the final product because of changes that were made. Thankfully, that has only happened that one time. I like projects where I am entrusted because of my past track record and the project fulfills what was in my mind's eye and everyone is happy with the final results. At times a client's suggestions might push you to do better work and the input has a positive result.

Of course, there are many now who have all sorts of opinions about typefaces. A lawyer I know wanted a logo and I fooled around with it for a time, but he needed it to be sans serif (he thought) because he wanted to show that his was to be a contemporary legal practice. I wasn't sure it needed to be sans serif and I am not sure what he ended up with. I designed a logo for my daughter's group and she wanted a more up-to-date sans serif than the one I was using. I was using Carter Sans which had just come out, so I told her you could hardly get more up-to-date.

I suppose there are some prejudices I have where I would refuse to traffic in typefaces I deplore. An example would be Pabst Old Style or Caslon Antique or any of those fonts that imitate badly worn metal type. Unfortunately, one sees too much of this to what purpose—giving off an aura of fake antiquity?

KS: Unfortunately, "fake antiquity" extends beyond typefaces: walk into Urban Outfitters and you're ambushed by pre-faded T-shirts, or go to Crate & Barrel and you discover one fake patina after another. Same goes for typography. My hunch is that consumers are attracted to this because they're looking for authenticity—meaning, history. For the graphic designer who stares at a screen all week in a cubicle, what could be more refreshing than picking up a composing stick on the weekend? I think that the kids who've grown up in front of the screen are bored, actually tired of the perfection and instant gratification of their 2D reality.

JG: Well, perhaps we are at a juncture where many styles coexist. We have retro cars like the PT Cruiser and we have the hybrids. We have high fashion clothes that harken back to Victorian ruffles and we have the new pre-worn jeans look with holes in them. We have period performance in classical music with gut strings and the use of vibrato forbidden competing with lush modern symphonic performance. And then endless arguments about what kind of pianos famous composers actually knew and composed for in their mind's ear.

And for nostalgia and escape from the overwhelming contemporary media we hear of movie stars knitting, urbanites with a flock of backyard hens, etc. And all the sudden interest in artists books and papermaking, new and old ways to bind books. In some ways, getting back to the use of the hands, the skill of the hands. Go for it. Whatever works.

In typography we have "allusive typography" and when you have a period piece, say Ben Franklin's writings, well then I could see using a decent Caslon with some swash characters if that is what works. Actually, years ago I had to handset foundry Caslon and I never really liked the fit of the letters and of the "Dutch" faces. I much prefer Van Krimpen's Van Dijck, though I have never used it.

KS: How did you come to know Jonathan Williams?

JG: I moved to San Francisco in 1963 and spent almost the entire year there. I needed a job and worked for a while for the post office delivering mail. This was right after they lifted a freeze in hiring and there was a large backlog of "shit mail" to deal with, plus the fact I was a substitute and was constantly given new routes. This ran me ragged and I decided to return to Bard and finish up school there.

Before I started working at the post office I had an inkling of a projected book by Jonathan Williams and wrote him at a time when he was living in England. The book project was one of interviews with English writers he was enthusiastic about: Basil Bunting, J.R.R. Tolkein, Mervyn Peake, and Stevie Smith. In the end only the Bunting "happened" and I published *Descant on Rawthey's Madrigal, Conversations with Basil Bunting by Jonathan Williams* in 1968. It was set in Goudy's Garamont and printed letterpress. I think it is one of two titles in a row (the other being the Meatyard book (*The Family Album of Lucybelle Crater*, 1974) where the asking price of the signed limited editions went for $17.50 and I've seen them now listed for $1,750!

That first letter started a correspondence that lasted until Jonathan's death in 2008. It was the beginning of a long friendship. I ended up publishing a number of his books after the Bunting: *Blue Ridge Weather Prophet Makes Twelve Stitches in Time on the Twelfth Day of Christmas* (1977); *I Shall Save One Land Unvisited, Eleven Southern Photographers* (1978); *Portrait Photographs* (1979); and *In the Azure Over the Squalor: Ransackings & Shorings* (1985). I also edited *JW / 50, A 50th Birthday Celebration for Jonathan Williams* (1979)—that was both a book by Gnomon Press and an issue of David Wilk's *Truck* magazine. He also wrote prose afterwords for two books I published: *Light at Hand* (1975), Guy Mendes' book of photographs, and *Presences of Mind, The Collected Books of Jack Sharpless* (1989). On this side of the equation I published some prose on Jonathan Williams including one piece that was in a magazine in the Canary Islands, in Spanish, and that is the only one of my publications I was never given at least one copy. And I also contributed a small piece for *The Family Album of Lucybelle Crater* by Gene Meatyard, one of the more collectible Jargon titles.

I also ended up designing a number of books by Jonathan published by others: the Duke University Press edition of *Blues and Roots, Rue and Bluets, A Garland for the Southern Appalachians* (1985); *Le Garage Ravi De Rocky Mount: An Essay on Vernon Burwell* (1988); *Eight Days in Eire: Or, Nothing so Urgent as Manana* (1990); *Jubilant Thicket, New & Selected Poems* (the text and the limited edition, but not the trade cover). And then the posthumous collection of Jonathan's edited by Jeffery Beam, *A Hornet's Nest* (2008), which turned out well, set in Stempel Garamond.

And then for the Jargon Society for a while I was their distributor and Dobree (my wife) was their treasurer, which was awkward for often Jonathan was short of cash and called Dobree for monies earkmarked (donated) for forthcoming projects. I designed a number of Jargon books including their "best-seller" and the only one to make "real money"—*White Trash Cooking* (1986). And I also ended up working on its first sequel as well for Ten Speed. They took over as publisher for Jargon who could not handle a big volume seller. I just recently received the 25th Anniversary Edition which proclaims "650,000 Copies Sold," but crazily this edition while still having my name on the copyright page as designer for the first time misspells it as "Johnathan."

Other Jargon titles I designed: Tom Meyer's *Staves Calends Legends* (1979); *The Photographs of Lyle Bongé* (1982); Mark Steinmetz's *Tuscan Trees* (2001); David M. Spear's *The Neugents* (1993); *Bill Anthony's Greatest Hits* (1988); Jonathan's Little Enis fold-out; *DBA at 70* (1989); Jeffery Beam's *Visions of Dame Kind* (1995); and then I helped in the production and designed the limited edition binding of Tom Meyer's *At Dusk Iridescent* (1995).

Plus we visited back and forth: Jonathan and Tom visiting here in Kentucky and us visiting them in North Carolina and England.

Plus at times seeing them elsewhere as well. And a rich wealth of mutual friends. A long, rich friendship.

KS: Could you break down the chronology a bit? 1963, you drop out of school to check out San Francisco. Did you actually meet Williams there? Who else? What was the first title published by Gnomon, and when?

JG: Let me start just a little earlier. The '50s as prelude to the turbulent '60s, for me personally as well as for most others. Late '50s I got involved in Civil Rights work and every weekend I was picketing Woolworth's or at rallies. My father called me a Communist, though this was hardly the case. Then in early 1960 after a lyrical walk in a drizzling rain in the Cloisters with my girlfriend, I came home to my parents waiting for an ambulance. My father had mysteriously spit up some blood. The start of his illness, which remained a mystery to me for too long. One uncle said I caused my father's illness by my political activities and that I better shape up or I'd be killing my father. Luckily another uncle (by marriage, not blood) told me what was what: my father had brain cancer, and of course I knew enough that different political beliefs did not cause cancer.

I entered Bard in the fall of 1960. For a projected six weeks starting January 1961 I was to work with Larry Eigner in Swampscott. His father drove us up to see Olson in Gloucester, but Olson happened not to be in. Hard to believe now, but Olson here and Duncan in San Francisco both were living somewhat on the edge and both did not have phones. During the Swampscott sojourn, I called Cid Corman from a pay phone in Boston Commons, but we would not meet until some years later. But Corman was a crucial connection in my life. The work with Eigner had to be cut short because my father had a turn for the worse and ended up dying on the twenty-sixth of January.

In the summer of 1962 my friend Chuck Stein and I went "on the road" across the country. He had a Plymouth Valiant station wagon and his father's gas credit card (gas then being around twenty-six cents a gallon). Often we slept in the back of the station wagon. At the start of the trip we met Olson for the first time. He suggested taking LSD and had a manuscript copy of Alan Watts' *Joyous Cosmology*. He was getting the LSD from Leary and Alpert, who were doing their research at Harvard. We had never heard of LSD and said we would try it, but the conversations heated up and went on until early morning and we never got around to the LSD!

We drove through Canada a bit, then dropped down to Chicago to visit my friend Manus Pinkwater (later Daniel Pinkwater, a children's book author). Then out west, up to the Canadian Rockies, Vancouver, then down the West Coast. I had a friend, Jonathan Eisen in Berkeley, and we crashed there for a time. We did have a good visit with Duncan in San Francisco. Then to Santa Barbara to see a woman I was in love with at the time. Then LA. Then back east with a memorable drive on Blue Ridge Parkway, a visit to Williamsburg, etc.

The West Coast had a liberating feel to it. So when I felt a bit of a roadblock at Bard, I jumped ship and spent 1963 in San Francisco. Jumped into a frying pan and got married young, had my first daughter. Was very close to Robin Blaser then, who lived a short hike up from Hyde Street where I was living. And also Duncan. Knew Jack Gilbert and others who were in the Spicer group, but that scene was very hush hush and I never caught sight of Spicer. My first wife went to a reading he gave down at the Civic Center, but I dutifully stayed at home never thinking we could afford a babysitter. During that year Chuck Stein came with another poet friend, Eric Felderman, and we all trundled up to the Vancouver Poetry Festival in July. Olson found us a place to stay (that was soon after raided for drugs). Back to Bard to finish up, all of 1964 through the spring semester of 1965. Then back to San Francisco until the move to Kentucky in fall of 1966. Kentucky the happy medium—or radical departure?

Robert Duncan, Fragments of a Disorderd Devotion
(Gnomon Press and Island Press, 1966)

Gnomon started in 1965 as a magazine edited with a friend, Bruce Marcus. Then in 1966 in San Francisco the first two books: Robert Duncan's *Fragments of a Disorderd Devotion* and Chuck Stein's *Provisional Measures*. I did the Duncan in cahoots with Victor Coleman and his Island Press and it was printed on an offset press I had bought in Toronto. Victor was supposed to be co-owner but never pitched in the money he promised. Strange to see all these years later Victor was involved in editing Duncan's *The H.D. Book* (2011) for University of California Press. That printing press I think later produced the anthology *New Wave Canada* (1996) and some other books. The Duncan *Fragments* (1952) had seen previous "light" in an edition of only fifty copies Duncan gave to friends, none for sale. So mine was its first "real" publication.

Chuck's book was printed by Graham Mackintosh. And then he printed the second and last issue of *Gnomon,* the magazine. But by the time that came out I was already in Kentucky where I also did an offprint of the Borges essay, "A Vindication of the Cabala," that was in that second issue of *Gnomon.* Strange, but some of those who contributed to the magazine never credited it in future books, as if it never existed—examples would be poems by Robin Blaser or translations from the Provençal by Paul Blackburn.

Then to circle back to part of your question, I don't think I actually met Jonathan Williams face-to-face until he visited Kentucky in January of 1967. For this it helps that J.W. sent me his letters with Guy Davenport, *A Garden Carried in a Pocket* (2004), where this visit is documented on page 87.

KS: Why Kentucky?

JG: Meeting Victor and Carolyn Hammer at the end of 1961 was a key to my moving here. And then I had met Guy Davenport and some poets as well, contemporaries of mine, and Wendell Berry. And on that first visit I went to Gethsemani, the monastery where Thomas Merton lived. Though I knew he was there it never entered my mind that a friendship between us would develop at the end of his foreshortened life. And that I had that job waiting for me in Kentucky at the University Press. Though I was never paid a decent salary, that I was given that job at all was a miracle in that I really did not have the credentials for it beyond on-the-job "John Dewey" training.

There was a small press circle around the Hammers: the Anvil Press, Joe Graves' Gravesend Press, and what would evolve into the King Library Press that I was involved with early on. There were type designers at IBM that I knew: John Schappler, Roger Roberson. And P.J. Conkwright, the great designer at Princeton University Press, retired to Lexington and Charles Skaggs for some years lived in Leitchfield. I knew them both and did some work with both.

And crazily, I wanted my "One Thousand Miles of Elbow Room" and not to be in a heated poetry environment where there were poetry wars—I thought for a while in San Francisco that I was the only one who conversed with Duncan and Blaser when they were at odds with one another—and many cliques bad-mouthing other cliques on the East and West coasts. I guess better for one's "career" to be in a coterie but it was not something I wanted. Living out on a hundred-acre farm doing farm work somewhat anchors you to the real world in a way the academic world most poets live in does not. But of course, "each to one's own" direction. Tropisms.

My first wife was from Kentucky, and though the marriage was short-lived, I stayed. And then I married Dobree Adams, who moved to Kentucky when very young and was here until college—Wellesley—and then various jobs on the West Coast before she returned in 1973 and we hooked up. On her mother's side about seven generations back, her family moved to Kentucky in 1779 and then a few years later were the first to settle in Scott County on two thousand acres acquired in a land grant from Patrick Henry. I also have Kentucky roots on my mother's side, but from more recent times. They were German immigrants who came to New Orleans, but moved to Kentucky in 1846 because of the Yellow Fever epidemic. So we both have family connections here, though that probably was not the deciding factor for moving to and then staying in Kentucky.

KS: Thumbing through Williams' *Portrait Photographs*—both editions, actually—it occurs to me that many of the writers and artists he liked lived outside of New York or San Francisco. Although the Jargon aesthetic is often described as "outsider art," I'm not sure that's accurate, at least according to my definition. How would you characterize the writers and artists you publish? Does Gnomon have an agenda, as they say?

JG: I used to think of a response to why I published the books I did (though I don't remember anyone ever asking before): They are books I just wanted to see on my shelves that no one else had thought to publish.

Williams as a sort of "trope" complained about being ignored by the mainstream art world, such as it is or imagined to be, and thought his living where he did off on a mountain hillside was the root cause of this. He thought that the art world was prejudiced against the possibility that anything of real interest emanated from the hinterlands and back roads. Serious art was done in the big cities.

Gene Meatyard, whom we both published (Gnomon in 1970, Jargon in 1974), was discovered years after he died (in 1972) and in this century has had the big city shows in New York, Chicago, and San Francisco. He earned almost nothing from selling photographs in his lifetime, less than seven hundred dollars. It's a story that has happened over and over again in American art. And writing: another case along these lines would be Lorine Niedecker, whom we also both published (but I got involved posthumously).

But then Jargon and Gnomon weren't "foolishly consistent"—we both published Robert Duncan's poems (Jargon in 1958, Gnomon in 1966) and would never think not to publish him because he was associated with the San Francisco poetry scene, though he did live in various other places: Woodstock, Mallorca, Stinson Beach, etc.

There's a strange phenomenon in the world: where many hunger for fame and where ironically the famous are often burdened by their notoriety. After winning the Nobel Prize in Literature, the Polish poet Wisława Szymborska found it hard to find that private space again in which to write poems.

KS: Could you describe your workshop and surroundings? What kind of press do you operate? Which fonts do you use most often?

JG: Well, I do own two presses, a Vandercook and a clamshell platen press, and once had a share in another, a flatbed Heidelberg. Gray Zeitz of Larkspur Press and I bought a lot of type and Monotype equipment when a Cincinnati printer was closing down its letterpress operation, but the 1978 flood hit and we never recovered enough to start up the Monotype. I have Perpetua type and I think Gray might have added to what I had bought. We also bought a good number of type cabinets, but I pretty much left that all for Gray's use and we only collaborated on one Gnomon book. He also published one book of mine early (*Quiet Goods*, 1980) and a broadside reprint of one of my poems.

But basically I ended up working from home and Gray is probably a fifty-minute drive from here on the other side of the

Kentucky River. In the old days I still used letterpress printers, especially Heritage Printers in Charlotte, North Carolina. I ran many jobs through that shop, both Gnomon and University Press books and also broadsides I designed. Early on they did not charge extra for Monotype setting vs. Linotype, despite the extra work involved. When Kingsport Press folded, Heritage augmented their type holdings and had a great selection. Later, Ed Rayher at Swamp Press bought some of these and now has quite a nice selection of Monotype faces. When I started design I was basically tracing type for title pages and envisioning what text would look like in such and such a size and leading. P.J. Conkwright could just freehand take a piece of paper and start in lettering in faces he was most familiar with, say Bulmer display, and then could scribe a page of 10/13 Caledonia! Amazed me to see this.

Nowadays, though, I am all digital. When I worked with Ed at Swamp Press on my small book *Hut Poems* for Mountains and Rivers Press, I took the digital version of Perpetua and compared it to the Monotype metal showing and adjusted the size by a few points to match.

Digital is not flashy, but I do appreciate the access to all the fonts now available, many of which were fairly hard to come by in metal. For example, Mardersteig's Dante, which is one I use often. Other types I gravitate towards and use more than others: Georg Trump's faces, Van Krimpen's Haarlemmer, Matthew Carter's Galliard, FF Scala, Adobe Garamond, and Robert Slimbach's Minion, at times with his Poetica mixed in. This off the top of my head.

My workshop is just our son's former bedroom with one fairly up-to-date iMac and one ancient Power Mac G3 which provides access to old Zip and floppy files. And two old Epson color printers I don't really use now since Dobree has a new Epson Pro 3800 in her office. We just printed a small thirty-two page chapbook of my poems here, only sixty-five copies, to see if we could produce a high quality book with just our equipment. For text we used Mohawk Superfine, for endpapers Canson Mi-Teintes, and a Red River paper, Aurora Art Natural, for the cover. Folding and sewing this reminds me of my earlier days when many Gnomon publications had to be put together after they were printed instead of getting a book from the printer all ready to go on sale.

KS: The home computer and printer have made such in-house productions possible, not entirely unlike the mimeograph in terms of domestic publishing. Do you think that today's presses compare to those of the golden era of the independent press movement, both in terms of the poetry and the overall aesthetic?

JG: There were many antecedents to household mimeos. For example, Leonard and Virginia Woolf setting up Hogarth Press in their dining room to print and publish two stories by themselves. Yeats had his sisters set up the Cuala Press to publish his work. And I recall a lengthy list in Bill Henderson's *The Publish-it-Yourself Handbook* of authors who published themselves early on. One could list William Blake, Walt Whitman, and on and on, to counter the stigma of self-publishing as only for minor writers. Take such a major figure as James Joyce and his publication history, his life of poverty. He had to underwrite the publication of the *Dubliners* which had been rejected by one publisher after another. And we all know Sylvia Beach from her bookstore Shakespeare and Company published *Ulysses*. Echoing the days when bookstores and "Stationers" were publishers.

It is just the means of printing that changed. I actually was involved with mimeo and worked in the printshop at Bucks Rock Work Camp in Connecticut, summer of 1959, under Julia Winston, who taught at The High School of Music & Art in New York. They also had letterpress equipment. We produced two literary magazines, one of which I have a copy because my mother kept it where I might have tossed it.

Bucks Rock was an important summer for me. I guess I was something like a "junior counselor" and lived in a tent with Joshua Rifkin who later made a name for himself in music (playing Scott Joplin rags on three Nonesuch records, orchestrating two important Judy Collins records, producing the *Baroque Beatles Songbook* and then coming up with a theory how to perform Bach's Cantatas). From working in the printshop, I went and worked in the "poetry department" with Alan Shavzin, who I think might have introduced me to the work of William Carlos Williams and Creeley, etc. And two writer friends I am still in touch with were campers there, Charles Stein and Laura Furman—with a strange bond that we all would lose a parent from cancer in a short time span of about three years. And Paul Lansky was there as a camper. Later he would head up the music department at Princeton, and he set a couple of my poems; there have been two recordings of those, plus another on his website.

A long answer, to a short question. But there has always been this impulse of a writer or group of writers taking over "the means of production" as their patience would be tried by the "powers that be" in the publishing world lacking an appreciation for their work. And that this now can be done at home or as an e-book or sent off to a print-on-demand printer. This makes sense in reducing the financial risk of publication, which has always been a concern. And of course in Russia there was *samizdat*, the mimeo and copying revolution there that was in a way parallel to the mimeo publishing in the States in the '50s.

KS: My next question is about the nature of artists books, about their relationship with poetry and private press editions, or their ability to expand common notions of what a book of poems or a well printed book might be. I think that Jargon, Coracle, and Something Else Press, for example, have published books that might fall into either "category" knowing full well that categories and definitions have their limitations. How would you describe your own practice in terms of the book arts?

JG: I tend to think of artists books in two distinct categories. One is the expensive productions such as Pablo Neruda's *Canto General* I just saw with an illustration by Diego Rivera. And many of the lavish productions of books produced in France where writers and artists collaborated. But I am sure we can go backward in time and claim Blake's prophetic books and perhaps a book like *Tristam Shandy* as well.

The other category I think of when that phrase comes up is the experimental private press productions with editions of very few copies. One friend here, Susan King, has run her Paradise Press for many years and has created many artists books in this realm. And years ago I met and traded books with Bonnie O'Connell of Penumbra Press who does exquisite small editions of poetry all with tasteful art elements. At times creative innovations in such books can influence mainstream publishing.

The first Gnomon Press book, Robert Duncan's *Fragments of a Disorderd Devotion*, has more of the look and feel of an artists book than anything I've done since. Duncan wrote out the text and illustrated it with his drawings. In retrospect, I see that I have worked on many books that mix photography and writing and at least one other that mixes art and writing.

And then of course I have worked on many books with cover art by many different artists and photographers. Plus I have published photography books and designed such books for other presses. And designed fancy limited edition of trade books for The Captain's Bookshelf, many featuring photographs by Dobree Adams. And Dobree has just finished her first artists book. Together we have now had a number of shows in which we collaborate: her weavings and photographs and my poems that interact with her art. And so far fourteen broadsides of her photographs with my poems and typography. Plus the signage for these collaborative shows.

[2015]

Alastair Johnston
Poltroon Press

Alastair Johnston was born in Glasgow in 1950. He grew up in Northern England and dropped out of college in 1969. In 1975, he founded Poltroon Press with artist Frances Butler, and he continues to publish original writing by contemporary authors in limited letterpress as well as trade editions.

Johnston edited *The Ampersand* from 1986 to 2002, and served as an associate editor of *Fine Print* magazine. Johnston taught Visual Studies, Typography, and Book Design at University of California, Berkeley and Davis from 1975 to 1986 and at UC Berkeley Extension from 1987 to 2011 where he was an honored instructor for the academic year of 2004. He served as a visiting artist in public schools from 1999 to 2011, teaching self-expression through poetry and book arts. He has designed books for The British Library, Oak Knoll Press, Crown Point Press, Harper/Collins, and Serendipity Books.

A prolific author, editor, and bibliographer, his books include William Loy's *Nineteenth-century American Designers & Engravers of Type* (2009, co-editor/designer); *A Discography of Docteur Nico* (second edition, 2012); *Transitional Faces: The Lives & Work of Richard Austin, type-cutter, and Richard T. Austin, wood-engraver* (2013); *Dreaming on the Edge: Poets & Artists in California* (2016); Max Jacob's *Omnia Vanitas* (2018, translator), as well as many books of poetry and a marvelous bibliographic trilogy on the Auerhahn Press, White Rabbit, and Zephyrus Image. He is also an expert on world music.

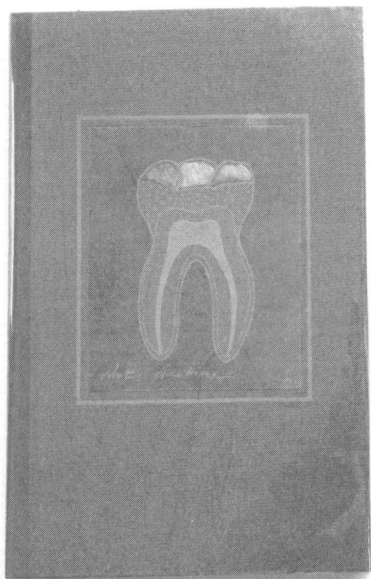

Lucia Berlin, *Legacy* (Poltroon Press, 1983), cover by Michael Thorn Bradley; *Safe & Sound*, (Poltroon Press, 1988), cover by Frances Butler

KS: Could we begin with some pre-Poltroon history, how you came to California, and what you were doing around that time.

AJ: How came I to be here? Chasing a woman! I was at college in London: a business major, if you can believe it. Passed the first year (economics, statistics, principles of English law, advertising, and marketing—only because there was no future in an art, music or literature degree) and in the second year there was a noticeable change in my class. All the long hairs had vanished, except me and a few others, and the suits were gaining the upper hand. I had started a literary magazine called *HEMP* (the college was on Hempstead Road) and had also spent the summer hitchhiking to Istanbul, smoking hash, listening to rock and roll, and growing my hair, which progress was interrupted by some border guards in Bulgaria who decided I was an anarchist and gave me a very bad haircut. Thirteen of us rented an old three-storey house from a Pakistani landlord. Two of the guys had been to the States and cruising through Santa Barbara, California had come to a stop light alongside a girl on a motorcycle and yelled "Where's the party?" at her. Follow me! She replied and took off on her bike. So they had spent a day with this hippie chick and she was coming to Europe and had asked them to meet her at Heathrow, en route to Italy. Problem was her flight got in at 6:30 a.m. but they gallantly picked her up and brought her to Watford and all thirteen of us were vying to catch her eye.

She and I got entangled and I gave some thought to what I was doing and decided to chuck it. We moved to Cambridge where my best friend was at university and rented a tiny flat where every fifteen minutes you had to put a shilling in the gas meter to keep the fire burning. I worked nightshift in a jam factory with all the psychos and outcasts. When her visa expired in January I proposed to her. We got married against my parents' wishes and spent our honeymoon in the American embassy in London trying to get me a visa. They were not keen to let me in but I did get a green card and came to Santa Barbara, sight unseen, took off my shoes and never stopped. It's odd because I was quite anti-American, still am against the naïve political mentality of this country. I spent a lot of time in the anti-war movement and the ban the bomb marches. We had a son and I spent a couple of years trying to get a decent job and trying everything from door-to-door sales (I was good at that because of my British accent), to gardening, shipping clerk (fired for an April Fool's prank), housepainting, bicycle mechanic, signpainter. At one point we were so broke we lived in a VW bus, but it was easy to barter stuff. I'd paint signs and get merchandise in return. Then by chance I got a job in a letterpress printing plant.

KS: So who taught you how to print at the plant? What did you do there?

AJ: No one taught me. I learned surreptitiously. Bill McNally was a modest publisher, half of the firm of McNally and Loftin, with a branch in Charlotte, North Carolina. He did job printing and published a few titles, local Santa Barbara-interest stuff by Walker A. Tompkins, a writer on the local paper, plus he had published *A Dashiell Hammett Casebook* by William Nolan that sold well. I was hired as office boy to do shipping and receiving, billing, dunning (a lot of deadbeat accounts, especially big firms like Baker and Taylor who were accidentally on purpose negligent of small publishers—a lesson I learned well), sweeping up. It was a small operation. There were a couple of Linotype operators and an old pressman named Morris. They all worked nights at the News-Press, the local Hearst paper. We also printed books for others. One of my jobs was to melt the old lead slugs and cast new pigs of lead, after it had been boiled, cleaned of dross, and toned. To get the impurities to rise to the surface you added a flux that smelled like sheep fat, then you ladled the molten lead into cast iron moulds to make the new pigs. I became really efficient at the office work so I could hang out in the printshop and be useful. I found this was what I wanted to do, something intellectually and physically challenging that was stimulating so at the end of the day you felt you had achieved something. I ran a galley proof press. It was electric and run by a foot pedal which made the rollers whir around, so it was easy to get mesmerized and almost run it over your hands. I even got to set correction lines on the Linotype and learned a bit about page make-up.

Bill McNally was a great boss, very paternal, and he encouraged me as I was hard-working. One Friday he gave me the page proofs for Ernesto Galarza's *Mexican-Americans in the Southwest* and told me to take it home and make an index! I wrote the index over the weekend and he paid me a little bonus. I proofread a UC Press book on the *Permanencia of Ruben Dario*. We printed a critical edition of Pérez de Ayala's *Belarmino and Apolonio* for UC Press, still one of my favorite novels. Working closely with a text really puts you inside it with the writer. You can almost feel him making word choices or laughing over a felicitous little sound.

One day cleaning up in the attic I found a box of books and opened it: they were all the early Jargon Press books which McNally had printed in Charlotte. Take any you want, he said. It was an epiphany for me. I had set my name in large Weiss italic and thought about printing my poems, but just one copy, to see it in print. These Jargon books showed a vision, determination, and real skill in making something tangible out of something so personal. I studied *The Darkness Surrounds Us* (1960), Gilbert Sorrentino's first book: it had a title from Creeley, a cover by Fielding Dawson. It was a small package of magic. I noticed Jack Spicer had dedicated a book to Creeley and that Spicer book,

Heads of the Town, published by The Auerhahn Society in 1962, was my favorite poetic discovery. Then I bought Creeley's *For Love* (1962) and though I also read crap like Brautigan's and Tom Robbins' novels (that friends pressed on me as great), I started to enter a whole world of American poets quite different from the contemporary English poets I was familiar with: Pickard, Raworth, Logue, Hollo, Tony Harrison, Brian Patten, the Liverpudlians, etc.

John Martin had just started Black Sparrow Press in Los Angeles. He hired Noel Young and Graham Mackintosh to design and print for him. They had a small boutique-like shop downtown on Anacapa Street, but they still only had a platen press so any big books, like Richard Grossinger's *Solar Journal* (1970) or a Robert Kelly epic, they brought to us. Graham became a kind of guru to me, though he was always drunk, but he would say these crazy things which I thought of as Zen oracles. Then he would hand me a little poetry book he had just printed by Ed Dorn or hook me up with some sign-painting job, so he was looking out for me. Through Graham I met Peter Whigham, who had translated the Penguin edition of Catullus, which was one of the most important books of my youth. This may sound corny but we had to sight-translate Latin in class ("My lady's pet sparrow is, dead, eheu!") and my friend Gordy went out and found this new Penguin translation and said, "Hey, look at these others poems about hard-ons and sodomy!" A group of six of us, teenage boys and girls, would get together at my house and read Catullus aloud. So it was mind-blowing to meet this guy, this brilliant translator, in a seedy bar who told me not to use his real name. He was night-clerk in a skid-row hotel and worked in porno movies as an extra. I don't think we had much literary discussion but they knew Bukowski, Henry Miller, and Lawrence Durrell, all heavy drinkers, and many other writers, and I was just an impressionable kid taking it all in. One night we were walking down State Street and Graham, drunk as usual, climbed on the flower box in front of Capra Press where he worked (it was Noel

Young's business) and pulled off the wood letters nailed to the fascia. He rearranged them and pounded them back with his fist so it read A CRAP PRESS.

But in 1972 there was a series of events that looked ominous: Kent State had been the prelude to police aggression, Attica was the next level, then the escalation of the Vietnam War. I was 1-A for the draft but I had a high lottery number. Still, I decided we should move to Canada. We got as far as Mendocino and our VW bus broke down, so at that point I decided to go back to England. But that was worse. I remembered why I had left: it was cold, you couldn't get a decent job. I ran an Army & Navy store with thirteen employees and still could have made more money on the dole. Again I had a series of miserable jobs and after a year found I would lose my green card if I did not go back to California. My wife was homesick and our son was still a baby so we came back to start over again, but she couldn't think of living anywhere but Santa Barbara. I met Teo Savory and Alan Brilliant of Unicorn Press, friends of Rexroth; they were about to relocate to North Carolina, and wanted a pressman to go with them. They were keen to have me come but I didn't really want to leave the West Coast. Graham told me the main small press scene was in San Francisco so I began thinking of going there.

I was writing a weekly column for the local free paper, the *News & Review*. I finally started getting the front page with a couple of stories I did: one on Nude Beaches (this was the beginning of the whole California Lifestyle hot tubs and healthy living epoch) and one on a Hells Angels funeral. I had two hot stories I was working on. First was about a guy named Gourgen Yanikian who was an Armenian writer that everyone knew. He walked around in a brown beret and a cassock-like robe, like a priest. He called the Turkish embassy in Washington and said he had some ikons that had gone missing from a church in the First World War and wanted to return them. He described these famous missing cultural treasures. The ambassador and vice-ambassador came to

Santa Barbara where Yanikian met them in the Miramar hotel and shot them both dead as revenge for the Armenian genocide. When they arrested him he was dressed all in white, even to the beret. He had told me about how his family had been wiped out, their land taken, etc. Now the state was taking away what little he had left. He had missed the slaughter because he was in Russia studying engineering and then in the Second World War he helped the Americans build bridges and got out to California and had nursed this grudge for his whole life. He also had some amazing theories about Christ that tied in well with my piece. I pitched it to *Oui* magazine which was a European-style men's magazine in Chicago and they were keen to see it.

My other story was even more apocalyptic. There was a hippie commune in Santa Barbara called the Brotherhood of the Sun, who had an organic farm and a couple of health food stores. I met some people who had escaped from there and they told me chilling tales of the leader Norm Paulson who was a lunatic visionary and how the whole thing was a great welfare scam and run like a prison camp. His philosophy was based on American Indian myths that also included a liberal dose of UFO-logy. They were stockpiling weapons and planning, at the "end time," to defend themselves and their land. I pitched it to *Rolling Stone*, which was also a relatively new publication, and they said they were interested. So I hiked up to San Francisco and met Smokestack El Ropo himself, in their 3rd Street office. I was a little taken aback when he said they rewrote everything, and I began to question did I really want to be a muckraking journalist. At that time Richard Parker, editor of the free paper, was offered a job as editor of *Ramparts*. My wife thought I was having an affair with one of the other writers (the *News & Review* staff were the only interesting people left in Santa Barbara so I hung out with them a lot) and so she went out and got involved with an old flame. I thought "OK I can do my own thing," so I walked out (which was rotten to our four-year-old son) and came up to Berkeley with Richard Parker. *Ramparts* didn't last, he went to *Mother Jones,* which was starting up and made a bundle in direct mail and I began to think my future in journalism wasn't so secure.

That was when I decided to try and get into the local small press scene. I went to Serendipity Books, because it was only two blocks from the *Ramparts* office on University Avenue to meet Peter Howard. "Jack will speak to you," he said. I thought he was being funny, because that was the slogan of the Jack in the Box restaurant and being a foreigner I couldn't get over how people would drive up to this clown and order food! But he was referring to Jack Shoemaker who had a platen press in the back of Peter's shop, and was printing Sand Dollar Books. Jack ran down the scene and told me there were three people I should talk to: Andrew Hoyem, Clifford Burke, and Wesley Tanner. I was staying with a cousin in Colma and it was hard to get around as there was no BART yet. I took a Greyhound bus to 7th Street in San Francisco and walked. The next day I walked to Commercial Street and climbed the rickety wooden stairs to meet Hoyem at the Grabhorn Press. I was wearing a black corduroy Mod suit that I had bought in England with a zipper instead of buttons and I had long hair parted in the middle and granny glasses (looking a lot like John Lennon did at the time). I talked about my proof-reading and indexing skills and he said, "Our apprentices work here for free then after a year if they work out we hire them." He asked me to repeat my name and said I reminded him of another Brit, Barry Hall, he had known years earlier (parenthetical exclamation point goes here, of course). Then I walked the three miles to Collins Street; it was a hot day. It took hours, all of it uphill. I got there late afternoon, it was a storefront on a quiet side street off Geary Boulevard and there was a lovely young woman (Cameron Bunker I think) in the window setting type. I introduced myself, then this dragon lady swept in to see who was there. It was Phoenicia, Clifford's wife (not her birth name, I think). "Oh, Clifford only likes *girl* apprentices," she said, dismissing me.

So next morning I did the mega-transit trip to Berkeley. I got there about 11 a.m. but Wesley was apparently still sleeping. We had this slapstick conversation through the door till I realized he was looking at me through the letterbox about eighteen inches off the ground, so I knelt down and we continued to talk in this ridiculous fashion. He got dressed and we went round the corner to a cafe, which had a sign that read "Working Man's Breakfast, Trucker's Lunch." Wesley was also a hippie type and we hit it off. He had come to Berkeley for the free love scene and been part of the Floating Lotus Opera Company. He got a job in a head shop on Telegraph but was busted for cannabis possession. So then he had gone back to printing, which he had studied in High School in LA, and worked a bit with Clifford. He said I could work for free, though he'd only had girl apprentices before, but did say he would give me a bit of pocket-money from any paying jobs. So I started at once. I learned the lay of the case by distributing type and he taught me makeready on the platen press. We printed bookmarks for Shambhala books, bookplates for The Bancroft Library, broadsides for Moe's, books for Sand Dollar and Stephen Kessler's Green Horse Press.

So I was happy I got to meet interesting people and be in the middle of the literary scene. Wesley even passed a spare girlfriend on to me! I met the Bolinas writers and the Berkeley Buddhists. McClure and Duncan would drop by. We printed Joanna McClure's *Wolf Eyes*. I couldn't afford the bus fare from Colma so Wesley said I could live in the shop. He moved to an apartment on Hillegass in Berkeley and I took over his sleeping loft. We bought day-old muffins and made tuna fish sandwiches. I spent a lot of time in the Bancroft Library reading (I read the Doves Press *Sartor Resartus* to see whether the typeface was truly legible or not: it was) and in the evenings I would go to the Pacific Film Archive, where Tom Luddy did the programming, and so I got a crash course in film history: Ozu, Renoir, Nicholas Ray, old and new German directors. If you look at the Arif Press bibliography, I imagine, you will see that between 1974 and 1975 he produced a ton of work. I did a lot of that. I set and printed all day every day for a year, but it took a toll on me. The concrete floor gave me bad varicose veins, I was severely malnourished. But we got along okay. We printed labels for pot growers and were invited to a fabulous harvest party at the Great American Music Hall. Pot was freely available. We listened to Bob Marley and heard the whole Symbionese Liberation Army thing go down on KPFA. We listened to freeform KSAN radio and went to poetry readings. We published Bobbie Louise Hawkins' first book of poetry which I printed and also got to design the title-page: it's the first asymmetric title-page in Arif Press' history. We stopped getting along. Perhaps I was outgrowing him. He seemed threatened by me and competitive and got very sullen, which most people thought was his mood anyway. Spiders attacked me at night, so Wesley let me stay at his apartment while he moved in with a girlfriend. I was saved by the arrival of Frances Butler.

KS: Frances Butler? The artist?

AJ: At the time she was Frances Butler, textile artist. She was the second person to show up at Arif looking for some letterpress instruction while I was there. First came Romilly Waite. Romilly was married to Kevin Power, an English writer who was getting a Masters or Doctorate at Berkeley in Modern American Poetics, I believe. He knew Duncan, Creeley, Jerome Rothenberg, etc. He was also very interested in the conjunction between art and poetry, so had interviewed these American poets about their connection to painting, you know, Creeley on Kline and Laubies, Duncan on Black Mountain painters, etc. Rom and Kev were both amazing, intelligent, articulate British people and I hit it off with them. Their plan was to start a press in France—Editions Braard—once Kevin got his degree, so Romilly wanted to learn how to do it. Wesley treated her meanly: he had her scrubbing rust off galleys, and cleaning a broken-down cylinder press he had bought, and then the old standby: distributing eight point pied type. So it was really through me she learned the rudiments of typesetting and printing.

Because they were married with small children, Romilly and Kevin lived in Berkeley's University Village and they invited me over for dinner. Their place was spartan but over the dining room table there was a poster-sized black and white blowup of an old French farmhouse, and that was Braard. They had bought a house in a little village called Loubressac near Romilly's uncle W.S. Merwin. Creeley had lived there in the '50s. It looked fabulous (and indeed it is: today, Frances is Romilly's neighbor and they spend a lot of time together, taking care of one another's animals, etc.).

Frances showed up because she had been offered a class in book-making at UC Berkeley's Bancroft Library. Roger Levenson had given an 1839 super-royal Albion press to Berkeley and he and Arlen Philpott taught papermaking, printing, bookmaking. The Bancroft had a lot of material from both John Henry Nash and the Merrymount Press (Updike's library had gone to the Huntington, his archives to Harvard, and his type to Berkeley, thanks to Roger). So there was stereotype equipment, hand moulds, paper, type, ornaments, even some old eighteenth-century Caslon foundry cuts! Roger was thinking of retiring and moving to Santa Barbara, so he asked Frances if she would like to teach the class. Frances had gone to the Library School at Berkeley (she wrote about Will Bradley and, separately, about Art Deco book design), then she went to Stanford and got a Masters in French Intellectual History. She was made a Woodrow Wilson Fellow, magna cum laude, all of that. She was teaching in the Design Department at UC Davis (Reagan had closed the Design Department at Berkeley where she had also studied and taught because that was where all the protest posters and banners were being made!) and her husband, Jonathan Butler, a polymath, was teaching Italian at Berkeley. Frances had studied calligraphy with Arne Wolf, made posters commercially and also made clothes. Her clothing was made by a collage technique which involved cutting out and sew-ing hundreds of little pieces of fabric until she had a better idea. Instead of the labor-intensive prep work, she drew the complex patterns and screen-printed them. She had silkscreen equipment for her poster-making so simply switched to fabric. There was a buzz, and people wanted to buy the running yardage; soon she had commercial representatives getting orders from trade shows and offers from department stores and big companies like Boros in Sweden. So she and her husband started a fabric silkscreening company called Goodstuffs Handprinted Fabrics on the top floor of a huge block-long warehouse in Emeryville. They got commissions from hotels in Asia, the Bank of America corporate HQ in San Francisco, etc. She went to Japan, one of her inspirations, and met Kiyoshi Awazu and got him to submit designs to her for screen-printed wall panels which sold very well. Frances branched out into textile arts, or fabric sculpture, and started getting gallery shows and cover stories in fiber art magazines while museums like the Victoria and Albert and the Bayer Museum in Germany wanted everything she made.

But then on New Year's Day 1973, a drunk driver plowed into their car, a VW bug. Jonathan was killed and Frances was in a coma for three months with every bone in her body broken. Her brilliant husband became a holiday statistic. I met her about eighteen months later, she was just starting to recover, and old friends like Roger were looking out for her. So she came to Arif to brush up on her printing skills (she had studied printing at Laney, the local community college). Again Wesley turned her over to me for instruction. We printed four broadsides together: "51B" by Catullus (in Peter Whigham's translation), a poem of Wang Wei, a poem by me, which Frances illustrated, and a piece from the notebooks of Leonardo which we printed by inking the forme, printing on the tympan and then feeding two sheets of paper so we got the imprint on the back of the sheet, reversed. This by the way was a couple of years before Bill Everson's famous *Granite & Cypress* which used the same trick to much acclaim. The upshot was Frances asked me if I would be her teaching assistant and help her teach the class in The Bancroft. She also offered me a job at her factory as a screenprinter and in a very short time I was living with her. She had a 219 Vandercook at her studio and a few drawers of Baskerville, Cochin, and Van Dijck. We bought a run of Spectrum and got into a period of intense collaboration.

For about four years, we screen printed during the day and in the evenings read, wrote, drew, and set type. Without her husband to run the business it was hard for her to keep it going, come up with a new line of wall hangings and running yardage every year and keep the employees motivated, so the textile business went into a decline. The reps wanted to dictate color schemes to her which was depressing and then she got scammed by a couple of New York sharpies, the Grossmans, who offered to promote her designs but basically stole them, taking them to cheap printers and producing a low-budget version of her work, thinking she wouldn't know about it. Some woman in the neighborhood started a rubber stamp company and just took her designs and turned them into rubber stamps, so suddenly she was spending more and more time with lawyers and less and less time creating art.

The press started to take off. We printed pieces by Philip Whalen and Spicer on the Berkeley Albion, but The Bancroft gig ended when James D. Hart, the director, gave us a really depressing manuscript by William Saroyan, a couple of obituaries he had written, and we rejected it, and instead printed a piece about typography by Emil Ruder that I translated. We bought a 10″ x 15″ C&P from a government warehouse that had been confiscated from counterfeiters.

Frances had a large library of graphic design books (she introduced me to El Lissitsky, Piet Zwart, Rodchenko), calligraphy, bibliography, and books on illustration, and then Roger asked her if she would be interested in buying his typographic library, so suddenly we had a ready-made research library on the premises. It's one thing to do research in a public library and look things up and follow a trail of footnotes into the stacks, where invariably the trail goes cold, it's quite another to have someone's carefully tracked-down collection that opens up vistas in all directions. As a teacher, too, Roger had bought important books to use as teaching aids, which was helpful. So in addition to Harry Carter and Graham Pollard's *Enquiry Into the Nature of Certain Nineteenth-Century Pamphlets*, he had actual Wise forgeries. In addition to books on Horace Walpole he had a Strawberry Hill Press book, and so on. Roger had major collections of historic type specimen books (Wesley stole some of the German ornament specimens from us, the creep), technical manuals going back to the eighteenth century, as well as dozens of Merrymount and Plantin Press books and ephemera which enabled me to study their work in depth. He also had Bruce Rogers and Goudy which didn't interest me as much, but so many other things. Minor presses I did not know about (Black Mack the Handpress intrigued me so much I tracked him down in Southern California, interviewed him and wrote an article for the *Book Club Quarterly*), shelves of Morison, Carter, Vervliet: the big guns. I read it all voraciously. I wrote to Carter and Vervliet and got replies (30 years later I still correspond with Dr. Vervliet). I got deep into the study of letterforms and because of Frances' interest in the vernacular and folk art, those became a passion with me too. Through Dawson's Bookshop in LA we built up areas of the library, with complete runs of *Typographica* and other key periodicals. The library became an entity we both cultivated.

From her time at Berkeley, Frances knew the faculty of the Architecture Department and they asked me if I would like to give a talk in their Fall lecture series in 1979. I gave a talk on the connection between vernacular letterforms, signage, and type design, and they were so impressed they offered me a job teaching typography in the Visual Studies Program. So suddenly there I was, 29 years old, a college drop-out, lecturing to some of the brightest young minds in the country, some of them my own age! I took night classes at Laney College in process camerawork and color photography. And we started a publishing program, lining up work by Raworth, Whalen, and other poets and writers whose work engaged us.

I also got work as a photo typesetter at the West Coast Print Center, which was formed with NEA money to provide cheap printing (in an old mortuary next to the Ashby BART station in Berkeley). It was the vortex of the Bay Area small press scene: all of us who worked there had our own presses and were moonlighting on our own projects. The typesetters included George Mattingly, Barry Watten, John McBride, MaryAnn Hayden, Johanna Drucker; Tim Hildebrand did the process camera work, Dave Bullen and Marjorie Kantor did prepress, and Don Cushman and Don Donahue were the pressmen. Later on people like Geoff Young and poet Steve Rodefer got jobs doing deliveries or running errands to get in the door. It was a scene.

Frances was on the Board of Directors, and she and I gave six free lectures on the history of design and turned everyone on to Jan Tschichold design basics. You can see it in the work of the print center. We had also bought a run of Sabon type from Stempel, so we had a big business providing repros and design work for all these many presses. I was a mentor to many of them as they were clueless about design. I designed all the early books of The Figures, Tombouctou, and many other presses, though quite often they would just ask me to do a cover or title page and then do the paste-up themselves and ruin it. There were many funny stories concerning books involving Jim Carroll, Harold Norse, and Jack Hirschman that are convoluted tales. McBride bought a bank of California job cases full of junk type and parked them in the print center next to a Vandercook. Johanna had not heard of Mallarmé or any of the Dadaists and so energized by this vision, decided to set all the junk type in McBride's cases into one epic book called *A to Z*. It was consigned to be melted down anyway so she ran every piece through the stick and put it on the press. She left town after writing this "tell-all" book. The funny thing was that no one could read it! At my suggestion she went to Amsterdam to get some real life education.

Another "scandalous" work at the time was David Benedetti's book *Nictitating Membrane* (The Figures, 1976). He had an early computer program that generated text randomly. He plugged in key words and names of all the local writers so the machine wrote this absurd book. "Geoff Young thought Summer Brenner's ass was ravishing"—that kind of fill-in-the-blank nonsense. Young's wife Laura Chester wrote a *roman-à-clef* about their scene called *The Stone Baby* that Black Sparrow published but it was quickly withdrawn when Gloria Frym sued. Steve Lavoie and Pat Nolan started a magazine called *Life of Crime* which was a mimeo gossip sheet about the poetry scene. The Language Wars had started and *Poetry Flash* was trying to stay neutral so Tom Clark and others (OK, me) started using *Life of Crime* to publish scurrilous attacks on the Lang Gang! They were great times but it ended badly. Cushman fired everyone and "stole" the Print Center. It turned out that while the NEA was paying for it, he was putting everything in his own name, and after he got rid of anyone who had been there since the start, he sold it and bought a house with the proceeds. It was meant to be a collective but there was no collective ownership and the NEA head Len Randolph had been feted by Cushman and Bullen who had wined and dined him at Chez Panisse and even published his writing. But that's off the story. I'm sure there's something more interesting to talk about.

KS: Certainly. Could you talk about how you conceived, wrote, produced, and distributed your earlier books, such as *Self Portrait with Several Beards against the Invention of Television* (1974), *Cafe 130 Charivari / Charlatan* (1975), *Unser Englische Reise* (1975), etc. And were others publishing your poems at that time as well?

AJ: I wrote poems in notebooks and then started producing notebooks that were like finished manuscripts, even drawing letterforms. I did a series of poems called *Crossing the Bay* and printed two copies on newsprint when Wesley suggested I put together a whole book, which was *Self Portrait*. He then generously put his imprint on it. It's minimalist concrete poetry. I gave them away. Same with *Unser Englische Reise*. I think I printed it at Arif, though now I don't remember. Frances did the calligraphy for the title, so maybe I had set the type and borrowed it to do the press-work at Poltroon. Again, I did a few copies and gave them away. *Cafe Charivari* was also set on the Linotype at Arif and *Partial Primer* was done from zincs and a title-page of metal Futura. They were two conceptual concrete poetry books. The bindery screwed up *Partial Primer* so there were only about 30 copies.

We did a broadside flyer, "Proletarian Books at Pig-elite Prices," with a picture of Chairman Mao on it, and offered them for sale at book fairs. I think Fred Cody had some copies too, but I never made any effort to market them. I sent out some of my poems to little local magazines in Bolinas or *Potrero Hill Literary Supplement*; there was a guy in Chicago, I think, had a magazine called *Bondage and Discipline: a magazine of shorter work*, and he published some of my haiku. The texts in *Confracti Mundi Rudera* (1975) were things in my notebooks (the title comes from Thomas Love Peacock: Frances and I would read Peacock aloud to one another and that concept, "fragments of a shat-tered world," struck a chord with us), but I never took my poetry seriously in terms of trying to get in print, just wrote things down and occasionally there seemed to be a thematic cohesion. I sent a book of translations of Max Jacob to Walter Hamady and he rejected it. I read at the Julia Morgan Center with Whalen and afterwards Kit Robinson said my poems were like failed advertising slogans. Funnily enough, he started writing just like that soon after! The Language poets killed the poetry scene, the camaraderie, so I gave up writing poetry. *Horror vacuui* (1986) was poems left over in my notebooks from *Habitual Own Way*. Now if I have a poetic idea I work it into conversation. This is mostly manifest in puns and other linguistic games. I still keep notebooks, as an *aide mémoire* for all the things I am working on, so on the most recent page I wrote down "Richard Watts 1816–44 Crown Ct, Strand / Bally Sagoo clash with integrity of Nusrat's voice"!

KS: So how does designing and typesetting someone else's poetry differ from working with your own text? That is, to what degree is the author involved with the book's design and/or production?

AJ: The author doesn't have much say. I don't give them type choices or anything like that. But you can't work in secrecy and then spring it on them (unless you know them really well, because this can backfire): you have to explain what you are doing or planning to do. I have been pretty lucky, often I will set some proofs and if the author says it looks fine, just print the whole book and give them 15% of the edition. An author like Tom Raworth has printing experience and practical typographic knowledge so you can discuss the finer points with him, but otherwise you have to bear in mind George Bernard Shaw's remark: "It's a mistake to think the modern author is insensitive to the qualities of a well-made fine press book—he positively hates it!" Most writers have pretty conservative expectations for their work: big margins, nice large letters. They tend to be more concerned with external matters like the cover art or color choices. Darrell Gray flipped out when I showed him the photos by Kathy Silva I wanted to use on *Halos of Debris* (1984). "You can't use those," he said, "it lays the poet's soul bare. How about some daffodils or sunflowers?!!" I used the photos anyway. The title-page is a failure, but otherwise that's a really nice book, I think, as is *A Dog's Life* (1978). I have more Darrell manuscripts I could print, but there's no interest in his writing which means I should do a very small edition, which in turn means it will be expensive, which means I will be accused of all those things I hate about Arion Press and Co: the Artificial Rarity market (actually the term, coined by Graham Mackintosh, is "Artifical Rarity").

I hired Graham to typeset my book *Habitual Own Way* (1981) on his Linotype because I wanted to use Linotype slugs which are easier to lock up at an angle. For that book (which, in my mind, became *Habit Your Own Way* then *Habitual Ennui*), I used all the ideas I had tried to use on other poetry books, but that had been vetoed by the authors: tiny type, small square format, 45 degree angle imposition, glossy paper printed to look like offset. I was just having fun, my text was an excuse to play. Graham got into it and introduced a few subtle typos which I didn't catch—single italic letters in a word, that kind of thing—so he was putting his own oar in there.

Habitual Own Way, cover photo by Shelly Vogel

Generally people hire me because they like my work and want me to be creative. In 1980 Jeffrey Miller of Cadmus Press in Santa Barbara hired me to print a book by Clayton Eshleman, *Nights We Put the Rock Together.* I hated the manuscript, so I set it in 16 point Van Dijck Italic which is pretty unreadable as a text face. Miller thought it looked fine. Eshleman made constant revisions and I had only enough type to do 4 pages at a time, so I was mailing proofs to LA and waiting for him to send them back, then sending revised proofs and so on, and it dragged on and on and became a real headache. To make matters worse Joanne Kyger was over at my shop and started writing marginal comments on the proofs also! Miller threatened me (he actually flashed a gun!) so I gave him the sheets and he had Mackintosh bind them and make the cover. An even weirder thing happened at the West Coast Print Center. As I said we were churning out scores of small press poetry books. I was handed a Jack Hirschman manuscript: it was written in felt pen on napkins. He'd composed it in Vesuvio Cafe and various coffee houses in North Beach in a mad rush (with Russian words, etc.), so I got the job of deciphering it and setting it in type. It was called *The Arcanes of Le Comte de St. Germain* (1977). I did what I could to make sense of it. McBride who was the office manager Xeroxed the galleys and sent them to the publisher for correcting, but the publisher decided he no longer wanted to publish it and blew off the Print Center. Jack got the galleys and did a paste-up and the book was printed offset from uncorrected proofs that had been Xeroxed. It was a mess and a classic exercise in desperation. I must get Jack to inscribe my copy!

When someone hires me though I stay detached from the content and other than suggesting minor changes of grammar or spelling I stay out of their writing (though I may employ little tricks of editing or kerning to obviate bad spaces, but these are trade secrets!). I've just finished a couple of books for a poet who tried to take over my life, I felt like he was stalking me, calling me at all hours to discuss changes and ask little niggling questions about it. He's a 60-year-old teenager: he'd be up drinking all night and then show up at 11 a.m. demanding whisky before he was ready to talk about the work. The work sucked (a brain-dead version of automatic writing: "I don't know where it comes from—I just write it!") and finally I told him to get lost. I need the dough but I don't need the grief. He acted innocent about all matters—typography, scanning, printing—a regular Mr. Skimpole, but would want me to explain the whole process to him so he could understand it. He wasted so much time I was afraid to answer the phone.

I have good friends who are poets whose work I have not (yet) printed. I'm thinking of Tinker Greene and Steve Lavoie, though I did do a little chapbook of Steve's in the Transitional Face series (9 *Further Plastics*, 1984). They both do their own books by Xerox and give them away. In the 1980s I had many long discussions with Bob Grenier about poetry and typography, and two of them were taped, transcribed and printed [in *Ampersand* vol. 6 no. 2, 1986, and *Dark Ages Clasp the Daisy Root* no. 5, 1992]. Bob had made Lyn Heijinian buy a font of Remington typewriter to print one of his books in her Tuumba series. I tried to point out the absurdity of limiting yourself to monospaced letters but Bob had a fanatical, numerological connection to his typewriter at the time. A bit like Aram Saroyan and the concrete poets who used typewriters in the '60s, Bob was extremely stubborn about it. I think mainly he liked having an opposing viewpoint and keeping the argument going. He lived with Larry Eigner, as his caretaker. Larry had cerebral palsy, and I had grown up in a school for spastics in England, where my dad was headmaster, so immediately I could relate to Larry and we became pals (for one thing I could understand what he was saying, and as a poet he was always frustrated trying to talk to people without full control of his facial muscles).

I would go over there at least once a week and hang out and drink Coors beer with Bob (the only flavor he would allow) and sometimes we would listen to African tribal music and we would talk all night. I printed a broadside of Bob's poem "Through the Manacle." I set it in Gill Sans which has an elementary look; Frances illustrated it in pochoir. It's a lovely print though Bob insisted it should have been done in typewriter. After Larry's death he moved to Bolinas (I suggested it as a logical place for him, and he lucked into a really nice spot) and he started writing in blank journals with colored markers. Again, he was pig-headed. He never thought about calligraphy as a discipline, in fact his writing is the opposite: it's cacography. I think Larry's manuscripts subliminally influenced him because they are completely illegible. Bob asked me about printing his

Steven Lavoie, *Nine Further Plastics* (Transitional Face, 1984)

notebooks and I refused to get involved. But he found a rich patron to pay for color Xerox and custom boxes. It's too much effort to try to decipher them, and I fear Bob has gone off the deep end. Partly his disappointment came from being undercut then annihilated by his protégés the Language poets. To make matters worse, Creeley persuaded Stanford to buy Grenier's papers for $50,000, so he sold them a bunch of these illegible scrawl notebooks and that encouraged him to pursue it further instead of either learning calligraphy or transcribing the poems on a keyboard and seeing them in print, legibly.

Since I stopped writing poetry, I have been working pretty consistently on my academic writing. Now I don't even bother with a draft, I open an InDesign document and write in the final form: typeface, type size, format: everything—and that way I can see the book take shape as I write it, and like James Joyce change the wording if I want to make a line-break or page ending look better.

KS: If memory serves, your *A Bibliography of the Auerhahn Press* (1975) wasn't written in InDesign, but in the stick. Your trilogy on Bay Area presses is quite exceptional. Could you talk about how, and why you took this approach as opposed to, say, a more conventional form like descriptive bibliography?

AJ: Ah yes, PC days, pre-computer. Actually each of those was done in a different medium. The *Auerhahn* in the stick but the revisions on the press were not that different from my InDesign fiddling; *White Rabbit* by photo-type and paste-up; and the *Zephyrus Image* digitally on my Macintosh, using Quark. I took a lot of shtick (no pun intended) for the *Auerhahn*, not just the content but the fact that it wasn't bibliographically sophisticated. I used Streeter's bibliography of Dorn, I recall, as a model. But the point is that the books were printed in the typical small press way, two-up on a platen press, hand-collated and delivered to the binder so there were no signature marks and any variants were accidental. They were free-wheeling presses without a set agenda, following their instincts, and so that was my approach to writing them up. Currently I am writing a biography and bibliography of Richard Austin, father and son, the Regency-era artists, and have been using the appropriate bibliographical notations for those books. In fact I have gone overboard, discussing minute variations and problems of collation in a way that most readers will not even look at. This is over-compensation I suppose.

I find when I finish one project I need to go as far as possible in the opposite direction. So after the *Auerhahn* came out and my name became mud among the old boys because I had dared to criticize Andrew Hoyem, I retreated to the sixteenth century and spent the next two years working on the Granjon book. The *Auerhahn* would benefit from a thorough revision. I should interview Andy, if he would talk to me, and let him have his say, because his website and any article printed about him always tells the same story that he was the founder of Auerhahn and printed those Beat poets because he wanted to see their work in print. That was actually the mission statement of Dave Haselwood and his partner Jay McIlroy: Andy was not in that scenario. Andy showed up with Paul Reps' book a few years later, and the previous dozen titles, by Whalen, Welch, McClure, Wieners, Lamantia, and Burroughs' *The Exterminator* are the important books of the press. Andy in fact alienated all those poets so the press no longer had work to print! First he fought with Spicer over *Heads of the Town* (the book that got me interested in Auerhahn in the first place) and then cancelled Duncan's *Book of Resemblances* after Duncan complained about the printing of the prospectus. They took the type and paper they had bought to produce that and printed a book of poetry by Andy. Then they fought with Diane di Prima. So the press was on the skids and Andy's solution was to go after the big money, doing a fancy reprint of Everson's *The Poet is Dead*, which approach altered the direction of the press and led to its demise.

You will notice between pages 48 and 51 of the *Auerhahn* there are lots of illustrations. I was printing it in formes so 47 and 52 were already printed and I had a change of heart and cut all the criticism and imputation of motives to Andrew. But then after my book came out Dave Haselwood told me "Andy is such a slut!" He didn't want to say anything negative beforehand for fear that I might print it, but he really feels Andrew screwed him royally. I walked into a hornet's nest. That was unexpected, but Auerhahn had been in existence only a decade before and suddenly no one would talk about it. In fact Clifford advised me not to write the bibliography but wouldn't say why. People critiqued the typography but I was screwed by Mackenzie-Harris who cast the type for me. I went back and made them recast the a and g because they were misaligned, but it still looks awful. Louie Mitchell (who ran the Monotype caster at M&H) told me, "Fred Goudy said it didn't look handset unless there were crooked letters." The good part of the story is I became friends with Whalen and found his unpublished "Prose Takes" in the press' archive at the Bancroft (which Andy had sold them). There are also great letters from Philip Lamantia there, but he refused to let me print them, saying "I wish to forget that period of eclipsed activity!" because they were from his junkie days in Mexico. I did get to tell the Auerhahn story again in the *BEAT: A Dead Horse* issue of *Ampersand* which is a good companion piece to that bibliography.

I corresponded with Brion Gysin, Burroughs, and Ginsberg just as the whole canonization of the Beats took shape, so people thought I was one of the Beat acolytes, but I really don't think much of the Beat generation as a whole, which is one reason I did the White Rabbit bibliography (1985). From Gysin I wanted to know about the Joujouka musicians and the Hashishim cult. Burroughs came by the press a couple of times. I printed stationery for him and sent him a Xerox of a nineteenth-century book on curing opium addiction. I introduced him to S. Clay Wilson. I wanted to do a book with them together but he was trying to fob off reprint stuff, the book that became *Early Routines*, at which point I decided to stick with younger less-established writers.

The White Rabbit poets were the anti-Beats. I am much more sympathetic to their writing. I did that one relatively quickly because I had access to Graham, but again it could be expanded with more interviews and a larger discussion of the books and their impact. When it was finished we organized a White Rabbit Symposium and Jack Spicer Conference in San Francisco. It was fantastic. There were panels at New College, a group reading at the Art Institute, a couple of book shows at libraries, and an art exhibit at New College Gallery. I drove all over the area borrowing paintings by Jess, Tom Field, etc. and then installed this show and discovered the gallery had no insurance. So I bought a padlock and every night would lock the door with this hasp and lock which anyone with a crowbar could have snapped off! I got everyone to sign the program, except Duncan who didn't stay for the reception. There was a great party at Ernie Edwards' house, which is stuffed with memorabilia of that time. Ann Charters came up to me and said, "What a great success, so who's next? Rexroth? Patchen?" She seemed to think if I had such a success with Spicer I would want to turn it into a business. I hate that mentality but that is how those endless Kerouac books and events keep getting churned out.

Zephyrus Image came about in different circumstances. I ran into Holbrook Teter one day and had lunch with him on Mission Street. He was doing social work and a letter-writing campaign about Pelican Bay Prison. The press was far in his past but I asked him if he would agree to do an event about the Zephyrus Image years. We set it up at the SF Center for the Book. I showed slides of his books and we chatted about the poets and artists and the times in general. There were people out the door, and afterwards I met people who had known Michael in college and lots of characters from the Hippie and Digger years. Again I made an

Ampersand article out of it and then suddenly Holbrook died of a heart attack, on New Years Eve in 1999.

A Bibliography of the Auerhahn Press (1976) and A Bibliography of the White Rabbit (1985)

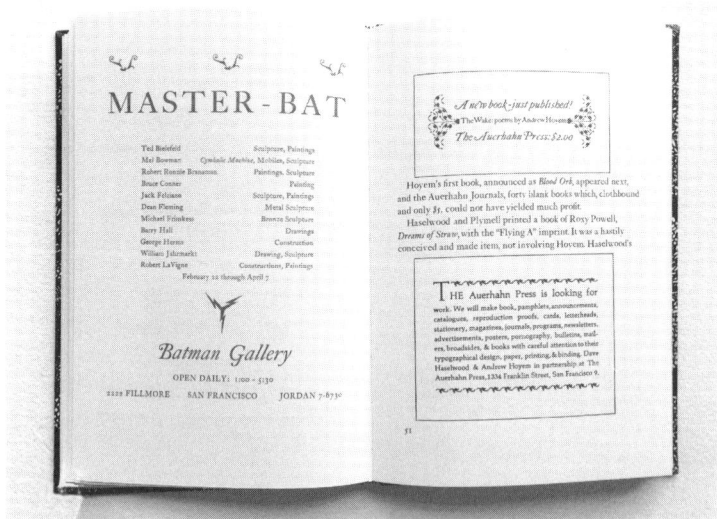

A Bibliography of the Auerhahn Press

Lots of people appeared from the past for his memorial service at the Starr King Unitarian Church on Geary. I realized I was the only one capable of writing about the press, not because I was around, but because I understood their intent and knew all the very different parts of their lives and work. I did a lot of the work by email as people are quick to respond electronically whereas a letter might sit unanswered for months. I called Fielding Dawson in NYC and he sounded a little fuddled and said, "Can you write all this in a letter?" I did but he died a couple of days later, so I never got his input, but I was fortunate to get Edward Dorn, Lucia Berlin (whom I had fallen out with), and others who have also died in the last couple of years. There was an archive but Steve Vincent had taken it from Joan Teter with the intention of selling it. In fact he was selling bits of it and pocketing the money. It took about a year to get it out of him because Joan is such a malleable character. She would go over there to take it back and he would say, I am still working on it. I would find rare proofs at various bookstores and they would say they had bought them from Vincent. When I confronted him about it he said the money was to pay his daughter for creating a computer database of the material. Of course this was never done. The two widows, Joan and Jenny Dorn, were both concerned about their husband's reputations so a lot of important stuff got deleted from the text to appease them. In fact it's "the widows' edition." Michael and Holbrook's relationship was a lot deeper than appears in my text but there are clues in there. Also I had to trick Jenny into talking about the coke use because that was such a major part of the story and she was anxiously sweeping it under the rug. I felt that the best way to tell these stories was to relive it, like a *cinema verité* account rather than an academic approach with citations and references. Partly because it was about a scene I had jumped into and wanted a bit of the background for myself, like tracing your family tree.

KS: I can't remember if I first heard the phrase, "Martha Stewartization of the book arts" from you or Walter, but it stuck with me. Could you elaborate on what MFA programs in writing and artists books have done to the fields and the relationship between the two? Also, any thoughts on how the history of book arts itself has been constructed and where these "fields of activity" may be bound as a result?

AJ: You would have heard "Martha Stewart book arts" from me, as I fed it to Walter, but I got it from someone else who would not want to be named as their job depends on this type of activity. That grew out of the book centers like Minnesota Center for Book Arts, Art Center and the Woman's Building in LA, Book Arts Centers in NYC and SF, etc. They found that the classes that filled up were the simple how to make a book with pretty paper and no ideas ones. These classes appeal to the bored housewives that are the Martha Stewart audience as a step-up from "scrapbooking," perhaps. They are not about to put a Kluge in their garage and start hand-setting their master's thesis on "Robert Fludd to Lawrence Sterne: Symbiosis and the Alchemist's Quest," or whatever. The MFA/Book Arts degree field is very narrow: there were only two schools, Alabama and Mills that were doing it as far as I know and Mills is reduced to virtual invisibility. Though of course there were things at Iowa and probably other universities that showed signs of life but I am not really qualified to discuss this. Kim Merker taught fine printing in the Art Department at Iowa but his assistant Kay Amert abandoned him and set up her own program across campus in the journalism school. So there's little continuity and a lot of factionalism, kind of like rock bands breaking up after their first hit and then they sink like a stone. I know Betsy Davids taught at California College of the Arts and Crafts (now California College of the Arts) in the English Department where they had a press and Walter Hamady at the University of Wisconsin-Madison in the Art Department in a similar setting, but Betsy's students never seemed to have a thorough grasp of the practical side of printing. I taught in the Graduate Book Arts program at Mills until it was disbanded; their problem was no one wanted them, neither art nor literature.

The few years that Mills was going (in the mid '80s) turned out a dozen or more book artists who became the next generation after Poltroon and Rebis. I mean people like Julie Chen, Ruth McGurk, Marie Dern, and others who took my theoretical typography class, along with practical classes in typesetting, printing, binding, etc. That's a wide spectrum of graduates: at one end are the structure fiends like Chen whose works are immaculate but pointless, and then at the other more focused literary printers like Dern at Jungle Garden Press. In the middle you have someone like McGurk and her quirky works. But Ruth McGurk is one of the few people I will take criticism from: you cannot diss my work unless yours is better. Some of the Mills graduates went into commercial design and quite a few only did one or two books before vanishing. I had a Vandercook in my graphic design class at UC Berkeley when I taught in the Architecture Department and Frances used a press in her design courses at Davis but they were very different from the handpress courses you would expect from Kentucky or a library school approach. Strangely when I went to college in Watford, outside London, there was a printing department, where students learned print production (for management training, I think) but there was a real printshop with Heidelberg cylinders, Monotypes, Linotypes, etc. Several of my roommates were taking graphic design and printing classes and would print up posters for our little revues. One of their teachers was Hansjörg Mayer. This meant nothing to me then, but I could have saved myself a lot of time if I had just been in a different program there!

That's all history now, like Fleet Street, but there is Camberwell with an ongoing program, but again I don't really know what is going on there, whether it's writing and book arts, or printmaking and bookmaking combined. Given that we have had a generation appear in the wake of this academic activity I am surprised there are no big names who are writers who have also been involved in innovative bookmaking. But then Walter Hamady had a teacher, and so did Alan Kornblum who was a student of Harry Duncan at Iowa. Kathy Walkup, who runs the Mills program, studied under Clifford Burke.

The problem of definition is paramount: "I say it's an artists book therefore it is," is the consensus. So we have books that are all about *livres d'artiste* (Riva Castleman, etc.). and others that are about democratic multiples, and most just pick and choose. Walter Hamady and Claire Van Vliet got left out of everyone's book until the latest one by Betty Bright and I would say they are the pivotal figures in the field, along with Hedi Kyle.

The artists book phenomenon didn't just appear suddenly with Ed Ruscha. You need to go back to pre-book structures (as Hedi Kyle has done) and come forward by devious paths through scientific books with moving parts, children's books, trade catalogues, advertising ephemera, photography monographs, Georgian *samizdat* pamphlets, etc. It's too vast to be encapsulated in the usual silly little books that just go through a shelf of recent work and tell you what's on it. I once heard a famous book artist lecture. She showed a slide: "Here's a nice slide..." (pause; next slide) "Here's another nice slide," etc.

And new stuff turns up all the time. I saw a bookdealer's catalogue recently and he was offering, for a vast sum, a book of photographs of LA Gas Stations. A unique work, from the 1930s. Someone had gone out and made these architectural studies of all the gas stations and glued them in an album. Ed Ruscha *ante litteram*. It's a chance survival but it's also good that this bookdealer found it because he will sell it for hundreds of dollars to an institution guaranteeing its survival and that it will get noticed, whereas there are other books like this that show up in yard sales and thrift stores and end up in people's hoards of *curiosa* (I have a few myself!). So the field needs a more thorough investigation. There are so many books—on Nature printing, Chinese varnish, mixing watercolor, *faux marbre* technique, grain painting, painting with wax, optics, dyeing, counterfeiting, patternmaking, color theory,

Japanese painting, blind reading—that are inspiration, source-books and forerunners of artists books that need to be investigated. The problem is that very few copies survived and there is no bibliographical reference, so it's serendipity. All of those examples by the way are in the latest Charles B. Wood catalogue, where I went looking for the gas station book, which was not there.

KS: It seems to me that many of the most interesting writers will publish in whatever little magazine or small press accepts or solicits their work. Many of the editors of these outfits have no background in design or publishing, but their hearts are more or less in the right places and sometimes the results are unexpected and wonderful. Disaster strikes too! In turn, the private press (as I understand it) tends toward authors whose work caters to "official verse culture." It isn't necessary to name names, but it's safe to say that Poltroon has introduced me to more than a handful of authors I wouldn't have read otherwise, i.e. if you publish it, I'll read it. Why? Because they're always great—okay, Lucia Berlin for starters and more recently Mark Coggins. There are a few other presses that I respect similarly. Could you talk in greater detail about where artists books meet the small press, private press, and the literary fine press and how you see Poltroon in this (enormous) spectrum?

AJ: I've lost touch with the world of little magazines. Not that I ever followed them closely. I always thought the functional-looking ones (*Stand*, *Granta*, *Evergreen Review*, *Chicago Review*) were the most serious. *Samizdat* is good, typewritten and multi-lithed or Xeroxed, but when the little mags start getting letter-precious or over-designed they lose their authenticity and urgency (*McSweeney's* comes to mind as a ready-made collectible like *Aspen*). Then the editors become this greasy eminence, to coin a phrase, I mean other poets are in awe of Cid Corman or Clayton Eshleman and revere their work. Even a character like Jonathan Williams, bless him, is a mediocre poet but wants impeccable editions of his work when others print it. There's an inverse ratio between the quality of the writing and the quality of the books in those cases. It's true the little mag scene is where you discover emerging talent (I first read Kapuskinski in *Granta*), but I prefer serendipity. Living in the Bay Area put me in touch with a vibrant literary scene. I met Tom Raworth and Ed Dorn through Holbrook and Michael. When Lucia Berlin started reading her work in public several of us, including Michael Wolfe of Tombouctou and Bob Callahan of Turtle Island were vying to get the first book-length manuscript out of her. We all discovered her simultaneously and we all eventually did books by her. I trust in my instincts and don't expect to make money at it. As soon as Lucia's work took off I relinquished the rights so she could go to Black Sparrow and get a bigger audience.

I am really proud of that book by Robert Gregory, *Interferences* (1987), his first publication. It was the only unsolicited manuscript I did. I used to get almost weekly manuscripts in the mail and would just skim the first page then put them back in the return envelope and drop it in the box on the way out of the post office (if they'd bought a Poltroon book first I would have become rich and they would have known not to send their stuff!). I read the first three lines of "Red birds carrying rain" by Robert Gregory and immediately thought, "Ah, real poetry." So I asked if he had more like that and he sure did. His second book was published by some university press and won a bunch of writing awards.

Coggins is a Stanford grad who took my book design class to self-publish. After the class he took me to lunch and said, "Look, I cannot do this, so I want to hire you to design my book and give me some pointers about getting it out." He gave me a Raymond Chandler first edition he wanted it to resemble so it was a fun project, and a challenge. As I was working on it I of course read it closely and by the time I had proofs for him I also said I wanted to publish it, so we were both happy. His third book I think has a New York publisher.

I was fortunate in my poetic education. I read avidly as a kid and my parents encouraged me. My dad loved T.S. Eliot and when I started wearing a battered top hat and an army great-coat he gave me a Beckett novel! When I was a teenager Tom Pickard started the Morden Tower reading series in Newcastle, where I grew up, and so I got to hear all this fantastic poetry, like Bunting reading "Briggflatts" with Scarlatti on reel-to-reel tape. That was Tom's great discovery. The visiting Americans and Europeans gave it an international scope, but the local lads, Tony Jackson, Tony Harrison, Barry MacSweeney, were all really interesting poets. Robert Bly gave out little pamphlets of Issa haiku he'd translated. Mine was stolen by Darrell Gray! I took a writing workshop from Roy Fisher and started collecting Fulcrum Press, Penguin Modern Poets, Cape Goliard. I loved the Penguins: *Children of Albion*, edited by Michael Horovitz, and *Poetry of the Committed Individual*, edited by Jon Silkin. And a book called *Love, Love, Love* that had a psychedelic cover and poets like Anselm Hollo, Pete Brown, and Adrian Mitchell. Those are all practical inexpensive paperbacks, though Goliard had some attempts at creative design. Then I discovered Trigram Press and Raworth; and, after I came to California, found the Bay Area small presses I have written about, and others like Divers Press that have great design combining good artwork with smart typography. That's what I appreciate and have tried to do with Poltroon. I don't pay any attention to the private presses (or "fine" presses—do they hold out their pinkies while they print?) that just reprint stuff or the gimmick-chasers which is where the idea of the artists book meets the fine press—Arion Press' edition of Ashbery's *Self-Portrait in a Convex Mirror* which is gauche or Peter Koch's lead book—but that's just my taste. Their work makes me ralph whereas others pay big bucks for it and eat it up. Fine presses, in general, are afraid to take chances which is why they will go for the Ferlinghetti reprint or the overdone binding. I see frightful stuff at huge prices, like Gunnar Kaldewey, and librarians think it's da bomb whereas I see shitty typography and ill-conceived design ideas. Those things are not books, they are marketing devices.

There's a connection between the little magazine and the small press in that we are almost interchangeable. Letterpress chapbooks are labor-intensive but a series like my Poltroon Modern Poets—or Toothpaste Press or Oyez! to name some others—is like a little magazine (very sporadic, esoteric, obscure work, etc). If you look at poetry bibliography it's the same crashing about in the darkness. Take Creeley, for instance. First book *Le Fou*: Columbus, Ohio, Golden Goose Press, 1952. I've never seen it but imagine it as a typical small press production, handmade, handbound. Then *Printing is Cheap in Mallorca* is his second publication, and you see where this is going. Self-published and immediately he has a circle and support network: Duncan, Olson, Blackburn, etc. Then in 1955 Jonathan Williams takes him on and the next year Henry Evans in San Francisco (who sold his type and press to Dave Haselwood); then Migrant Press in Worcester (England, not Massachusetts) does *The Whip*— that's Gael Turnbull—but it's printed by Mossen Alcover in Palma de Majorca. From Majorca he stands astride the world: one foot in Black Mountain and the English avant-garde scene under the other. It takes him a decade but with a little help from his friends he scores Scribner's in 1962 and is on the landscape as a major American voice, not yet 40. This network is important because you then see the connection to other poets with the same or similar publishers. With Duncan it goes back to Bern Porter, an important figure on the American scene and an early exponent of artistic books.

But it changed when Black Sparrow came along. That was more a marketing venture. John Martin collected D.H. Lawrence I think, but got Duncan, Bukowski, and Tom Clark to pick titles for him, so the esoterica (John Fante, Fielding Dawson) comes from their taste. I imagine Ecco Press is the same and some other later ones. Not that it's bad to get suggestions but it lacks a singular mind, an individuality. Martin's books are truly ugly but he had this concept: 26 lettered and signed copies, 100 numbered in cloth, and 1000 trade paperback. All his titles are that way.

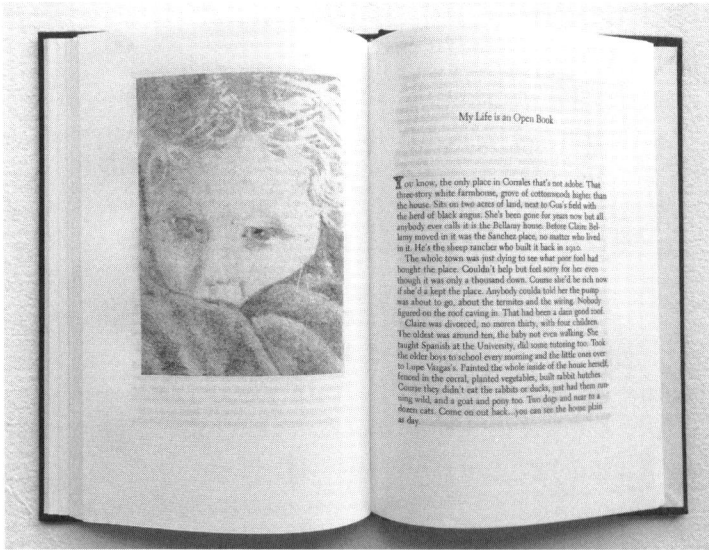

Lucia Berlin, *Safe & Sound* (Poltroon Press, 1988); illustration by Frances Butler

He even did a signed Gertrude Stein by buying a collection of her checks and cutting out the signatures and mounting them in the 26 copies! That's pretty inspired. But it's a marketing mentality, he just switched from office furniture to books.

Art Beck's translations of *Luxorius* (1990) is the only instance where I think I made a successful artists book and literary work in one, well, maybe *Muted Hawks* (1995) by Tom Raworth. I make no claims for the literary merit of the books I wrote that Frances illustrated—*Confracti* (1976) and *New Dryads* (1980)— they are more typical artists books in that there is an obvious imbalance between the structure and art and the "literary" content. My texts are really just filler, though if I can persuade her to finish *Western Excess*, Frances' book on boundaries she has been working on for twenty years, I think it will have both meaningful content and great imagery.

The curators determine a lot of where the artists book movement is headed. I was fortunate to be acquired by Marvin Sackner and Clive Philpott, and that's a seal of approval I want. But the contemporary scene seems to be the same wherever you are with maybe the Dutch as the best in all classes. There's a show of 13 German Book Artists at the San Francisco Public Library right now. I walked in and my first impression was it's exactly like the PCBA members' show, maybe a bit more upmarket. The German books seem better made on the whole, though there are the same goofy ideas about structure and materials.

My place in all this? I don't know. For me artists books are throwaway gestures, almost private. I teach artists book classes to elementary school kids in the inner city and they love it, the magic of discovering that books are not just commodities to buy. I make little one-offs for my own amusement or to give away. The books I write I want to get out to a big audience; those I publish I try to conceive as real books that are affordable, will function normally and last.

KS: A final question: Have you begun the restoration of your Stanhope? And could you describe other projects in the works?

AJ: I have finished the restoration of the Stanhope! I made a trial impression last week and it looked awful so I am pondering the next step. The dealer who sold it to me lied and said it was in working order. Still, he did not know the value of it, so I figured I would lose the $1,000 cash deposit I had sent him and I had flown to Florida to get it, so I just decided to go through with it. It took over a year to get the rails welded back together. They had snapped at the bolts (I suspect he lifted it up with a forklift). The guy who welded the broken parts is an expert metalworker who rebuilds old motorbikes but he had to contemplate it for a while. Then he had forgotten what he was doing so came back to look at it. During the year I cleaned it thoroughly, with small metal tools—make-up rule and tweezers—and a toothbrush, gouged out the rotten wood in the base and poured in a gallon of marine epoxy. When we put the rails on we broke a bolt that holds the ribstay in place, and he offered to make me a new bolt. After a couple of weeks I went over to his shop in Redwood City and picked up the parts. He had drilled them out for a ¾″ bolt, which I bought, cut off to length with a hacksaw and pulled the two bits together. With a little effort it all clicked back into place beautifully.

It's an incredible machine, very transparent technology and brilliantly designed. I look forward to doing all my printing on it soon (not the jobwork, unless I find some rich patron). I had to get a frisket frame made and it's missing four small plates that bolt onto the bed to hold the chase in place. I asked a friend to make them for me from bronze and I drew up a new wooden handle which should arrive in a day or two. The frisket had a double layer of felt nailed onto it, which I replaced but clearly that's a bad idea (hence the blurry impression), so I need to look at Richard-Gabriel Rummonds' book and the Allens' book and figure out what would make a better packing. I have a vision of a book in my head using wood type and the full 20″ x 30″ forme but I will probably start out slowly with smaller projects. Maybe Charles Pasley's letters to Wordsworth if I can get permission to do them. I haven't planned any new books in a while, I have been too busy researching and writing the Austin biography, and now starting work on the Loy book on nineteenth-century American type I am doing with Steve Saxe. Meanwhile my book on vernacular letterforms is sitting on a publisher's desk in London, so either I will have to rework it or send it to someone else who is more excited about it, so I don't want to get too involved in anything else while I have these three things up in the air.

I am hoping to do a type specimen facsimile with an introduction by Nicolas Barker, but that's been in the planning stage for over a decade: his brief intro turned into a full-fledged biography so it may have outgrown my idea. However now I can do it on the handpress. I hope you will see a combination of letterpress and laser- or inkjet-prints in the future and it will work well together.

[2007]

Johanna Drucker
Druckwerk

Born in Philadelphia in 1952, Johanna Drucker is a prolific poet, book artist, and scholar. Drucker earned her BFA from California College of Arts and Crafts in 1973 and became immersed in a lively community of poets, publishers, and artists living in the Bay Area. She went on to pursue a doctorate from University of California, Berkeley and has since served as a professor at Columbia University, Yale University, and the University of Virginia. Drucker is the author of a wide range of scholarly works, including: *Theorizing Modernism: Visual Art and the Critical Tradition* (1994); *The Visible Word: Experimental Typography and Modern Art* (1994); *The Alphabetic Labyrinth: The Letters in History and Imagination* (1995); *A Century of Artists' Books* (1995); *Sweet Dreams: Contemporary Art and Complicity* (2005); and *Graphesis: Visual Forms of Knowledge Production* (2014). Drucker has also created over fifty artists books, many printed letterpress with handset type using her own illustrations, produced under the Druckwerk imprint. Her artists books have been collected and exhibited worldwide. A master printer, Drucker is the inaugural Breslauer Professor of Bibliographical Studies in the Department of Information Studies at UCLA. She is recognized internationally for her research on the history of graphic design, typography, experimental poetry, fine art, as a pioneer in digital humanities, and the history of visual information.

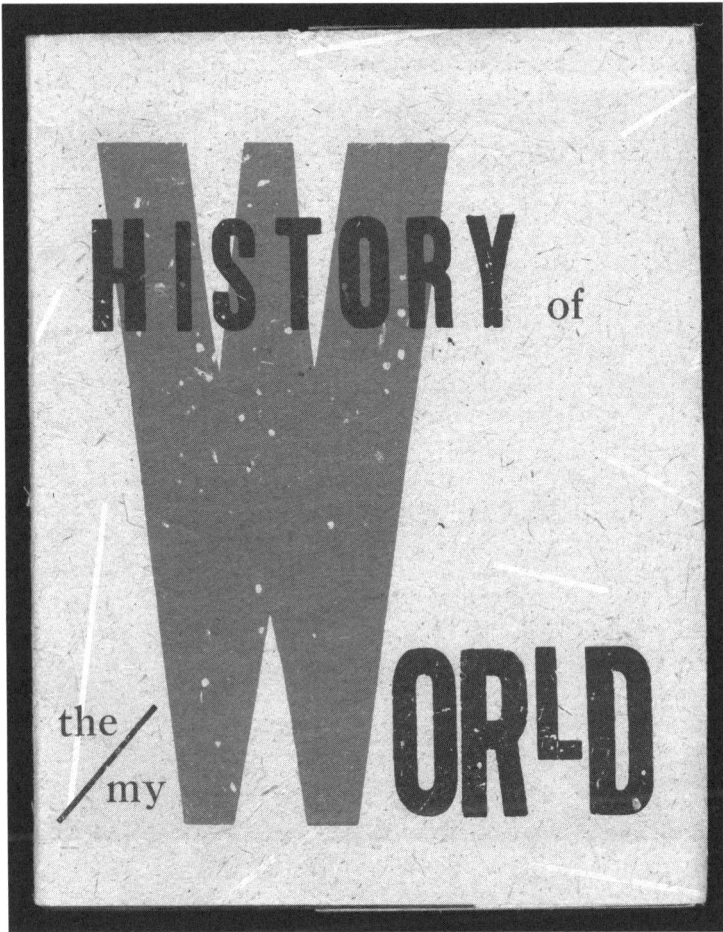

Johanna Drucker, *History of the/my Work(l)d* (Druckwerk, 1990)

KS: Interviews can be somewhat predictable; they often begin with the interviewer asking a question about the distant past and work their way toward the present. I know that you've recently relocated from Charlottesville, where you were the Robertson Chair of Media Studies, and that you're back in California, currently in residence at Stanford University. Perhaps you could begin by discussing your current writing and research projects?

JD: I'm in transit this year, with the privilege of being the digital humanities fellow at the Stanford Humanities Center. The project for which I got the fellowship is titled "Diagrammatic Interpretation." This is a historically-informed critique of information visualization as it is appropriated from empirical sciences into humanistic studies. My argument, as yet to be developed, is that the epistemology of "representation" that underpins most data visualization is not appropriate to the interpretative methods of humanities scholars for whom point of view and historical subjectivity are essential factors. My critique actually goes a bit farther than this, suggesting that the concepts of self-evident identity and stable relation between image and data are themselves suspect within the frameworks of post-Structuralist and cognitive studies approaches to knowledge as co-dependent and emergent, rather than static, fixed, mechanistic.

This research extends work I did at Virginia, most of which is about to be published in *SpecLab: Digital Aesthetics and Speculative Computing*, due out from University of Chicago Press in spring 2009. Watching humanists cede intellectual authority to the exigencies of computational methods pushed us to provocative projects. I teamed up with book experts Jerry McGann and Bethany Nowviskie and set up SpecLab to introduce aesthetic concerns and speculative, non-mechananistic principles into our projects, even if this made them difficult to realize. One of these projects was "Subjective Meteorology," which I was able to develop while a digital cultures Fellow at the University of California, Santa Barbara in company of Alan Liu and his circle. That project also had a book form, which can be seen at www.artistsbooksonline.org—the online artists book collection I built at the University of Virginia.

My creative energies have largely focused on getting my artists book *Combo Meals* (2008) perfected. I used Amazon's CreateSpace to do a print-on-demand edition of this and learning how to work with the transformations from on-screen PDF to finished object took some—not a lot—of trial and error. And now, my chief project has been the ongoing manuscript *Poetry Wars*, which traces the lived history of avant-garde poetry through a *roman à cléf* from 1975 to the present, though broken into several volumes.

Making the shift of institutions—and life—from Virginia to Los Angeles is also a major project since my teaching focus will change from media studies and literature to information studies and history of the book. While there is considerable overlap, the constituency of a professional graduate program is not the same as that of an undergraduate one and the charge to the Breslauer professor involves considerable attention to special collections materials at UCLA. Needless to say, the treasures there are beyond the reach of single lifetime's teaching dedication, but the task is one I am very happy to contemplate taking up. I'll also be moving my little Vandercook and skimpy type collection, so setting up a new shop on the campus with which to inspire another community of designers, scholars and creative writers will be a factor in what unfolds as well.

KS: I've heard many references to *Poetry Wars*, but I'm still not sure that I understand exactly who was involved and what was at stake. I'm also curious why you chose to write a *roman à clef* rather than a memoir?

JD: I think a memoir pretends to fidelity—to actual persons and events—while a novel presents itself as fiction. I chose to write *Poetry Wars* as a novel, derived from impressions of real events and experiences, but meant to tell a story of a generation, a time, an era and a history of avant-garde poetry from a distinctly personal point of view. The book has a long time span. It begins with early struggles to understand and define a poetics, continues with professional achievement—including academia and critical success—and then examines the effects of fame and success in a highly mediated world. We could not have imagined that world in 1975 because it did not exist and the attitude that poetry was "other" than the realm of media spectacle was so absolutely entrenched.

The "wars" in the title of this multi-part project has several meanings, but above all refers to the struggle over ideas of poetry—what it means to write experimental work in our (my) generation, how poetry can offer an alternative to the administered and spectacularized world, provide other ways of thinking about experience and being. These are real struggles, real "wars" in our lived lives. But the central idea of the book—what is the value of poetry and experimental work in particular and how did it change as the world changed—is the main question I am addressing. But I am also interested in the links between particular beliefs and the character of individual people and how these have an effect on the fate of ideas. Some people adapt and change, others rigidify into orthodoxy, and oddly, so do the ideas they have.

By writing a novel, a work of fiction, I am turning away from accountability to individuals as themselves, giving myself permission to change and alter at will to suit the story. The portraits in the book are synthetic, usually hybrids of various persons I've known, some more or less fully invented, others closer to an actual model or individual, but in no sense are these characters "real" persons. However, all ideas live in people, and social relations are an essential aspect of the ways ideas come to have power. I have always been interested in reading about the Bloomsbury circle, and the Surrealists, and the Russians, and getting a glimpse into the human relations that helped shape the wrestling of ideas. *Poetry Wars* is, in that sense, in the tradition of the novels of H.D. or Djuna Barnes—women's recollections of scenes witnessed and known and lived. If I were to write a straight memoir, then I would feel constrained to a very limited portrayal of people as themselves. This is not about people, but ideas; it is a work of cultural criticism and personal history, not an exposé. Persons inclined to project themselves into any fictional character with whom they have the slightest resemblance will have ample opportunity to do so—but it will be projection, insofar as there are portraits here, they are meant as appreciative recollections of aspects of very complex people whose ambitions and strivings were sincere and engaged in a deeply committed investigation of important intellectual and aesthetic issues. But they also lived these ideas, we all did, and do. At the end of one of the early chapters, when Dawn, who is about as un-idealized a portrait of a young woman who could be me, a character resembling my own chubby, unformed and naïve self at the time, meets another major figure named Will, the narrator says, "You don't meet poetry. You meet poets." I think you can't separate ideas from individual characters, personalities, beliefs.

I think the notion of the avant-garde as a resistant instrument is an idea that aligns with particular character types. I've never believed in resistance or difficulty for its own sake, as political acts, for instance, and in that I differ from many of my colleagues in the critical, academic world, in the art world and in the poetry world. My sense is that the function of aesthetic activity is the transformation of experience or thought or sensation into form. The possibility of giving form as a cognitive and social act is powerful; inventing new forms of thought is a way to reimagine the world. This is a profound and essential part of human capability. But politics—instrumental, applied and transformative work—is another matter. The idea of avant-garde resistance that we absorbed in the 1970s was a residual legacy of late modern responses to fascism, totalitarianism and the rise of a consumer culture that seemed to have equally terrifying features. It was an idea formulated by Theodor Adorno and Max Horkheimer, by Clement Greenberg most famously in "Avant-Garde and Kitsch" and, to a lesser but important degree, in the work of those Russian Formalists for whom the modes of conventional realism were considered an instrument of false consciousness.

Poetry Wars is not didactic. It is elegiac, descriptive, commemorative and meant to be entertaining and engaging. It is an attempt to recall a lost world and time of the 1970s, then 1980s and early 1990s, in the later parts. Above all, it is written as a novel because I want to tell a story and tell it for an audience not entirely composed of people looking to see if they are in it. That aspect of the project, the search to self-identify or recognize people or partial profiles, is trivial, irrelevant to the larger challenge of trying to understand the way we are produced as subjects of history as well as in history. That, too, is an old theme—not my own, but one I've worked on in other creative books. The artists book behind this project is *From A to Z*, the book printed in 1977 from 48 drawers of type, as a summing up of two years of work at the West Coast Print Center as printer and technical support.

None of us has exclusive claim on historical events wc have lived through, or the impressions we leave on others of our selves and lives. This book is no different from most of the other creative books I've worked on—it is an attempt to turn experience into form, aesthetic expression, for the sake of communicating some insight to an audience beyond myself. The only difference is that unlike *From A to Z*, which contains much information, it is not in code. The spell under which the prohibition to write fiction

From A to Z (Chased Press, 1977), hand-set and printed at the West Coast Print Center, Berkeley, CA held me since those days is broken, in part by the act of writing about the original scene in which that taboo was so deeply impressed upon me.

KS: Because the edition was necessarily limited, I know a lot of people have read about *From A to Z* or seen it at Artists' Books Online, but haven't had the opportunity to actually read it, to spend time with the book itself. Will *Poetry Wars* be released as a trade or limited edition? And is it an artists book?

JD: I've written *Poetry Wars* as a straight novel, with the idea that the audience will be broader than the insider scene, even if it holds particular interest for others who shared that time and the development of a particular strain of late avant-garde poetry—so I would like it to be published as a trade book. I thought about doing something more artifactual in the design, but it gets kitsch-cute so fast once you do that. I have all sorts of letters and notes from that period, and some might be used in endpapers or cover designs, but I deliberately wrote the text to be legible in a conventional mode. No tricks, no devices, no experiments except in the poems and prose pieces within the book that are writings by the poets, who are characters. I have thought about doing a small book that would anthologize these and calling it *Everybody Else's Writing*, but even that seems a little silly, though it could be fun.

I think I might do an annotated *From A to Z* in facsimile. I have all the scans, so this would be easy to produce now and could make a good counterpart, as well. But my focus is on getting *Poetry Wars* published, and that has enough challenges in it for the moment. I'm not sure I even know how to find a trade publisher or agent, as my experiences in the past have been mixed and without any success. I've written quite a few other novels that are unpublished, but nothing of this scope or depth before. The character who narrates *Poetry Wars*, Dawn, wrote another novel a few years ago, titled *Like Totally*, which is very funny—a meta-chick-lit book about two adolescent girls competing for erotic experience as a route to enlightenment. I tried to find an agent for that book but wasn't successful. I think I have to be much more persistent. I've gotten used to academic presses and success with my critical work and with artists books, but that doesn't translate into mainstream publishing circles.

KS: Your writing, art, and research cover a lot of ground, cross a number of genres, disciplines and mediums. For instance, as a scholar, you've written on media studies, poetry, fiction, art history, graphic design, feminism, philosophy, critical theory, and let's not forget artists books, a discourse that you've pioneered. The list goes on, and within those broad categories, you've addressed a staggering range of specific topics, brought fresh insight and ideas to the table and made important connections between seemingly disparate artistic and intellectual communities. What are some of the questions that help you find continuity in your scholarly research, and are they the same questions you ask in your art?

JD: All my work is united by a few key themes. My academic and critical passions are driven by a fundamental belief in the power of aesthetics as a form of knowledge and knowing. This was sparked early on in creative work as well by a conviction that the visual properties of language were essential to meaning production. That simple, single idea arose from my printed book work, but also became central to the research for my scholarly books *The Visible Word* (1994), *The Alphabetic Labyrinth* (1995), *Figuring the Word* (1998) and the book with Emily McVarish, *Graphic Design History: A Critical Guide* (2008), as well as for the art historical and digital projects.

That inquiry continues in my work on diagrams, which itself extends the projects in "Temporal Modeling," "Ivanhoe," "Subjective Meteorology," and other graphical projects. I think my understanding of epistemology has become better informed, so the notion of knowledge has shifted from older, mechanistic ideas of "things" "known" to a probabilistic and co-dependent situation of knowing. A few key references put this in context: the radical constructivism of Ernst von Glasersfeld, Heinz von Foerster's second-generation systems theory, and the truly inspirational work of the biologist of cognition, Humberto Maturana. In all of their work, as in the world of numerous critical philosophers, the idea of a post-Cartesian idea of knowledge emerges. I'm still passionate about visuality and increasingly interested in mapping a theory of aesthetics grounded in these ideas of radical epistemology. The diagram project is a step in that direction.

My creative work takes up other themes, particularly narrative and women's lives, reflections on language (visuality, constraints, generative possibilities) and reflections on the state of the world. If you look across the artists books I've done, they fall pretty much into those three realms. I write as a way of knowing, to figure things out and to make experience over into form, to have experience. All of these draw on critical sources in the study of feminism, art, media studies, graphic design and philosophy of language, of course, but they are not didactic works; they are aesthetic projects.

Does that framing provide a bit of coherence?

KS: It certainly does, though I must say that the tension between your eclecticism and specialization is quite unlike most of the poet-scholars of your generation. Could you talk more specifically about the relationship between aesthetics and epistemology in your creative prose and artists books before you began publishing your critical writing? When you were entering graduate school, did you fear that enrolling in a PhD program might detract from your attention to your artistic practice, and if so, were there any particular moments where you could pinpoint the influence or presence of your academic environment in your artistic practice? Conversely, I imagine that your thesis, "Ecriture: Writing as a Visual Representation of Language," did not address your own art directly, as some creative PhD programs permit students to do today, but that you were, on slightly different terms, enriching your practice as an artist.

JD: I think perhaps eclecticism feeds specialization, but I also think that my driving interest in visual knowledge production—in writing, graphical forms—is so outside of most disciplinary fields that it requires a broad base. I'm still struck by the fact that only a handful of scholars in the humanities take a serious interest in visual epistemology. I'm equally struck by the absence of a place in the academy for the history and theory of writing and inscription/notation. My goal is to produce some synthetic work in this field—the diagram project is part of that—to open some insights into this rich realm. The treasures of historical legacy alone are enough to entice the eye and mind—look at the work of Robert Fludd or Athanasius Kircher as dramatic demonstrations of visual knowledge production, chart the distance between these seventeenth-century figures and the beliefs of the Encyclopédistes, and you see the cultural universe shift.

The challenge is to find the focal point of expression within the expanded field of perception. Process is the means to articulate this relation, though I am nowhere near able to do so to the extent I would like. When I was quite a young writer, I only thought about the associational capabilities of prose. Density, distillation, and double-triple entendres, a grasping at recollected phrases twisted and parodied, the inventory of what I'd read, forms adopted and torqued—knowing was only in writing, making experience into language. That would have been true for the early, early books—*Dark* (1972), *Fragile* (1977), *As No Storm* (1975). With the 1976 book, *Twenty-six '76*, a whole other level of self-consciousness about form and language registers became part of the visualization. That book was conceived as a pictorial landscape with space and depth, and the typography was meant to distinguish found, narrative, overheard, and meta-language about the book itself. Typographic style as individual voice became one of the motifs of *From A to Z* (1977), as well as book format and structure as ways to organize a field of social relations. I won't go on and on, but each of the books I've done has

twenty-six

'76

LET HER's
not a matter of permission

2:J&B

Twenty-six '76 (Chased Press, 1976)

had a considered graphical format that informs—that is, creates a semantic structure in—the work.

I didn't go back to school until 1980, and by then I'd already done *Experience of the Medium* (1978), *'S Crap 'S Ample* (1980), *Jane Goes Out w' the Scouts* (1980), *Netherland: How (so) Far* (1978), and was working hard on the writings and drawings that became *Against Fiction* (1984) and *Just As* (1983). I made a very conscious decision not to blur the boundaries between creative practice and scholarship. I wanted to learn things that were new, and also, I did not want to study literature or poetry since I felt that was too close. I didn't want the self-consciousness of trying to position my work in relation to critical discussions of literature. That was a bit naïve, and of course I did immediately start to see intersections and exchanges between what I was studying and what I was writing. That was particularly true of critical theory—and Structuralist, post-Structuralist, and feminist strains of language and approach became a part of the final versions of *Against Fiction* and *Bookscape* (1986–1988), both from the mid-'80s. And *Tongues*, one of my favorite pieces of that period, was a procedural work that came right out of the theoretical discussions that were all over the architecture department and film studies at Berkeley in that period. *Through Light and the Alphabet* (1986) and *The Word Made Flesh* (1987) were both direct responses to Derridian deconstruction, demonstrations of materiality in play.

The dialogue of historical work and creative practice remains central to what I do, and I'm always aware of the timing that makes an academic book coincide with a creative one. *The Visible Word* and the two books just mentioned happened at the same time, and that makes sense, for instance—or *Damaged Spring* (2003) being written with *Sweet Dreams*, or *Testament of Women* (2005) coinciding with *Graphic Design History: A Critical Guide* (2008), the book I did with Emily McVarish. *Combo Meals* is the other product of that period, and it has the most vivid presentation of my painted imagery of any book to date—partly because the technology of print on demand allows color reproduction in new and affordable ways. And "Subjective Meteorology" is a direct outgrowth of digital work, even had a digital form, so definitely fits with *SpecLab* where it also is featured as one of the projects.

Right now I'm steeped in diagrams and would love to write something creative about the amazing Annie Besant, but it will have to wait. Instead, I'm trying to do a small demonstration of the principles of probabilistic materiality in a creative piece for *Parallax* that will show some of the principles I'm writing about

Damaged Spring (Druckwerk, 2004)

in *Diagramming Interpretation,* the critical book I'm scribbling away on. I think I am fortunate in having developed various skills over the years so that I feel a certain fluidity in moving from drawing and layout design to the craft of prose while drawing on scholarly work. Of course I always feel I am just at the beginning and that the most synthetic and interesting work is ahead. I'm excited that I'll be able to teach the history of the book, typography, information visualization and other topics that I have not yet been able to teach now that I'm the Breslauer Professor in Bibliographical Studies. But at the same time, the idea of being in Los Angeles and seeing lots of vibrant contemporary art will be invigorating as well. When I look ahead, I see an inexhaustible array of possibilities—more things to write about and work with than I will be able to manage in this lifetime.

[2008]

AGAINST: As IN, LEANS, Is OPPOSED TO; a Dependent CONFLICT, The REFU-tation and the support. Gratifying hook

INTO ATTENTION AND OBLIVION. AN OUTGROWN FORM, ADDICTIVE, SEDUCTIVE. OPENinG WitH ALL I CAn RECALL Of -- The Drama, Forces and Fate, As an Inevitable Configuration. No Lost Time In The Narrative -- Plunges Deliberate. The traditional obsession with categorical order required the unities of time, place and character, one room after another

AVAILABLE TO PLAN, SECTION AND ELEvATION AS IF THEY HAD BEEN CONSTRUCTED FROM IT. 'AS IF -' ELIMINATIvE SUPPORTS. INSTEAD: The corner of the room gaped wide open, just as she imagined it would standing there yesterday with a grin in her hand and a paper across her face stating the conditions of occupancy. The issue of shelter had become a melodrama wide open to the air. And the social climate so full of abuse there was no way to formulate those grand statements -- that this was the stock from which the ancient races had sprung -- and no way not to. Vitality put up strong resistance. Decay was the active component. The force of communication was no longer contained within wires, but flew through the open air, wild, exciting, and slightly disturbed by the random quality of noise.

AGAINST. Lean. Force. To no immediate, linear resolution, no neat artifice opposed to the aCtual. Real. The bullet grazed God's shoulder. **Make directly,** make a correspondence to, or make an independent conceit. Not deeply, just enough to burn along the surface of the flesh, leaving a red hot welt. **Riding the line between the specimen figure and its activity, ground.** He didn't flinch; the muscles of his torso tightened and gleamed where they were exposed from the shining emerald costume. **Invert them, make their organic struCture inTo a CodifiEd formaliTy.** I could see nothing of his face, of course, behind the painted mask, but the heat inside it caused the fluid in the fake eyes to glow intensely. **ThE program so displayEd ExTEnds iTsELF Through digEaTiOn; WhaT NEEds TO bE EaTEn is a WAy inTO fOrm.** Then smoke began to stream, quietly, threateningly, from his jaws. It was terrifying. This had gone beyond being a game, so far beyond that I began to have serious questions about the success of the group's pursuit of cult power. Against all rational instincts I wondered if they hadn't surpassed the natural limits and touched into something beyond . . . What else could explain the control this Being had over himself and the group so conspicuously forming a nodre around him. The plaster front of the building blew open from the small explosion. The whole flat facade collapsed forward on its face, and the heap of bodies that fell out on top of it in that instant, gems pouring out of a burst casket, glittered with paste jewels on tan flesh, running with blood from the ritual wounds. They weren't dead, only exhausted from the frenzy, orgiastic rites of ceremonial pain. They lay sweating, baubles piled all over each other, slightly dazed. What a day at the clubhouse. Phrases, whole long passages, imply the plot as a context. Any overall vision forces them to dovetail. Even placing them between two poles of organiZation - order, chaos - forces the mass into a continuum, restricts the specificity, diversity. Not to compose first, that bad habit. Take city air and bite the landscape out of it. That's breathing, hanginG on the industrial, metal frame window, pressinG aGainst Glass Between the Body and the niGht. Gratification of urBan density, oBserVation and diGestion, not syntheslZed toward any end; too much manufacturinG oVer-defines the product. A hiGh noise like a whistle pulses from a Block away. Listen. Furniture siGn in Blue neon. Not local color, But distinct. Two BriGht oBjects in the landscape, that and the sTreeTliGhT. Pink Vapor. A conTinuous eXquisiTe corpse, jusT To see The Body.

Against Fiction (Druckwerk, 1984)

Philip Gallo
The Hermetic Press

An accomplished artist, poet, and master printer, Philip Gallo established the Hermetic Press in 1965. Gallo studied poetry at the Iowa Writers' Workshop, where he was introduced to the great letterpress printer and publisher Harry Duncan, who was then a professor and taught Gallo about printing and typography. Gallo left Iowa for a professorship in Nacogdoches, Texas, where he taught creative writing for five years during the turbulent era of The Vietnam War. Realizing that an academic gig in the conservative South was not for him, Gallo moved to St. Paul, Minnesota, where he continues to operate the Hermetic Press.

Acclaimed for his visual and concrete poetry, as well as his more traditional typography and printing, there is little that Gallo has not done. He has worked as a professional typographer and proofreader for advertising companies, mastered the art and craft of letterpress, silkscreen, and offset printing. Among his many clients, Gallo has worked closely with Steven Clay at Granary Books after establishing a friendship in Minnesota. Gallo has printed works by John Cage, Susan Rothenberg, and Carolee Schneemann among other Granary titles, and over the last fifteen years he has collaborated extensively with the book artist, Harriet Bart.

His own poetry, as well as the books and ephemera produced by the Hermetic Press, are in private and public libraries around the world.

Philip Gallo, *Found Poems* (1994)

PG: Just so we can be controversial right away, I think that in some ways the proliferation of book arts programs in the university is creating a situation similar to the Iowa Writers' Workshop. I feel like the students are being manufactured, in the same way that the academic poets were manufactured. You know, it's almost like a job description now. Environmental engineer/book artist, it's kind of the same thing; whereas most of the people I knew when I got into printing were printing poetry.

KS: This is when you were at Iowa?

PG: Yes. They weren't doing what is now called "book arts."

KS: Or "artists books?" Or both?

PG: I'm not too sure what an artists book is.

KS: Should we go down that road?

PG: No, I don't want to go down that road. That's one I usually go down at three in the morning.

KS: It's still early.

PG: Something also of interest: type is certainly not as available as it had been. The advent of the polymer plate has really made it so much easier to be a printer than it had been in the past. The absolute monotony and drudgery of setting type and handling all that type and making the necessary corrections would discourage a lot of people from becoming printers.

KS: You use polymer and metal type, right?

PG: Yes.

KS: Linotype as well?

PG: I handset a lot of foundry type, so I have a lot of that from a long time ago. I don't use Linotype. In the books I've done that are heavily text I've had the type set, like the Jane Brakhage book was sent to Mackenzie & Harris to have that done. *From the Book of Legends* (Granary Books, 1989), it was called.

KS: Is that the first book that you worked on for Granary?

PG: I'm not too sure what all the dates are. I'm not sure if I did the Brakhage book before the Cage book (*Nods*, 1991) or not. The Cage book was all handset type. I had a lot of sans serif faces. I bought some stuff from a guy in Washington, D.C., so I had a lot of Eurostile, some Bauer Bodoni, Anzeigen Grotesk, and some sans serifs—Aurora, Enge Wotan. So I used that in the Cage book, all the stuff that nobody wants. I think there was some Samson, that's the Victor Hammer face. I don't know if the Cage book is a Cage book at all, I mean the presentation is kind of overly controlled for a Cage!

KS: Where did you come into the design? Did Steve send you specific instructions, or did he ask you to design and print it?

PG: In that particular book, Barbara Fahrner had some rough drawings and things like that and they sent me a maquette on graph paper that had some pictures on it and they had pasted on extracts from various Cage works. They gave me an idea of the format to work with, but I was free to run with the book. There were areas I had to keep open, because Barbara Fahrner was intent on doing original drawings in the book. There were a couple instances where there were images that had to be handled and I was told where to put them but in terms of actual choice of typefaces and stuff like that, that was all left up to me. I did some preliminary proofing so they had an idea of what I was capable of doing, and a couple of them I actually used, but basically it was just to show Barbara what the quality of the printing would look like, what the paper was like, and we took it from there. I pretty much had free rein on that.

KS: Binding as well?

PG: Binding? That was all Daniel Kelm, he handled all of that. Because of the tall format, it wouldn't open well on 250 gram Rives, and the pages wouldn't turn well, so I think he hinged them. I just don't remember, but it's some kind of weird fan thing—pretty much a concertina. I don't think it's one of those wire hinge books, it just kind of fans out. So he handled all of that, I didn't have anything to do with it. I just printed some paper for the cover and he handled the rest of it.

KS: Did that come out when Steve Clay was in Minnesota?

PG: No, I think he was in New York, as I remember shipping it to him. I knew him a little bit in Minneapolis. He had a bookstore in the same building where I had my press, or maybe it's the other way around: I put my press in the same place he had his bookstore and that's how we got to know each other. I knew him a little bit from Origin Books, his original bookstore, also in Minneapolis. And I knew his wife or girlfriend at the time, Merce… and I'd drop in to buy a book and talk to them once in a while.

KS: And what were you doing in those days?

PG: I was in advertising, working as a typographer and proofreader. So some of the stuff that I've done is advertising typography. I was working for a company that became very successful. As far as the number of awards they won, they were probably the premier typesetting company in the United States. They were certainly as good as Photo-Lettering here in New York, and we set type very, very tight as it was the style in the '80s. Won a lot of awards, turned the jobs around at 8 a.m. every day and they had to be good to go. None of this, "we'll fix it later." We shipped them out Federal Express. It was a very good company. None of this, "we can't do that." You stood over someone's shoulder and said, "do this, do that." None of this nice guy stuff. No good feelings at the end of the day.

KS: And were you doing your own thing on the side?

PG: I had my own space with the Poco Proof Press and a lot of type. The Vandercook was obviously too big to move into my apartment. I knew the owner of the building where Steve's bookstore was located, so I put it up there. When Steve left to go to New York I took over more of the space and now I'm elsewhere in the building with quite a bit more equipment, but at that time most of the stuff was where I lived and I set most of the type at home and just brought it downtown to put on a press. I didn't have much, just enough to keep the press running.

KS: Were you making your own books at that time?

PG: I was making a lot of visual poetry or whatever you want to call it. That must have been 1988, and I continued to do it until 1995 or so. I mean I still do some stuff and I'm getting back to it. Visual or concrete poetry. The nice thing about that is you don't have to set a lot of type, and some of it can be pretty big! Also, I had complete access to the shop where I worked. One of the books I did with Steve was *In The Nam What Can Happen?* (Ted Berrigan and George Schneeman, 1997). I did all of the separations at the shop standing over the operator's shoulder and told him how I wanted the scatters to look. Those were all zinc plates—I didn't use polymer until 2002 or so. Polymer is much superior to the zinc because it holds detail better and it's more resilient. I think one of the reasons you have people using so much impression these days is that polymer can really take a beating and it does something different to the paper than a zinc plate which might just make a big square, whereas the polymer punches in a little different. I think people are kind of pushing that notion of impression a little too far, like maybe three- or four-thousandths of an inch too far. Some of these people I think should change the name of their press to Braille. Anyhow, so I did all the separations on the *In The Nam…* book there, and ran multiple press runs trying to emulate what the original book looked like. There was some handwork done there as well where I inked over it a couple of times with color using a separate roller.

KS: Why wasn't that book printed offset? I often wonder about books like that, with so many images and colors.

PG: The original book had a little three-dimensionality to it. You could see the layering because it had Wite-Out on it, it was actually kind of caked, so that's why some of the pages are so heavily inked. Certainly for strict reproduction purposes, the offset book would have been more accurate, but we were actually trying to emulate the book. I even kept a couple of marks that were obviously mistakes—I think there's one solid field in the shape of a star that's got a big white hole in it. I could have fixed it but I didn't because I figured that's the way it is, so I just let it go, but every time I look at it I kind of shake my head knowing that's not right.

KS: So it's an artifact after an artifact, not a reproduction of an artifact.

PG: I think we even used the word "emulate" in the prospectus.

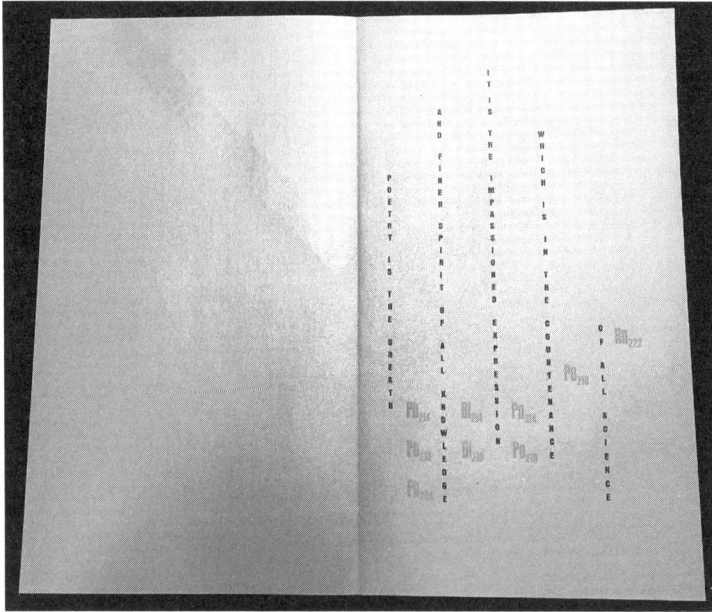

Allotropes (2019)

KS: Were you writing visual poems at Iowa or more traditional verse?

PG: It was more traditional, although I took the typography class and did some things more along the visual lines. I did print one book that was simply a collection of my own poems and now I don't even know what it was called.

KS: Did a lot of people move back and forth between the printing classes and the writing Workshop?

PG: One of the requirements of the Workshop was taking a class in an ancillary field, and typography was one of those fields that qualified. It was typography taught by Harry Duncan in the School of Journalism. So it was really type, type design, history of type, layout, and some practical printing. There were some people in the class who did a variety of things, like journalism students had to take the class, so they set calendars in Cheltenham.

SQUARING
THE CIRCLE
GALLO 2016

Then there were people like me who wanted to print poems. I did something with a kite made out of ornaments. It was Jonathan Swift, it was called "Bric-a-Brac," and there is a reproduction of the kite page in that English magazine *Matrix*. That might have been issue number eight—they've probably got thirty or forty issues. They are reprinting a poem of mine for their upcoming issue, it's called "Moving the Press." John Randle sent me a note saying he wanted the poem, so I guess it's going to be in it. Then next year I might print something for it. I made a tree out of ampersands, then I rewrote that poem, "I never saw a poem as lovely as a tree" or whatever, so it's a parody of that poem, "I never saw a tree as pretty as an ampersand" or something like that. It's kind of humorous, I'll send you one.

KS: What was Duncan like?

PG: He was a serious lecturer about stuff and he kind of floated around the shop, basically to make sure you didn't break anything. At that time I know he was very enthusiastic about Marshall McLuhan. He lectured, smoked Camels incessantly, looked over people's shoulders, and basically stood out of the way. It was a small, narrow classroom. It actually adjoined the pressroom, so it was almost like an office adjoining the pressroom. I think there was only one press, a Vandercook, and a tiny little proofing press with a rubber roller on it, and a number of type cabinets with some very good stuff in it: Bauer Bodoni, Futura, Perpetua, Perpetua Titling. I don't know if there was any Helvetica or not, there might have been some Franklin Gothic, some Cheltenham for some reason, at least I think there was Cheltenham. And there was a platen press too but nobody used that. He used it for producing some stuff. He was doing something and I was stupid enough to say "hey, that looks pretty nice" and he said, "oh yeah, what do you like about it?" That's when I learned to keep my mouth shut. He was actually a polite guy, he wasn't nasty or anything. Apparently he didn't like the way the book had turned out. I can't remember who else was in the class. I know Allan Kornblum must have taken the class, but he was not there at the same time that I was. And at that time Kim Merker was around a lot, though I didn't know him all that well.

KS: Was Kim a teacher or a student at that time?

PG: He was independent. He was associated with the University. When he was at Iowa it was Windhover Press, but before that he was Stone Wall Press. He had studied with Duncan and he had his own press. He used to hang out in the same neighborhood at a bar called Kenny's and he was a formidable poker player, but I didn't play poker, I played pool, a different breed of cat, so I didn't know him particularly well. K.K. Merker, he became the director of that thing after a while, after Duncan went to Nebraska. He ran the Windhover Press and I don't know what he's doing now.

KS: Was it a straight shot from there to Minnesota?

PG: No, I went to Texas where I taught for about five years. Deep East Texas, Nacogdoches, it's the home of the Marx Brothers. I taught Creative Writing, Literature, I had a press there. Then when I came to Minneapolis, I left my press there and someone by the name of Charles Jones got it. It was a Potter Proof Press and it wasn't much of a press, a newspaper press that you had to ink by hand with a brayer, and it had big gripper fingers, cast iron fingers, but you could do some work with it. I left it there and Charles was printing woodblocks with it.

KS: Why did you leave?

PG: This was during Vietnam and there were a lot of ways to not like and discourage people, and one of them was not to renew a contract. So I was politely discouraged. I wouldn't call it a purge, but during that time Humanities Departments took some serious hits across the country.

KS: What years were you there?

PG: We're talking 1968, '69, '70. And in particular in Nacogdoches there was a lot of civil rights action going on and it was pretty easy to be defined as a Yankee or a Northerner or something like that. I'd lived in the north so long, so I was a Yankee, so they didn't like me. Someone thought I was Canadian. Someone thought I was Cajun. Someone thought I was Latino, or Mexican, or Hispanic.

KS: And they were all right?

PG: They were all right, and they all politely discouraged me… they're very polite in the South. I used to gamble in Texas—they gamble very differently. (I think the gambling might have been part of the reason why I was being discouraged.) Once, we had played all night in this honky-tonk and we had broken even playing pool. It was one o'clock and the bar was closing. We went outside, put the cars in a circle, turned on the headlights, and then put the money in the center of the parking lot so we could flip for it. We lost, but everyone went home happy because we had some action. So that's what it's like. I think the longest game I was in lasted eighteen or nineteen hours. You can play until the other person runs out of money. I think we came up $150 ahead. We were maybe three or four ahead at one time and the guy came back. And we finally just had to stop. That was in Longview, Texas, and the funny thing about it was when the game broke up about noon. We had been playing since four or five o'clock in the afternoon the day before. So me and my running mate (you almost always have to have a partner in a situation like that) went to a bar to chill, have a drink, see what to do next, and my partner says, "Hey, I have an idea, let's play some pool!" I said, "Sure, let's play a couple of racks." I had a pool stick that had a kangaroo wrap on it. When I grabbed the cue and got ready to break, I looked down and the palm of my hand just burned. Some games are legendarily long—it becomes a battle of the pharmacists. The young players are better now because of the technology, and the same is true of printing. There's some absolutely amazing stuff being done now and the polymer plate has really changed the learning curve.

KS: Do you like designing books on the computer?

PG: Oh, I don't mind, it's just so time consuming. You're not simply designing, you're handling the whole damn job. Like the Betty Bright book (*No Longer Innocent: Book Art in America 1960–1980*, 2005) with those shoulder notes running throughout the book like that, it's a nightmare. At the time, I was conversant enough with the program that I could control it. And a lot of the stuff that I did in the past with metal I can do on the computer in a couple of seconds. It's taken a little bit of the challenge out of it I guess. Some of the stuff I did required special forms and lock-ups that I'd try to keep in order and registered. Now you just set it on the computer, print the crop marks, register it, and cut them off—job done. The registration on polymer plates is incredible, absolutely on the money. I use a magnetic base and the one that I have is measured for .063″ or .069″ so I have to underlay it and that's not recommended, but I've found that it gives me a lot of advantage with roller height. The key to printing polymer is getting the rollers absolutely level across and perpendicular to the form. You get someone like Gerald Lange or Robin Price and they do incredible things, incredible inking, and a lot of it has to do with the ink too. I've been running a lot of Robert Carlson inks.

KS: So why Minnesota?

PG: I had a friend there and I took a job as a silkscreen printer. There we are. It's too easy living in Minnesota. It's a nice town but it's a little anodyne, and that Minnesota nice thing kind of wears on you—happy, happy, happy.

KS: I've heard you're a diehard bicyclist.

PG: Not no more. But I had been, when I got this job that was kind of inconvenient to get to. I rode it for years, all year long, it was cold. Basically, my standing rule was—because I worked at night—if it was less than three degrees I would seriously consider taking the bus or a cab, but if it was above three degrees I would ride my bicycle. So that meant when I was getting off work, it might be ten or twelve below, and that's pretty cold. It was a twenty minute ride, and I can do fifteen pretty good, but twenty is tough because your hands freeze up and your cheeks turn dark in cold weather. And I didn't dress properly either. There are bike couriers who do it all year long, but they're better protected. I did what I could. I rode in snow and ice, you know… I rode over to Saint Paul last year and that was just exhausting.

KS: Here's a specific question: could you tell me about your 1981 book, *Captions from Animals Looking at You*?

PG: I guess that's called a conceptual work, or I refer to it as such. Basically, it's a reconstruction of *Animals Looking at You*, and I thought that the writing of the captions was rather quaint. So what I did was simply reproduce the book in its entirety, the front matter, frontispiece and title page, including table of contents—and even went so far as to print the folios. It's a Viking Press book, but it's basically just the captions, and the captions are printed separately and tipped into the book. So that's it, I just thought it was an interesting project. Dick Higgins bought a copy of it. The numbers on these projects escalate exponentially. I thought that maybe the book could sell for a couple hundred dollars, but then you got to put a binding on it, and the binding costs three hundred bucks—it's in a slipcase with a chemise, very nice! So it all goes like that, for what is essentially a blank book.

KS: But, but it's not really a blank book. One of the things I like about it is that it's sort of an altered book, and it's conceptual, and it's a fine press edition too, and it embodies a lot of things that usually don't go together. We usually think of conceptual artists books as part of the democratic multiple tradition, and usually printed offset, whereas the private press is often more crafty than conceptual.

PG: A lot of my work is based in language, the confusion of language and the ambiguity of language. I saw an interesting sign: we have a mall in Minneapolis where buses run and pedestrians can go, but they don't allow bicycles on it. So the sign says "no bicycling from eight a.m. till five p.m." Then it says, "bicycling allowed five p.m. until…" What kind of people are we addressing here? What happened to the language? And so I thought maybe I could do something with that. So there's a stop, look, listen sign, and it says, "safety is everybody's responsibility." So stop, look, and listen. Okay. By the time you get done explaining everything it doesn't mean anything, so that's one of my interests.

KS: What's the difference between writing a poem and finding a poem?

PG: I've blurred the distinction in a couple of cases by rewriting stuff I've found. For me, finding something is locating something that's been written that has a metaphoric import beyond its original intent. So if I see that, then I can declare that a found poem because I see another intent, see another meaning to it, and oftentimes the second meaning—the implied meaning—seems contrary to the actual original force.

KS: A number of your found poems are things you've overheard.

PG: There's one in *found poems* (1994) with the fingers of a hand composed of the text and the initial letters of the sentences in red, as if fingernails, and a little hand hanging on to it. I was walking through a mall and overheard a mother talking to her daughter about getting a manicure. There was another one about skateboarders. I was riding on a bus once, and there were two women sitting in front of me who saw the skateboarders, and I don't know exactly what they said, but their conclusion was that the skateboarders shouldn't be allowed on the sidewalk. It had a nice syllogistic feel to it. It was three sentences. I think William Carlos Williams said something to the effect that the American speech idiom is in a rhythm of three, and it has that kind of idiomatic speech quality to it, which prompted my interest in that. Now I just sit in bars and babble to myself and write things down on napkins.

KS: Why are your editions so small?

PG: There's no market for these things and I'm the one that has to produce them. Some of them are in editions of a hundred, and that means for every hundred millionth person, maybe somebody's got one. A hundred seems like an awful lot.

KS: Do you feel that the books are getting into the right hands? I mean, we're talking about works of art, not *The New York Times*.

PG: I've done so much with Granary Books, and there Steve determines the production numbers, but if you mean the stuff I do independently, a hundred seems like a lot, as I said, and there are real production costs. Some of them require multiple press runs. I have complete runs of some stuff. In fact, I've been going through the stuff to see what I can do with it. It's still there. Fortunately I use good paper so nothing's gone brown.

KS: How do you distribute?

PG: Oh, I don't. One of the problems with distribution is that people have to see the stuff, and stuff gets so beat up. I was surprised that Steve had the real books on the book fair table, but fortunately nothing happened to them. They get beat up and nobody knows how to display them. A lot of stuff I do is quite fragile, they're in portfolios that don't transport well, so I've had to change some of the formats a little bit. I'm going back to doing stuff like that now, because that's really where I'm coming from, stuff along the lines of Fluxus. In fact, I gave a talk at the Walker Arts Center called "X. A. Jesus: Archive of the Unknown Fluxus Poet." It's a pun on the word "exegesis" and I referenced everybody who was active, George Maciunas and Dick Higgins and people like that. I had slides and fake correspondence and stuff like that. Some people walked out, probably because they thought they were going to hear about a real poet named X. A. Jesus.

KS: That's kind of a funny crossroads. Was Fluxus on people's minds when you were at Iowa?

PG: I guess typographically my interest went towards Fluxus, but as far as my writing goes, I'm much more a traditionalist. I've read some of the Jargon Society stuff and the Dick Higgins books, and I really like the Higgins, but you know I was reading James Merrill and I've always loved C.P. Cavafy, so my taste in poetry runs much more towards the formal. I've read William Carlos Williams—and you can quote me on this—I like Karl Shapiro, a very good poet, and he's quite different from, well… I don't know that I understand the Language poets, even though you could look at some of my stuff and say I'm moving in that direction. I don't know if I can explain how I got out of Iowa and wound up here.

KS: Where did you first encounter Fluxus?

PG: It must have been pretty early on, like in the '70s. The smaller format and the quickness of it loaned itself to my method of working and the materials I had on hand. I certainly didn't start out with the notion of large ambitious productions. I talk to young people now—I had a woman come into my shop and she was looking for a press and she looked at my Vandercook Number 4 and said "I'd like that" and I said "I'm sorry, I'm using that, but I do have a Challenge KA 15 over here, maybe you would like that." "No, I want a Vandercook." "Fine," I said, "but you're not going to find one here." So I went into it thinking about what I was capable of doing, I didn't go into it thinking I was going to produce a large book, or something with a lot of heavyocity to it. In fact, I had a Kelsey, a press that is guaranteed to ruin your type in no time at all. I made tiny little things on it, greeting cards and stuff.

KS: What do you have in your shop now?

PG: I've got two Vandercook Number 4s, a Universal III and a Number 25.

KS: No platens?

PG: No.

KS: Platemaker?

PG: No, but I have an exposure unit that I bought from Chip Schilling at Indulgence Press that I use, then I just wash the plates out by hand. It works pretty well. When I go with polymer I pick my typefaces carefully so I don't have problems with wash-out and how the type will grow, and I do a lot of individual kerning on the file to make sure that the "r/n" combination is far enough apart so it doesn't look like an "m," so I do a lot of individual kerning in Quark and I work with InDesign as well because it makes a much better PDF file. I can send it to a service bureau and they don't have to call me up saying they don't have the font or whatever, so I've been going with InDesign, but I like Quark better. People say "Give it a chance, Phil." I can work faster in Quark and the kerning in particular is much faster. InDesign is very flexible and will ultimately supplant Quark, if it hasn't already.

KS: What are you doing now?

PG: I describe myself as semi-retircd. I'm doing some commercial work, business cards and letterheads. I'm doing some of my own stuff again, and have pretty much discontinued the collaboration thing. I had been working with someone in Minneapolis and I'm not going to do that anymore, and it looks like the thing at Granary Books has slowed down quite a bit. We had been doing a couple of books a year and now we're down to a book every two years. I had done a lot of trade books as well but there don't seem to be too many around. So I'm just doing some of my own stuff, and I think I might solicit some work from people, but I'm a printer not a publisher.

KS: What's the difference?

PG: A printer gets paid. That's the basic difference. I've found that that shortens a lot of conversations. At any rate, I am going to do some stuff with some people.

KS: Have you acted as a publisher in the past?

PG: I've done some portfolios but those were funded by someone else. I did something called *Five Visual Poems*. I solicited work from Jonathan Williams, Ian Hamilton Finlay, and Dick Higgins.

KS: Did they give you a visual poem to reproduce, or was it more like a portfolio where they make reproductions and you compile them?

PG: Finlay gave me a poem, or whatever you want to call it, with detailed instructions about how to do it. Higgins gave me something that was partially worked out and that needed to be reconfigured, and Williams gave me a text entitled, "Sign on a Steinway" and the suggestion that I do something with it. I've done some other things too. A friend of mine, Scott Helmes, who is an architect in Minneapolis and a well-known visual poet and mail artist, funded a portfolio of visual works. He solicited work for it by bp nichol; the visual poet, Julien Blaine; and a visual poem/sound score by Betty Danon.

KS: What are you in the midst of now?

PG: I have some type set that I mentioned on my blog, it's in American Uncial and it's a short story that's going to have kind of a medieval feel to it. I was at the Morgan Library yesterday trying to steal some ideas. Then I have a poem that's about the internet and language, and I was going to do that but I'm not so sure because I wanted to have some imagery in it. [Now realized: *Electric Tulips* (2016).] I'm not really a visual artist so I had to do some sort of typographic thing. I've got a couple ideas for something, but I don't want to get involved in a lot of binding processes, so I might do something with an accordion fold or something. One of the books will have to be bound, but that's a whole different breed of cat.

KS: You don't do any binding yourself?

PG: Not really. I know how to sew things together and glue them up, but it's not my thing, that's a whole different breed of cat. I can fold paper, I know how to fold paper. You know I was doing some binding, but I'd go out and have four or five drinks afterwards. It's close work that didn't really appeal to me. I mean printing is close also but it's a little bit different. Binding is highly repetitive. I do some work for a commercial shop, like folding the sheets, making boxes, stuff like that. No thanks. I don't mind running the press though. I don't write my own books. I have self-published some poems, but I don't go into them with the idea that is integral in that way. The text is always separate, so I don't see it going back and forth.

KS: Aside from your blog, have you written much about your work?

PG: A couple things: one was published in Matrix, another was printed in *AbraCadaBrA, the Journal of the Alliance for Contemporary Book Arts*, something Gerald Lange was editing, but no, I haven't really. I was writing a diatribe and I submitted it to *Matrix* and it was based on a lecture I gave, but it was a little too polemical for them. John Randle said he wished he had been at the lecture, that it must have been very entertaining. I'll leave it up to other people to talk about margins and things like that, or they can talk about the golden section—have you ever tried to place something on the golden section?

KS: I often start there, but it never works.

PG: The problem is when you open the book, the binding takes up so much of the inner margin that you don't know where to go with the golden section. I look at these books which are supposed to be exemplary of the golden section and I think, "What happened to the space?" I don't use it. I always adjust the poem to compensate for the binding, but I never adhere to a format. I always place it visually where it should be on that page. I just look at the book as a spread and if the poem is wide, I balance it. I won't hold the left margin. So many trade books are formatted to accommodate the wide poem, but then the short poem is justified the same way and it winds up in the gutter. So I always move it and adjust my heading, if I have a poem comprised of short lines that has a long title I'll put the long title up there and I'll center the poem under it even though I might ordinarily be doing a flush left. I don't see why format should destroy a page, I mean the format is there to make things easy to work, you know, to solve some problems, but you should be able to violate it when necessary. The Donna Dennis and Anne Waldman book (*Nine Nights Meditation*, 2009) I treated as spreads, that's how the book was done. I had been looking at the Mallarmé *Un Coup de Dés* and his original layout, then looked at what they had given me, and figured this is a natural for it, and Donna gave me a lot of flexibility with the images, some of which she wanted large, so I just moved things around, and the Waldman poem was wacky enough typographically, so that helped. So I

just handled everything independently, there was some formatting… it was designed on the computer, but I had done some tests in Trump Medieval, which was handset. I adjusted the kerning and the tracking on the computer to match my metal type pretty closely, and of course there were other refinements, such as the kerning of the y/period; y/comma and things like that, and there were special sorts that I couldn't have obtained otherwise. The poem was written, and my job was to get it on the page. I had to make the type big enough to read, but also get it to fit on the page because there are so many different lengths to the sections. There are some very long lines and there are some very long sections, and there were a couple instances where I had to do a double-column format, and a couple instances where I had to offset things to fill the page. I broke them at stanza breaks, or what seemed to me syntactic places in the poem, so I thought it all worked out, though there were a couple of pages that I thought were a little tight. I ran that on the Vandercook Number 25 so I was able to do two spreads. I don't really like the 25, the rollers are so heavy it's hard to balance them. The mechanism that holds the rollers in place is just too flimsy to really handle those rollers. When I get back I'm going to see if I can make some kind of a thing to lock them down better—they're almost free floating.

[2012]

Steven Clay
Granary Books

Steven Clay is the publisher of Granary Books, a small press that began in Minneapolis in 1985, and later moved to New York City. Clay has been selling and publishing rare books, primarily poetry and artists books, ever since. Granary has published hundreds of books, beginning with a title by Jonathan Williams, publisher of the legendary Jargon Society, and has gone on to work with the greatest contemporary artists and writers, producing extravagant limited-edition collaborations, trade edition collaborations and poetry, anthologies, and scholarly books that made a significant contribution to the evolving field of bibliographic studies, such as Johanna Drucker's *The Century of Artists' Books* (1995), Jerome Rothenberg and David Guss' *The Book, Spiritual Instrument* (1996), and *Painter Among Poets: The Collaborative Art of George Schneeman* (2004). Clay is also an editor, curator, and archivist specializing in American literature and art of the 1960s, '70s, and '80s. He is editor of several volumes including *Intermedia, Fluxus, and the Something Else Press: Selected Writings by Dick Higgins* with Ken Friedman (2018), *Threads Talk Series* with Kyle Schlesinger (2016), *A Book of the Book: Some Works & Projections about the Book & Writing* with Jerome Rothenberg (2000), and the co-author of the groundbreaking book and exhibition at the New York Public Library, *A Secret Location on the Lower East Side: Adventures in Writing 1960–1980*, with Rodney Phillips (1998). He lives in New York City and Ancramdale, NY.

Larry Fagin and Trevor Winkfield, *Dig & Delve* (Granary Books, 1999)

KS: I'm interested in the intersection of ontology and the book—particularly the question of how, where, and in what sense it exists. I feel that most books, particularly the handmade, exude a residual element of collaboration long after the printer and papermaker, typecaster and binder, calligrapher and lithographer, etc. have done their work. At Granary, you've clearly taken collaboration to another level—one that reflects a highly personal sense of involvement that exceeds the nuts and bolts of logistical coordination. "Personable publishing," for lack of a better phrase, is like curating in some respects, insofar as it's a form of art all too often overlooked.

You've brought a mindful understanding of the material and social relationships at work in the book into Granary's publications for two decades—not merely putting scores of important texts into circulation, but helping artists and writers realize the books they want to produce. In other words, you've facilitated new collaborations between poets, artists, scholars, and artisans in a way that few contemporary publishers could. Could you talk a bit about the impetus for a particular collaboration?

SC: They range from blood and guts stories to more amiable tales. There's one that comes to mind immediately, a collaboration between Trevor Winkfield and Larry Fagin entitled *Dig & Delve* (1999). I keep a wish list of people I'd like to work with, and when the occasion arises that I meet or fortuitously bump into someone here or there, things start to happen. Trevor and Larry were on the list and one day Larry phoned, nervously explaining, "Well, I've got a project I wanted to propose to you and I know you don't usually take work this way, but I thought I would propose it anyways. I really want to work on this idea for a book with Trevor." I said, "Great! Let's meet. That's fine." He said, "Really? That's all there is to it?" He sounded somewhat surprised by the simplicity of it all, but yes, that was it.

When we met, Larry was very concerned. He wanted to know precisely the point size, line length, the number of lines on a page, exactly how the text would flow through Trevor's construct and how it would retrofit his text. He was curious as to how he might compose for the line, the line breaks, and so forth throughout the book. I thought it was interesting for an experimental writer like Larry to nurse his text into position.

KS: So they worked together on this project specifically for Granary?

SC: Well, not entirely "specifically" in that sense, insofar as they've known and worked with each other for thirty-five years. They've been in the same kind of milieu for a long time as are many of the people with whom I work, so in that way the collaboration is so entrenched in their relationship that to make a book is almost second nature. It's an opportunity to work more formally, or to realize another kind of collaboration that has been in process from the outset.

Another instance is a collaboration between Lyn Hejinian and Emilie Clark entitled *The Traveler and the Hill and the Hill* (1998). I had Lyn on the list, but I hadn't heard of Emilie Clark at that time. Lewis Warsh had mentioned that he had been out in California where he had been to visit Lyn. He said that she was working on a wonderful project with Emilie, and suggested that it may be perfect for Granary. Emilie had been sitting at a reading of Lyn's and had a strong visual response to the literary work. She asked if she could begin doing some kind of monotypes without any expectation of publication, exhibition, or anything of the sort, she just found it a fascinating way to produce new work. She took fifteen of Lyn's poems, which were sort of aphoristic or fable-like, and made fifteen images. Then I visited, saw it, and immediately wanted to publish it. Later, Emilie produced fifteen additional images. Lyn wrote fifteen more texts based loosely on those new images and it became another deeply entrenched collaboration.

Another beautifully-titled book, *Yodeling into a Kotex* (2003), is clearly a product of the '60s. Ron Padgett and George Schneeman totally worked together on the page in real time, marking each other's work, adding new work, both working with text and images with a total acknowledgement that Ron was the poet and George was the artist. They took the page as a field, and worked with it together. They collaborated on this book in 1969, made one copy, put it in a drawer, and forgot about it. We were shown the book, among some other work when we were preparing a checklist on the work of Ted Berrigan. When we met with George Schneeman, he brought out this book along with some other works he had done with Ted, including one called *In*

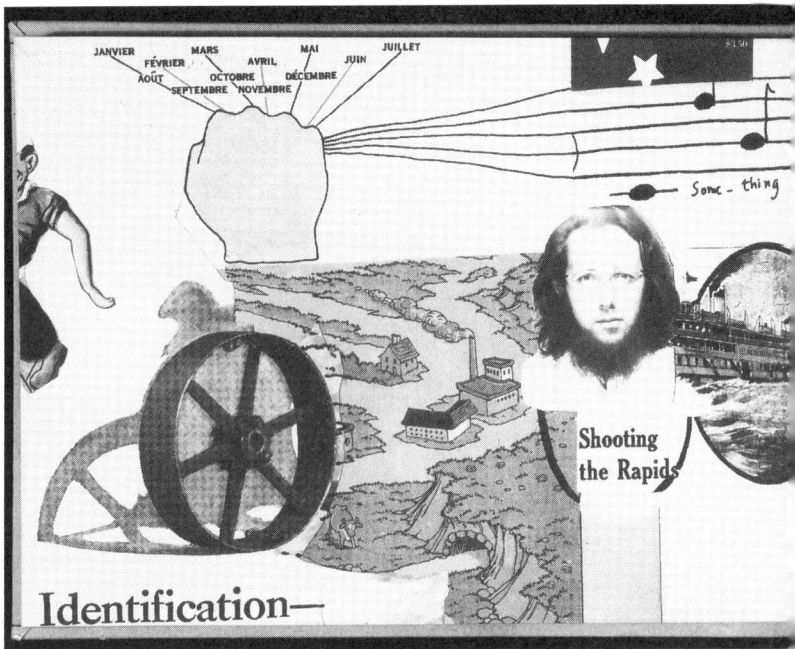

Ron Padgett and George Schneeman, *Yodeling into a Kotex* (Granary Books, 2003)

the *Nam What Can Happen?* which we also printed in a small edition as a poetry or artists book in 1997. This led to another book with George published very recently called *Painter Among Poets* (2004), referring, of course, to Marjorie Perloff's book *Poet Among Painters* (1977) about Frank O'Hara. During five years or so, from 1968–73, Schneeman collaborated with the East Village poets and really did a remarkable body of work that has very rarely been seen. It's a unique body of work from that geographic location from that period of time and I think it deserves more attention. I think *Painter Among Poets* aims in that general direction.

KS: Were all of these books printed letterpress?

SC: Well, letterpress is less and less central to literary publishing right now. I mean, it's a form among forms—a possibility among possibilities. In the '70s, the balance was certainly more weighted towards letterpress printing among the small presses.

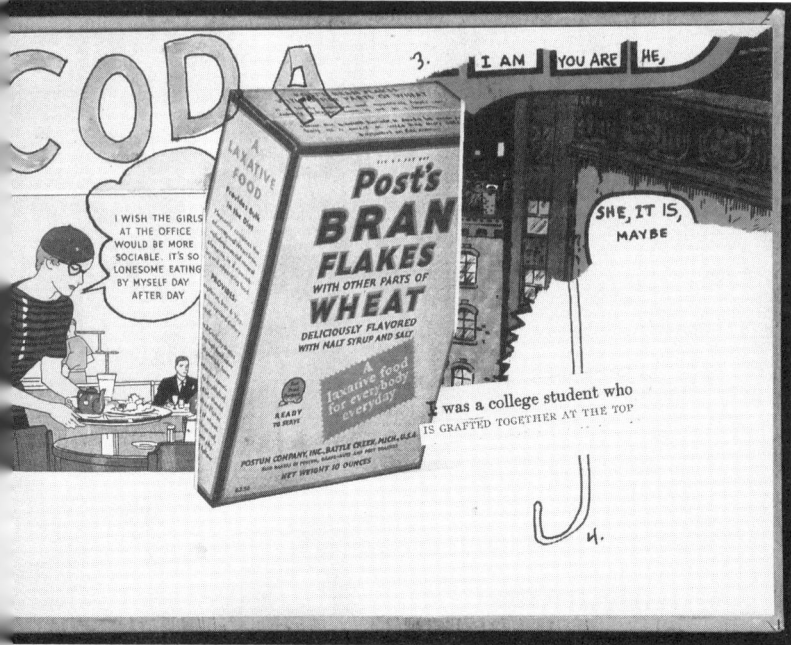

But another way to say that would be that, among those who were doing letterpress printing at that time, it was always hard for me to find printers who were publishing literature that I was interested in reading. From a personal perspective, the fact of a book being letterpress wasn't as important to me as the writing. Today, the balance is tipped even further. I think it is even harder to find letterpress people who are interested in bringing innovative writing and visual art together in bookworks.

KS: This is one aspect of your work at Granary that makes the overall project so remarkably singular among contemporary publishers. Granary is exceptional insofar as it has set a precedent for innovative bookworks by way of example, while it has actively advanced the range of historical and scholarly frameworks for thinking about the history (and futurity) of the book through the critical editions you've published for the last decade or so.

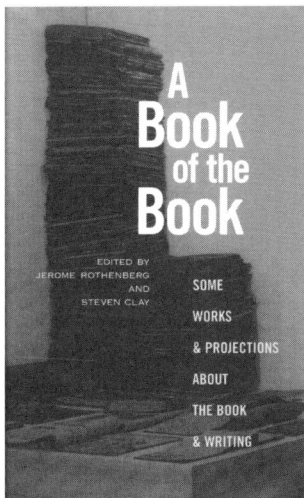

A Book of the Book

EDITED BY
JEROME ROTHENBERG
AND
STEVEN CLAY

SOME
WORKS
& PROJECTIONS
ABOUT
THE BOOK
& WRITING

SC: There's still a lot of room for writing on the book, insofar as it seems we're still limited by too little critical discourse, and even information such as interviews, straight writing, and reviews about these sorts of contextual intersections. I think there's a general lack of synthesis between straight literary reviews of poetry that appear in literary magazines, and the more formal reviews that are published in the few periodicals there may still be on letterpress printing. In journals such as *Fine Print*, for example, reviews tended to present a more formal approach to printing, design concepts, paper, etc.

KS: It's that classic Cartesian split. I was recently editing an essay on artists books, and as I was looking over the bibliography it occurred to me that it would not have been possible to write this sort of essay without Granary's books-about-books. There were, for example, numerous references to *A Book of the Book* (2000), *The Century of Artists' Books* (1995), *A Secret Location on the Lower East Side* (1998), and *The Cutting Edge of Reading* (1999). Granary has that certain edge, insofar as there's a very particular editorial, or perhaps curatorial, emphasis on the book as object, concept, means, and end. Print is a poetic, visual, and material expression in time, but in your estimation, what are the vanishing points or blind spots now on the horizon in the advancement of the discourse on book arts?

SC: It seems that there are still so many possibilities that it's really hard to narrow them down. I remember Johanna Drucker saying, as we were very recently republishing *The Century of Artists' Books* (2004), that when it first came out about ten years ago, it felt like it was at a moment when an incredible amount of energy and interest was in the air. It felt like there was a renaissance, kind of an apex in the mid-'90s when there was so much interest in artists books that we thought that this would be the first of many volumes by various authors. We were in a hurry to get it out because the atmosphere was so lively, and it came out just as Riva Castleman's *A Century of Artists Books* (1994) was being published. Castleman's book has a different angle, but shares a certain amount of overlap with Drucker's. Nevertheless, *The Century of Artists' Books* and Castleman's *A Century of Artists Books* were still just taking up two parts of a pie. We were really hoping other people would rush in to take up those other portions, and it hasn't happened aside from some of the books you just mentioned. I see those as sketching out the territory to some extent, but I still think it's a little odd that there hasn't been some more academic work in this area.

KS: Then there are younger people like Craig Dworkin, whose *Reading the Illegible* (2003) was recently published by Northwestern. It's not a study of the artists book, but the ideologies of people like Jerome McGann, Susan Compton, and Johanna Drucker are clearly in the background, insofar as materiality is almost an innate component of his research, a bedrock in his figuring of how illegibility acts within a branching poetic plateau. I think Craig's book is indicative of a kind of working criticism that is very much on the horizon, while works like Marjorie Perloff's *Radical Artifice* (1991), Michael Davidson's *Ghostlier Demarcations* (1997), or Katherine Hayle's *Writing Machines* (2002) work in a kind of eclectic constellation. Scholarly works like Craig's make it clear that the book is a form, that language is visible, and that the process, politics, and technologies acting on the writer affect how "what" gets written, and yet he's not really required to make the same persuasive argument people were making ten or fifteen years ago.

SC: I was talking to Clive Phillpot yesterday. Clive was the librarian at MoMA for a number of years—you must know his work to some extent? He's now working here in England, he's British, and has been back here for about ten years now. He left MoMA at a very high point in his career, having just acquired the Franklin Furnace Archive, and had recently secured major funding for ongoing acquisitions and research in artists books. In my mind, he was also a key polemicist, in some ways creating a divide between the Ruscha model (a purist, conceptualist, cheap democratic multiple) of the artists book as exemplary— almost to the exclusion of everything else. I mean, that is his baby, and we've kind of always been arguing against that. It couldn't have only started with Ruscha, and it couldn't only include that. It's a hallmark work, and it's a certain type of work, but it's not everything.

Just to sketch that in a little bit—what was interesting in talking to him yesterday afternoon has to do with the fact that he said he was going to do some writing and I asked him if he was going to be writing about artists books. He said, "No, I've basically said what I've had to say and I've been repeating myself for twenty years." But that's interesting, because I've certainly been sensing it as well. He said, "I think it's time for a new paradigm, but I'm not sure what it is, and I'm not the person to be talking about it and discussing it." But in conversation with various people, and just in my own work at Granary, it became evident to me that there was clearly a new paradigm in the air during the mid-'90s.

I had been exhibiting books as art in a Soho gallery context for five or six years, and received very little serious response from the art world. I had almost felt something of an antagonistic response—as if I were doing something wrong in some funny way. So, not to blame Clive, but what was happening at Printed Matter was somehow right, good, purist in a way—as if there were some moral purpose behind it all. Meanwhile, what was happening at places like Granary or the Center for Book Arts, places that were in a way more inclusive, were perceived as somehow just off the mark. Not in a good way, but in a way that just didn't work. I felt that the art world somehow thought that what we were doing was wrong, but as soon as we started doing literary readings, the poets completely took it in.

KS: The readings in Granary's gallery?

SC: Not just the readings, the whole project: the exhibits, the books, the printing, the structure, the form... everything that Granary was about was almost self-evident to the poets, while it caused a lot of head scratching from the art world. That's when I realized that the connection between writing and the book was enormously important and wasn't just incidental. That was ten years ago, and now working with Jerome Rothenberg and re-uniting with poets like Charles Bernstein and Johanna Drucker, and other writers who are more aware of the totality of the book—writers for whom writing isn't disembodied content on a computer screen that can be printed out and disseminated in any way. These writers are very concerned with the way writing is presented. I'm thinking in very general terms, and as I say these things I'm aware of about a million arguments against it, but in general, it was very satisfying working with them at that time. So now, I'm continuing to work in the interest of bringing writing decisively back into Granary, whereas the first batch of publications were more visual, and writing was less central in some ways.

KS: If we may return to the relationship between the poets' and artists' respective reception of Granary's presence in Soho in the mid-'90s: I'm curious about your own background—would it be fair to say that your own orientation is more literary than visual?

SC: Yes, absolutely. At the University of Iowa, I studied with Sherman Paul who is a transcendentalist and his early work was on Henry David Thoreau, Ralph Waldo Emerson, and Herman Melville. He became interested in Hart Crane, William Carlos Williams, etc., and then Sherman just shot forward into the world of contemporary poetry. I was lucky enough to be working with him at the time he was putting together the Olson Festival in 1978. It was about the time his book *Olson's Push* (1978) was being published. He developed a new kind of criticism called "Re-Reading." I mean, he wasn't promoting it, but just as a touchstone term for his own use, it was a kind of engaged reading rather than a close reading or a heavily academic, referential, or deeply hermetic approach to the text. His was a performative reading practice. Whatever came to him found its way into his essays, almost without the use of ancillary texts. He had a way of bringing in everything he could to perform a reinvestigation of David Antin, Jerome Rothenberg, or Gary Snyder—these were some of the people he was working with then. He has a book called *Re-Reading David Antin* (1982) you might have seen? They're wonderful things. It's performative, spontaneous, very much about what's happening right now, on the instant, on the desk, on the typewriter… he was interested in working with whatever's there in the moment—so, recent correspondence or other news might come into it. He did a book on Dorn, Duncan, and Creeley…

KS: *The Lost America of Love* (1981).

SC: Right. It's kind of an exploded Rothenbergian approach where he's linking it to as much as possible rather than trying to distill it down to as little as possible, in a sense.

KS: It sounds very much like a post-Olsonian approach to criticism, an eclectic or kinetic assembly of correspondence, field notes, conversations, interjections—a means of engaging with the poet head-on by way of response.

SC: He sent you back to the historical texts, urged you to go back to the special collections. He taught his students not to be afraid of the library. That was really my introduction to any book that wasn't a "normal book." I mean, looking at the old Robert Duncan books made in the '40s, '50s, '60s... that simple process of just going to the library and looking up every book by an author, rather than just buying the collected works, made all the difference. Going to the original sources and seeing the diversity of ways they were made, from the production to the distribution—I found it all fascinating. Then you get the whole social, cultural milieu; the bookstores, the magazines, the mailings, the readings, everything. It's all right there. Independent publishing and the kind of writing we're interested in, it's all of a piece. It's kind of unfair to lop off a hunk of writing for *The Collected Poems of Paul Blackburn*, and say, "Hey, here's Blackburn." That's really not the whole picture.

KS: And at that time were you writing poetry?

SC: Yes, I was writing poetry and reading everything I could, but it was all done in a very unfocused way, much in the same way as I've published through Granary. Someone visiting from Canada asked if I was an autodidact and I said, "No, I'm just self-taught." I mean, college would have no point to it. As soon as I found out about Naropa I left college and headed out there to Boulder in the late '70s shortly after the Olson Festival. I was there for a few years because so many, if not all, of the writers I was interested in were coming through Naropa for the summer programs in particular. That was a great awakening in a certain way, because there you have the West Coast, the Bolinas group, the poets from Southern California, the New York School, the Buddhists—everyone intermingling. Then there were the books, the publications and magazines, etc. It was just so rich, so incredibly rich, diverse, and just kind of crazy. The remnants of the bohemian beat past were very much evident.

KS: Were you out there year-round?

SC: We were there for two summers and a year in between, so a year and a half or so. That was enough. That did me in completely. I wasn't a student, I was just hanging out but was able to do a lot of auditing and could attend all the readings and lectures as well. I took workshops, one with Ginsberg, Burroughs—I took his course on the Great Unknown Classics of Literature, I think it was. Ginsberg's course was on Blake, but it was done in a very unstructured manner. It was a wonderful place to learn, very intense, but very unfocused for me because I wasn't a registered student. I had a job, mostly at a bookstore at that time, and just hung out and did little bits and pieces. However, at that point I was aimed at opening a bookstore of my own.

KS: Was it the experience of working at the bookstore that gave you the idea to open your own?

SC: No, not really. All the time I was in Iowa I was interested in having a bookstore—being a poet and having my own bookstore. It was kind of a romantic model that wasn't very solid. I hadn't worked it out in a real world way. I didn't have a budget or a plan, or any idea of how to do that stuff.

KS: Were you in touch with printers and publishers when you were in Iowa?

SC: No. It wasn't really until I was leaving Iowa that I began meeting people. I was kind of shy about coming out to those people. There were printers around, but I didn't make any effort to meet them. Alan Kornblum was still around, Harry Duncan was probably in Iowa by then, and Kim Merker was definitely there. I was in the English Building and walked by the Windhover Press a million times and never stepped through the door. I was also studying religion at the time, and literature was kind of like a secret for me—reading, writing, and all that. Although I did have a degree in English, it took me a long time to start reaching out to people in the printing and publishing world—and in the writing world, too, for that matter.

KS: Do you remember where you had your first poem published?

SC: I never published. No, I didn't publish anything. I sent out a couple things but didn't continue. I worked at it into the '80s and it gradually fell away. It just wasn't what I was doing and the more I got involved in putting the bookstore together, the less I wrote. My interests were always very divided, and the more I got into the history of publishing—not that I couldn't have done all of it, but somehow the way it unraveled, the writing fell away and the other activities became more dominant. After Naropa, my then-girlfriend and I drove to Chicago with a U-Haul full of books, where we intended to start a bookstore. I spent every penny I had on books for an imagined bookstore. We were in Chicago for a while, but it didn't seem quite feasible, so we moved to Minneapolis where I lived for about eight years, and did start a bookstore.

Merce Dostale and I started a bookstore called Origin Books, and that was primarily a poetry bookstore although we had a little bit of everything: a few cookbooks, a few children's books, a little bit of this and that. At that point, I became aware of who was around locally, and started making some contacts with those people and quickly became affiliated with Granary Books, which already existed. It was an offshoot of Bookslinger, a distributor, and the man who was running Bookslinger, Jim Sitter, had a little side distribution thing called Granary under whose umbrella he distributed for Harry Duncan, Toothpaste, Windhover, Copper Canyon, and so on. Granary distributed a few of the literary fine presses then in operation, but their holdings were quite small, perhaps a shelf. That was Granary circa 1980.

We got involved, thinking naively that it would be a way to bring economic feasibility to the poetry bookstore, somehow. Of course, that was a ridiculous idea. Through distribution, through the continuity and the stability of an ongoing distribution thing called Granary, we imagined that this would be a way to reach out a little. So we were the exclusive distributor of Abattoir Editions, Windhover, and eventually Red Ozier. At one point, we had over two hundred presses in stock from around the world, and that peaked when I moved to New York and started attending the Frankfurt Book Fair. I began buying from continental presses, and we had perhaps thirty English presses, twenty or so from Germany, France, Italy, and a few things here and there from Australia, New Zealand, and Japan. At the peak there were a lot of presses represented, but it was also at this juncture that I realized there was a lot of work in circulation, though most of it was not really what I was interested in. I realized that I had all the pieces to the puzzle. I knew offset printers, lithographers, mimeographers, binders, papermakers, everyone. I even knew writers and had a sense of what I would want to publish.

The germinal seed moment for me was when Alison Circle, Charles Alexander's ex-wife with whom he ran the Black Mesa Press, came into Origin Books one winter day. She was a friend and she asked me, "Steve, if you were going to publish anyone, who would you publish?" and I immediately said, "Jane Brakhage." I had been reading Jane's work in *Rolling Stock* magazine, she was married to Stan Brakhage at the time and was writing this column called "Lump Gulch Tales" in *Rolling Stock*.

They were bizarre little Steinian stories about freak happenings in the mountains of Colorado. They were passed on stories, made up stories and so forth. I was surprised even to hear myself say that, but I didn't forget and eventually we published Jane's *From the Book of Legends* (1989). This may have been Granary's third book. I was distributing for Charles Alexander, he had split up with Alison by this point, and she was in Minneapolis where she was intending to continue doing Black Mesa, but I don't think she did anything more than a broadside or two. Charles was then in Tucson, where he was running Chax Press and we had talked about doing a book together which became *Firebird* (1987) by Paul Metcalf.

KS: That's terrific! It was Charles who put Granary's first book to press?

SC: Yes, Charles designed and printed it, and a friend of mine, Mary Beaton, made the paper out in Oakland at the Magnolia Paper Mill. The irony of it, thinking in the context of the publishers I was distributing, was that so few of them were publishing the work that I wanted to publish. We had that Paul Metcalf manuscript in hand, and we later learned that Red Ozier had also had a look at Paul's manuscript and they rejected it, and they were a press I was distributing. So conceivably, I could have been very happy to see that Red Ozier had published *Firebird*, but in a way, I found it quite amusing that they had turned it down.

But then there were also some little projects with Jonathan Williams at that time. We did a couple of little items, like *Noah Webster to Wee Lorine Niedecker* (1986). To be quite honest, it was rather terrifying to be in touch with Jonathan at that time. Really. It was a moment of much stretching on my part to be on the phone at that time because I revered him in a way. Well, he was just a person who was doing some interesting stuff. We had produced a catalogue of Jargon Society books for sale because we were selling books at that time, and had sent it to Jonathan just so he could see what we were doing, kind of as an homage—just to let him know that someone was interested in keeping an eye on what he was up to. Somehow, he found our number and gave us a call at the apartment much to our surprise, thanking us for sending the catalogue and we had a great conversation.

KS: He's always been very giving of his time and information...

SC: A wonderful guy, absolutely. Then I asked him for a little poem and he sent something and we printed it letterpress. That's why letterpress was so important for Granary at the outset. It was kind of built in from the outset, and there was a certain awareness that the perception of letterpress as being elitist, in a way, necessarily made the books more expensive than they would have been if they were printed in any other way. I remember the first time I had ever found a letterpress book by Robert Creeley—at the University of Iowa bookstore in Iowa City, up on the shelf published by the Toothpaste Press.

KS: *Later*?

SC: Yes, *Later* (1978). It was three dollars. I thought, three dollars? That's way too much. I can't buy this. There was always that sense that it was a little out of reach, and I've never really gotten over that, and rightly so. But at the same time, as Bernstein points out, no one is being deprived of Charles Bernstein's work if occasionally a letterpress or more involved version of his work comes along.

KS: I consider it an extension of the writing in some ways—it's just another form of experimentation. Reading Bernstein and Susan Bee's collaboration *Little Orphan Anagram* (published by Granary in 1997), for example, is very different from reading Charles online or in an old mimeo magazine, while another collaboration with Susan, *Log Rhythms*, which you published at about the same time—the modesty of the format gives it another feeling altogether. It's really a fascinating textual, or textural, transmission.

Would it be too simple to suggest that the greatest difference between Granary Books and The Jargon Society is Williams' affinity for the rural culture, the handmade or provincial way of life—while your own editorial direction seems to be more inclined towards an urban or metropolitan culture? Williams was accustomed to seeking out writers who were off the mark, at least geographically, celebrating and supporting the writing of people like Olson, Creeley, Niedecker, etc. That was always his preference in a sense. While Granary is quite cosmopolitan and international in its scope, it shares in what Williams would celebrate as the local, that sense of making use of those people and resources in one's immediate environment, locale, region, time, and vernacular.

SC: Exactly. I'm sure that's a factor. It was always fascinating to hear Jonathan and to know that he always had a desire to be accepted by an urban community. There was always talk, or a complaint: "I could have gone there to have lunch at the Harvard Club, or this or that, but I chose this other thing." It's an easy split, but I really noticed it yesterday when listening to Harry Gilonis at the Small Publishers' Fair, the person who read before Simon Cutts. As I was listening, I kept thinking what an interesting, fascinating, and bizarre outsider he is; highly intellectual, very articulate, very able. Somebody that would be perfect for Coracle, perfect for Jargon, a real outsider in the best sense of the word.

It kind of struck me then that there is a very particular kind of refinement that Jargon and Coracle were always interested in. They share a lot, and although Coracle is often urban, it is also very much outside of the dominant urban conventions, and very much interested in what was not mainstream. Simon and Erica are very interested in what is not being shown in the mainstream or published elsewhere, and that was certainly the case with many of the writers you just mentioned. When Jargon published them, they were not available in other forms. But there was something about the style and again, I come to that word "refinement," the way Harry Gilonis was so beautifully refined but just completely off the radar. I mean this poet was just really,

really interesting. It would be perfect for Coracle. They have published him of course, and Jargon has published Simon and Thomas A. Clark and others who are bridging this gap: somehow rural without becoming pastoral.

I think of the work of Thomas A. Clark and Laurie Clark, for example, which has found its place within the more radical side of publishing and writing communities, and publishing communities and readers—but why wasn't this work picked up by the Whittington Press? They lived in the Cotswolds for thirty years, they were just a few miles away from these people, but they seemed to have framed this pastoral, very charming word and image context into another field, and I'm really curious how they managed to do that. I was talking to Simon about it when we were out in Ireland, and he used this word "refinement." It's a different kind of refinement that they're getting at, and for that reason it just wouldn't show up on the radar screen of a press like Whittington. Whittington was doing very similar kinds of engravings, little drawings of moments and pastoral scenes with writing that may appear to be similar in tone to Clark's, but that's not the case at all.

There's really a divide, just as Ian Hamilton Finlay wouldn't be mistaken for the work of this other direction within letterpress, craft-oriented publishing. It's an area that I find really fascinating, how that sorts out, and could you breach that? Could you cross over to the other in a meaningful way? Or would each be lost? Are the differences so powerful that the two could never converge harmoniously? That's what's fascinating to me about what you're doing, and what I always found problematic about the earliest part of Granary when I was a dealer. It was as if I was coming close, but not quite in alignment with what I found interesting about writing.

KS: Looking back, what changed when you arrived in New York in terms of whom and how you were publishing in Minnesota?

SC: It really flourished in New York. Before New York the publishing was just an item or so a year, and then after about two years in New York we did the John Cage book *Nods* (1991), and from there it really went from two to five books a year, then to ten, then to twenty, and from then on it was just crazy. It became evident in that context that I had to vastly limit the number of books

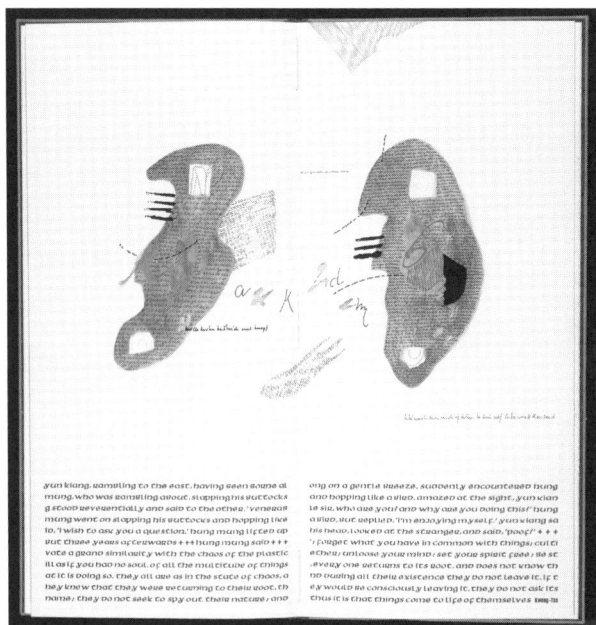

I was distributing because I had so much of my own work to do as a publisher. I also realized that while traveling and showing the other publishers I was representing, that I would tend to show the same books repeatedly. I would show what I was most interested in at the time, and a lot of it really languished, and I wasn't responsible to it in the way that I really intended to be. It quickly boiled down to a handful of works that were important to me, those by Timothy Ely, Barbara Fahrner, and Red Ozier for a short period of time. They went hand in hand, paring down on the role as distributor and concentrating on my role as publisher, which is what I really wanted to do. The other things just sort of fell away.

KS: What was the first trade edition?

SC: *The Century of Artists' Books* was book one in a series of trade paperbacks and critical editions. It was the first time we had done anything other than these elaborate, limited edition, special books by artists or occasionally by writers. Shelagh Keeley, Pati Scobey, Toni Dove, Buzz Spector—all of these books preceded *The Century of Artists' Books*, and the irony, among many ironies, is that *The Century of Artists' Books* actually sold quite well at the beginning, and I was imagining that there may have really been an audience for this sort of thing. The second trade book we did was *The Book, Spiritual Instrument* (1996) which I was shocked to discover as an issue of *New Wilderness Letter*. There's another example of being preceded by Rothenberg in so many different ways. I would think of something and of course, Jerry had already thought of it fifteen years earlier. That was kind of the most earth-shaking example on a number of different levels. I had nearly every issue of *New Wilderness Letter*, but not this one.

KS: How did you come upon it?

SC: I found it at Carolee Schneemann's as I was helping her sell her library and I just couldn't believe it, I just absolutely could not believe that they had done this in 1982. I set about trying to find a carton of copies to send to people and wrote to Jerry, wrote to Charlie Morrow, wrote to David Guss, the co-editor, and even wrote to many of the contributors, most of whom had never even seen a copy. Many had never realized that it had been done, and this was in 1995 or thereabouts. I couldn't even find a second copy, never mind a box of copies, so I contacted Jerry and Charlie and asked if it could be reprinted and I thought it was going to be enormous, like the Americans liberating Baghdad or something, like we were going to be met with flowers, and hallelujahs! But in fact it was quite the opposite. There was some interest, but not really.

KS: But people weren't critical of the book, were they?

SC: No, exactly! That's where you get to a wider audience; this book was about Balinese books and performance, it was all over the place. I think in the end we sold five, six, seven hundred copies in ten or twelve years, where we have ten thousand copies of *The Century of Artists' Books* in print, so it reached a different audience and I want to keep returning to it... that's why *The Book, Spiritual Instrument* led directly to *A Book of the Book* (2000). We subtitled that book, "Some Works and Projections About the Book and Writing" because we wanted to keep writing central, always central to even the high conceptualists of Clive Phillpot's world. Books are largely writing and documentation; that's the new paradigm I'm thinking.

[2008]

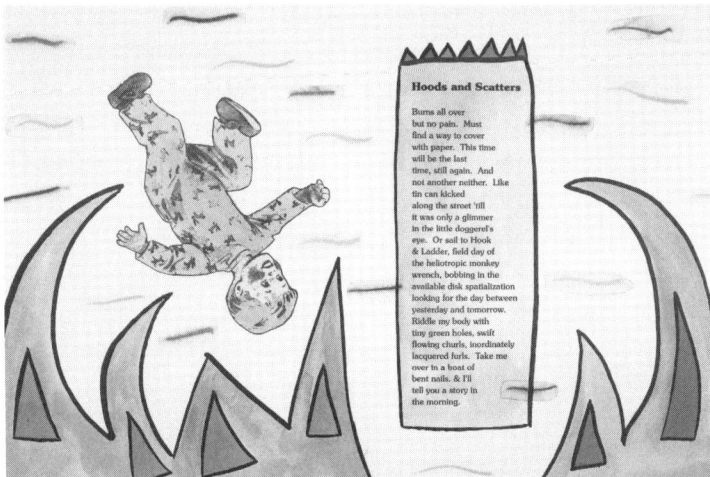

Susan Bee and Charles Bernstein, *Little Orphan Anagram* (Granary Books, 1997)

Charles Alexander
Chax Press

Charles Alexander (born 1954) is an American poet and director of Chax Press in Tucson, Arizona. Alexander went to Madison, Wisconsin where he studied and wrote poetry, and later typography, with the legendary Walter Hamady, who taught him the art of typesetting, printing, binding, and making paper by hand. It was there that Alexander began to produce expertly crafted books where form and content were in direct dialogue with one another.

Alexander founded Chax in 1984 when he moved to Tucson. Jackson Mac Low's *French Sonnets* (1984) is the book that bridges Alexander's second imprint, Black Mesa Press, with Chax. The presswork began in Madison and the book was finished in Tucson in an edition of just 250 copies. Chax published relatively small, handcrafted editions until the '90s, when they began to amplify and diversify publishing formats by introducing trade editions.

In three decades, Chax contributed over 200 carefully crafted books of innovative poetry to our community, ranging from one-of-a-kind artists books to large offset editions and all the spaces in between. Since its inception, Alexander has been dedicated to finding harmony between form and content, while continuing to write his own poetry, teach, travel, lecture, and sponsor countless poetry readings. Chax archives are housed at the University of Arizona.

From 2014 until 2018 Alexander headed the University of Houston-Victoria Center for the Arts, and taught letterpress printing and design to undergraduates. In 2018 he returned to Tucson, Arizona, where he remains engaged in publication and poetry projects of many kinds.

Maximum Ostentation

Hyattecture is all strut and stage
and a cheap high to move through.
The inner space is hollowed-out egyptian
and although the Egyptians
were not squeemish about slave labor
their engineers wouldn't have created
a structural episode like Kansas City.

In this franchise,
the most worn-out lobbyist
drinks from the cup of absurdity
because there is Forever
one more drop of it in the cup.
A dollar bill glued to the floor
will arrest half the parade.
From that clue I take it
Dobro Dick is somewhere around
grinning through the foliage,
inside the cocktail well,
a copy of *Hobo* in his chaps.

A distant background audio
of blowing out of pipes and flues
spreads like gas
through the Titan scale of the lobby.
Dizzying verticalities of glass
launch themselves as from Cape Canaveral.
Single, sharper sounds penetrate
the gas, as if just arrived
from galaxies found only in The Catalogue.

Through this half-tone crescendo
debauch the footpassengers
from the Sheraton to the quartzy elevators
visible as ants bound for the Van Allen Belts,
only to return in the grip
of their ionized bagatellas
raincoats & umbrellas
shock smeared across their kissers.

Out comes the book.
The crowd stares at the bill
stuck to the floor.
Dick promises to levitate the money
and with it the floor
of the surrounding dynastic structure.
The grins tighten around the mouths
the fingers around the briefcase handles.
This audience is educated.
Dobro's theatrically darting eyes
set the moment
when the bill rockets into his flat hand
with the stinging snap of the rubber band.

Edward Dorn, *Captain Jack's Chaps or Houston/MLA* (Black Mesa Press, 1983)

KS: I'd like to stump you with the first question: *what is Black Mesa Press?*

CA: You stumped me. Black Mesa Press. Black Mesa Press was the first press—actually, it was the second press I founded. It was the one I founded *after* learning typographic skills, printing and bookbinding with my then-partner Alison Circle, who subsequently moved to Minneapolis. We ran the press together in Madison, Wisconsin from 1981 to 1984 when she left for Minneapolis and I moved to Tucson. At that point, Black Mesa Press ceased to exist and Chax Press began. There are several Black Mesas around the country, at least a couple, but the one I was thinking of is in the Oklahoma Panhandle. It's the highest point in the state of Oklahoma, which is not particularly high, fairly austere, but geographically, a really interesting place. I was very involved in geography at that time. I was intensely reading Charles Olson and Carl Sauer. I was also interested in some of my own roots, which don't necessarily go to the Oklahoma Panhandle, but do go to Oklahoma. It was only later when I was considering moving to the Southwest, the year before I did move to Tucson, that I went to Black Mesa and camped.

I did take one book in-process with me to Tucson, and that was *French Sonnets* (1984) by Jackson Mac Low, which came out as a Black Mesa Press book although I have frequently referred to it as the first Chax Press book because in my mind that's what it is, even though it doesn't say that on the title-page of the book.

KS: What are some of the other Black Mesa books?

CA: Edward Dorn's *Captain Jack's Chaps or Houston/MLA* (1983); Mary Oppen's *Mother and Daughter and the Sea* (1981); Toby Olson's *Sitting in Gusevik* (1983). Let's see, Jesse Glass Junior's *Man's Wows* (1983); Lucy Tinkcom, who is an old college friend who translated a set of poems from the Carmina Burana, and Donald Wesling's *American Sentences: The History of West Seneca, New York* (1981). That's probably the bulk of it right there. Might have been a couple more. Do I remember every book that I ever printed? There you go. Few if I'm unprompted. There were numerous broadsides published by Black Mesa Press.

KS: Including?

CA: Including one by Theodore Enslin. One by Joel Oppenheimer. One by Helen Adam. I'm getting a little confused in my mind because a lot of these broadsides were done in conjunction with a literary center in Milwaukee, Woodland Pattern, and I kept doing broadsides for them even after I moved to Arizona, so it changed to being Chax Press broadsides at that point. The one we did by Robert Duncan, I have a feeling was—I'm not sure if it was Black Mesa Press or Chax Press. Probably still Black Mesa Press because—no, probably not, because I didn't go hear Duncan in that reading. Which means, I can't imagine not going had I been sixty miles away, while I can imagine not going had I been 1,900 miles away. I had published two small books as a student both by myself. One titled *To Turn Over* and one titled *Hack's Song* under the imprint the Pared So Thin Press. And that's why I said Black Mesa was my second press. And you may never see those books. They may have one in the Poetry Collection in Buffalo, but I'm not sure.

KS: Were those your first two books?

CA: The first one absolutely. Actually, yes, both of them. And the next, the first book of mine published by anyone else, was by a fellow printer and typographer in Madison, the Copper Ogham

Press of Beth Grabowski. It was titled *Third Light Poem*, and in some ways it was very much indebted to certain strategies I associated with Jackson Mac Low. If you know Mac Low's work you know he uses source texts. While my methodology was out of Mac Low my source text was Ronald Johnson's *Ark: The Foundations*.

KS: My understanding is that Black Mesa was mostly, if not all letterpress?

CA: All letterpress. All of my work was all letterpress from the period of 1979 when I first printed little broadsides as a student until 1990. Probably a couple of books that came out in 1990 were in the works in '89. So, even the first five years of Chax Press were all letterpress works too.

KS: Do you find harmony between traditional methods of printing and binding and avant-garde or experimental poetry? Wouldn't more conservative verse complement the tradition of bookmaking by hand?

CA: I can't publish anything I don't want to read, Kyle. There are many things I learned from my teacher, Walter Hamady, and I think one of them was learning traditional arts and fine craft methodologies. We lived in the twentieth century and now we live in the twenty-first century, so you don't want to repeat something that was done between 1450 and 1800 or something. It was absolutely important to attune your ears and mind and hands to work that captured your imagination, and the work that captured my imagination was by writers that I guess have come to be called avant-garde, although I think when I first started encountering such writers they were just the ones that turned me on. Also the ones that I liked. And now as I become more aware, there are certain things I've done with books with particular projects that pushed the edges of book structure a little more in non-traditional ways that seem to meet some of those texts where they stand. Not all books, because I think you have to do what's right project-to-project. One thing I really have been happy about is the fact that Chax Press has never had a house style. I don't think we've ever had a logo. We haven't been interested in branding in that kind of way. We are more interested in taking a project on and doing what that project needs.

KS: Do you associate a pressmark with branding?

CA: It would be something that would be consistent from book-to-book-to-book, and whenever I think about having one, I think, oh yeah, that would work with this book by Lyn Hejinian but would it work with this book by Myung Mi Kim? It would be something that is static. I am not sure I'd want to be limited in that way.

KS: Did Black Mesa have a pressmark?

CA: No, no. Never had one. The closest I've come to that is with Chax Press or something I've done with mixing typographical fonts in a way I like. I've used that more often on things like business cards and paraphernalia, but I've actually never printed that in a book. One of my favorite mixes, as you put it, of conventional typography and bookmaking with possibly unconventional poetic text is the one we discussed earlier, *French Sonnets* by Jackson Mac Low. I think of Jackson himself and his work as actually poised between this classically-minded philosophical soul and this wonderful avant-garde experimenter. So I designed that book to look like it could have been printed in the seventeenth century in certain ways.

KS: Not the shape.

CA: Not the shape, no, but the choice of fonts, the choice of colors, the choice of papers, the choice of the particular cloth used in the binding. In the seventeenth century it would have been leather I suppose. I didn't have to supply the avant-garde part because Jackson does plenty of that himself. I hope there is a little bit of surprise in that book for someone that might open it either not knowing his work, or suppose from the other side: someone who knows his work might be surprised at the form of the book. I do like to do things with books that hopefully just a little bit jar someone into thinking or into asking questions. *Why was it done this way? What is this mix of form and content?*

KS: *French Sonnets* always feels fresh when I open it. Certain typographic or aesthetic trends get dated very quickly. Jackson's work always looks fresh, you never read it the same way twice and *he* never read his poems the same way twice. The classic elements do the work justice. The oblong shape of the book is very theatrical.

CA: It's theatrical and yet it's also a function of the line. You know the poems themselves have extraordinarily long lines and I think we set them in 14 point type. They do extend, yet even within the line, also go on to give ample and comfortable margin reading room, so there's that too. And I do like it when the book is designed, as I like to say, from the inside out. Beginning with the text you start making decisions based on the text, whether those be size decisions, whether those be more imaginative decisions of color and possible illustrative or illuminative material or whatever might be.

KS: But why would you want to do that when it's so much more efficient just to make every book the same?

CA: Sounds like why make books at all? If you want efficiency go work for Gillette.

KS: But City Lights is pretty streamlined. New Directions is fairly streamlined.

CA: The irony of these things I'm saying is that I love City Lights. I love the look of their books. And Green Integer, I can slip 'em in my pocket and carry them with me and those are great. Every once in a while I look at my own bookshelf of works created by Chax Press and think, what a strange jumble. And yet when I look at the individual book, I usually still like what happens there. I don't know if I have any answer other than that. People who know me best, people in my family, will tell you I'm not all that efficient to begin with. I'm likely to make decisions that are sometimes not very efficient. One book that we did by Lyn Hejinian and Ray DiPalma was called *Chartings*. I had not printed a letterpress book in a couple of years because I was running the Minnesota Center for Book Arts, which was a big enough job. So when I got to it again, I thought I wanted to do something small and simple. And I thought I was going to do this project with Lyn and Ray that was oh, you know, maybe a 6″ x 8½″ book. Nicely printed, maybe on some Oriental papers, comfortable binding that wouldn't particularly call attention to it as an imaginative piece of book art. I printed most of the book that way and then decided that was not the right thing to do for those poems and trashed those pages and started all over again.

KS: Did you tear them up and use them in the book that we know as *Chartings*?

CA: No, no, no. I literally started all over again, printing poems on Mulberry paper and hand-tearing them out, which is where I'm sure that you might have gotten that idea. Then pasting them into oversized pages that have large, random numbers and letters in the background and envisioning something that seemed to be hinted at in the text of the poems. I think there's a line in the poem, something about *meaning carved in and out in space*, or something like that, and I wanted to activate that space. While that was time consuming, it wasn't difficult. It was a lot of fun. I had Jesse Seldess, who you probably know, doing an internship with me in the studio while that was going on, and he was helpful on that book. I regret spelling his name wrong in the colophon, but things like that happen once in a while. I often had student interns, and for a while there were some particularly gifted people who came with a lot of ideas and interests. You know that to me, having Jesse in that studio was a high point. I think within a year of that I had Trace Peterson and Heather Nagami in my studio and that was another high point.

KS: **Duncan, Creeley, and Blackburn were some of the poets Hamady was publishing when the Perishable Press was first starting out. I know you like their work very much, but I don't get the sense that you and Walter sustained a similar view of literature—his own writing is very different from yours. Did Walter's take on poetry have any influence on you?**

CA: He certainly gave validation to some of my literary ideas. Compared to people who were on the faculty in my PhD program in literature, which I did not finish partly because I discovered bookmaking. We shared a lot of affinities. It was an opening for me to find Walter who was conversant with and had even published some of the people I was reading. He knew about some of them, maybe even most of them. But you are right, he had been changing in some directions and we didn't agree on everything by any means, though we didn't really fight and argue about things. I think there were times I tried to educate him. I think I wrote a little essay on Robert Kelly at one point.

KS: **I found that in Walter's archives!**

CA: In Walter's archives? He actually taught a class, probably the second class I took from him beyond just the basic. I don't remember what the number was, Bookmaking or Typography or something, but he taught a class he called Book Illustration. It was more like, let's get together and read some books and have discussions about what illustration would mean in conjunction with these books and what kinds might be appropriate and what kinds might not be appropriate. I think in that class was my first, or at least one of the early times I read Paul Metcalf, who is not someone that Walter ever published but was someone that

Walter was reading. Walter also published George Oppen and Diane Wakoski. He never lost his loyalty to Blackburn, certainly, who he thought of as one of the great friends of his life. He was still publishing Joel Oppenheimer when I knew him. Compared to anybody else with another press, there was some crossover and some not-crossover. Walter was not anybody I ever had a difficult time disagreeing with, and he was certainly not anybody who ever had a difficult time disagreeing with me. I thought, actually, we had a pretty good relationship in that way. We would needle each other fairly often. As difficult as Walter could be, he really liked having some people around who didn't take his shit, and I was happy to fill that role as well as someone who clearly learned a lot from him and was willing to let him know that too. Since I left Madison I've had very little contact with Walter. I've seen him once in the last twenty-five years and have only talked to him three or four times in that period, and yet he's definitely a lingering presence in my consciousness. I maintain much closer ties to many of the other people who studied with him. Here in New York is Ruth Lingen, a delight as friend and collaborator. In Portland, Oregon, Kathy Kuehn directs the Salient Seedling Press, and is one of the ongoing presences for me, someone I always like to see, though we have not been in as close contact as I'd like. Pati Scobey. Penny McElroy is probably the one I've seen more than anyone over the years, partly because of geographic location. She is at the University of Redlands, which is about a six-hour drive. If I find myself going to Los Angeles, I stop and see Penny on the way. She published a book of my poetry after I was already in Arizona.

KS: Did you know Mary Laird?

CA: Yes, very well. They split up not long before I left Madison. Most of the time they were together, and I spent Thanksgiving at their house at least twice. I remember splitting wood with Walter one winter, which sounds so terribly Paul Bunyan-esque, but he had one of these automatic log splitters and all we had to do was lay the logs in. Eating Mary's wonderful cooking was a pleasure. I'm also very aware that everyone thinks of the Perishable Press Limited as Walter's press, but a lot of the typesetting and hard work that went into that was Mary's work. San Francisco, of course, is one of the places I've visited many times in part because of the vibrant poetry community and people I've published from there. Mary, when she left Wisconsin, went to Berkeley, and I've stayed at her house in Berkeley and we've maintained a very close friendship over the years.

Primarily, there were fourteen people that were part of a year-long seminar [in Madison]. Some of them had had a couple of years of study with Walter, some maybe one. He handpicked people to create a museum-scale exhibition of book arts or artists books. We weren't too worried about the terminology at that point. We went all over the country trying to find activity in bookmaking and putting together an exhibition: me, Pati Scobey, Kathy Kuehn, Stephanie Newman, Penny McElroy, Beth Grabowski, Ruth Lingen, Nancy Andrews, Susi Schneider... I'm missing some but I think those were the people that I at least kept in touch with enough to follow their careers. Walter Tisdale, of course. That was a fun group, and actually a lot of people in that group were strong-willed. I remember one moment in particular when Walter was proclaiming about somebody's slides we were viewing—I don't know if Walter thought that he was really going to make the choices here, but it was sort of made clear to him, when—I believe it was Penny McElroy—shouted: "Shut up, Walter!" He really had created a group that felt empowered. I think, if you put it to him, he would admit to being pleased to have created a group that felt empowered in that way.

KS: Were you one of the more literary people in the class?

CA: And I still am! I came to this work as both a poet and literature student, and actually, to go back a step further, I was coming out of meeting Robert Duncan and Robert Creeley and

Ed Dorn, Nate Mackey, and some others at a conference in Iowa on Charles Olson in 1978 when I first saw some handmade books by the Windhover Press at the University of Iowa and by Allan Kornblum's Toothpaste Press. I was in graduate school at the University of Wisconsin, Madison and had gone to Iowa City with the blessings of Merton Sealts who was a Melville scholar in the English department that I was teaching for as a TA and he actually gave me, or loaned me, a big notebook of his years of correspondence with Olson. But besides maybe confirming some of my literary directions in that weeklong event, I also was just so impressed with the notions of these small press handmade books. I actually came back to the University of Wisconsin wondering if there was any possibility of learning how to make such things. I ended up in the Art Department talking to Walter Hamady, not having a clue who he was, and asked if I could take his class. I had to get special permission from my English Department to take that class and I did.

KS: And then they lost you.

CA: They would probably never let anybody take that class again. I know that at the University of Arizona, creative writing students were printing things in the Art Department and doing some interesting books and broadsides and the Art Department just kicked them out and said, "No, this is for art majors only." Today, colleges are a little more proprietary in their various departments than they were in the late '70s.

KS: The University has absorbed some of the rhetoric of interdisciplinary arts, but when it actually comes to letting people wander, well—that's another story.

CA: Another interesting thing about that period for me is the Comparative Literature Department. I took a course from a terrific scholar named John Brenkman who was editor of *Social Text*, which was an important leftist literary journal or artistic journal.

In 1978 I took a course on Black Mountain Poets, reading them vis-à-vis the Frankfort philosophers, particularly Habermas and Horkheimer. Right when I left, there was a huge teaching assistants' strike and the faculty member that supported the students was John Brenkman, who was denied tenure as a result, or at least that was our suspicion at the time. His scholarship and teaching were great, but his politics and social organizing went against the grain of the University. Subsequently, he had absolutely no problem getting a job at Northwestern University. So I wasn't the only one to leave an academic program at that time, and maybe that has something to do with it beyond just being catapulted by my own interest in bookmaking. I think maybe a bit of dissatisfaction with academia as a way of life steered me toward art classes, which I never took thinking I would be an art professor. I just wanted to learn about making books.

KS: Did you want to see your own work in print?

Paul Metcalf, *Golden Delicious* (Chax Press, 1985), illustration by Wendy Osterweil

CA: That wasn't really much of an issue for me at the time. I was beginning to publish work and like most of the students, I did print some of my own work, but from the beginning I had in mind that I would print and publish other people's work. Since those early student days, there have been fewer than a handful of times that I printed and published my own work, from 1981 until now. I might do it again, though. I am thinking that the next book I publish I might be vain enough to think I can do it justice as a designer.

KS: What are the drawbacks to self-publishing?

CA: Right now, I don't think there are any. If that was what one person was doing to the exclusion of doing almost anything else—I wonder. I think part of the reason for doing this has to do with building community. Part of the reason for being involved in poetry, part of the reason for starting journals, part of the reason for starting presses, part of the reason for talking to you sitting on this bench right now, is all about building something together. We're not necessarily always conscious of just what we are building, but the language we work with is social material. We share it and we build relationships and ultimately other kinds of community. In fact, I think I learned to make books partly for that, partly to enter relationships. William Everson printed a lot of his own work, didn't he?

KS: Sure.

CA: But he printed Patchen and Jeffers and other people's work, too. Sure, there are plenty of people especially in that grayer area of artists books who self-publish. One of the things that led me in the late '80s to consider bringing out some books that were not printed in letterpress was the desire to get more texts into circulation, and we have continually done that ever since. Now, in a typical year Chax Press might publish eight trade paperback books and would be lucky to get out one letterpress book.

KS: Why is that?

CA: Well, once you start publishing books like that I think most people want you to do more, for one thing. If you are, as I am, interested in publishing a number of younger writers who aren't that well published you're not helping them a whole lot by putting 50 copies of a letterpress book out into the world, whereas if you can put 500 copies of their work out and get it around to the libraries, people, and reading groups you are, in that sense, building community. People start sending you 150-page manuscripts instead of 25-page manuscripts and you start thinking, do I really want to letterpress this? In part, this was a response to what seemed to be demand, not thinking of economic demand, but social literary demand in different ways. I enjoy getting those other kinds of books out and pretty quickly began to think of them as design challenges. They're creative projects in somewhat different ways. Particularly after I had a stint directing Minnesota's Center for Book Arts, in a certain way, it freed me from the letterpress—from feeling like I needed to do two or three or four letterpress books a year, feeling like I needed to produce them in large editions of 150, 250 in some cases. And keeping them at what I felt was a fairly accessible affordability level wasn't easy. A lot of books cost between 30 and 75 dollars at one point. Now I want to challenge myself artistically or technically in some way and I'm not too worried about what the ramifications of that are going to be in terms of the size of the edition or the price, because I have the trade editions, which I find fulfilling. In the letterpress books, when we make a book in 25 copies, I often wish there were 100 more available. That said, I know what it took to make that limited edition and it didn't make sense from the standpoint of labor, materials, and such to make more. And it didn't make sense in terms of the project to do it in a different way.

KS: Do you enjoy making books on computers?

CA: Do I make books on computers? I have yet to make an e-book. Or, what's that kind... Kindle book? But designing books on computer? Yes, I do. I enjoy the actual programs. I enjoy the back and forth with authors, and sometimes I'm amazed at how fast it can go having been trained in these letterpress arts which don't go very fast.

KS: Do you think you approach the software differently than people who have never worked with letterpress?

CA: You mean the way I think about the digital construction of leading and margins and what you can do with type, even the terminology? Yes, I do. I also think that I look at it differently in the sense that I've cut paper by hand and thought about the physical relationships of types sizes, paper sizes, and book sizes. I think I bring that consciousness to the computer, though I'm fairly self-taught, so I know I do things more slowly than people who have studied in art programs or design programs. On the other hand, I also have come to know at least some instances where I think to do things that they don't think to do because nobody told me I couldn't.

KS: Why don't we talk about your studio in Tucson? How do the nuts and bolts of your practice dovetail with or oppose your philosophy?

CA: Is there a philosophy?

KS: There is always a philosophy. Do we understand it? Now, that's another question.

CA: Let me start with coming to Tucson. Why Tucson? When Black Mesa Press ended I felt the need, for various personal reasons, to move on and move away. I had always had good feelings about the American Southwest desert and my sister lived in Albuquerque. I was done with school, as done as I was going to be. I got a loan from the bank for $1,500 to buy a press. I got some type and started a studio. I spent part of the summer in Santa Fe and Albuquerque when my brother-in-law encouraged me to look into Tucson. He said it had maintained more of its history than some other places in the Southwest, particularly in urban areas during the '70s where so much urban renewal came along and neighborhoods were transformed. I think he was right. To be honest, Tucson was also one of those places where I could find adequate studio space very inexpensively. I barely knew anybody. There wasn't a poetry community in Tucson of which I was aware (though of course there was quite an active poetry community which I would eventually come to know). Nor was there a book-making community. In other words, there were few distractions.

KS: Of course that's changed, thanks to you.

CA: Thank you.

KS: How do you know what to publish?

CA: Part of my insistence on knowing is in the talk I'm giving tonight, but I'm just going to be full of clichés on this, Kyle. I mean, you know, Emily Dickinson said poetry is "something that takes your head off." Donald Davie just hated that line. I remember him saying, "I would not want to have a lobotomy in order to understand…" But, it is something that somehow strikes you in the way that you like it, and in my case, I think I'm somewhat challenged by it. I remember, early on as a child, maybe more like an early teen, moving away from the so-called young adult books— reading people like Vladimir Nabokov. Things which, at the time, I knew I didn't really get, but there was something exciting about it—and even about not getting it. I think often when I read some of the poetry that's been endearing or enduring to me it has been something that I felt I hadn't understood or mastered right away. But it had something that made me want to try, so that's part of it. I'm conscious of Chax Press publishing work that in my mind has its antecedence somewhere among the area of Objectivist

Poetics or Black Mountain Poetics or New York School Poetics or Language Poetics or increasingly some mixes of those, which I think are current, particularly in poets in their forties and younger. Although, I'm not scared of lyric; I like to sing.

I often like poems that are conscious of the sound of the poem in various ways—some things I might call lyric somebody else might call anti-lyric, but it's playing off of that in some way. I think if you look at Chax Press books there's a fairly wide range. On the other hand, there are areas that I don't publish and probably tendencies that I do have. I know locally in Tucson I feel like I was one of the very first people in that community to bring a consciousness of Language poetry, and in certain quarters I got branded as that and certain people won't talk to me again and others are forever glad—neither of which I think have a total understanding of where I was coming from.

KS: Yes, someone once told me that Chax was the press of the Language poets and I told them I couldn't agree with that.

CA: No, but, I think from a perspective somewhere outside of Language, maybe outside of what we might call experimentalists or avant-garde altogether, Beverly Dahlen looks like a Language poet. From my perspective she does not look like a Language poet. There are fine tunings within these positions, certainly. I guess most of the people I have published, or at least talking to the Language poets, are not totally antithetic to that. Ron Silliman— let's name a Language poet. Ron Silliman is a Language poet, and he once defined Chax as—I forget if he used the term "experimentalist" or "avant-garde" poetry, but with strong humanist tendencies. I'd have to sit down with him and ask what he meant by that exactly, but it sort of sounds right. I'm still interested in the human in the work even if I'm not interested in personal narrative and its complications.

KS: Maybe that brings us back to my earlier, somewhat ironic question about the relationship between a traditional book form or printing technique as a medium for experimental writing. Do you think that the humanist elements in the poetry, even procedural work like Jackson's, are somehow illuminated or augmented by the warmth of the handmade book?

CA: It's a humanist quality and also, let's not forget the tactile. I'm interested in the tactile in the way that the book feels. Somebody will probably come in someday and find me lovingly running my hands over the type. I don't know, and wouldn't know, how to make an argument about how that might be important to the book and what somebody takes out of the book, for most readers, but certainly, it is of interest to me, and I hope there is some kind of relationship between the content of the book and some of those specific tactile possibilities. I've always been interested in making the reader aware of the act of reading, which is physical—unfolding, pulling something apart, and peeking in. There are various kinds of things you can do with the structure of the book that activates qualities in the reader that are not just about turning the page, and not just about the text as a disembodied substance.

KS: Also in the writing itself—there is a double reflection or hinge that connects the materiality of the language and the material book. Both are forces, objects, not necessarily poised in the same direction, but necessary and present.

CA: Yes, that's exactly what I'm saying.

KS: And you've been saying it beautifully for years.

CA: Thank you.

[2008]

EFFICIENCY WITHOUT REASON IS DESPERATION

the host invaded by
her tenants (maybe)

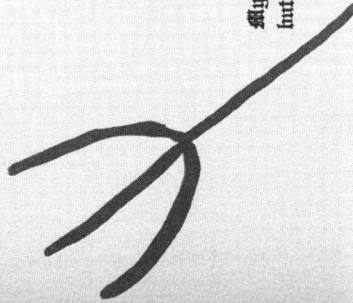

My memory is short
but my anxiety is rapacious

locust leaves
hold the bowls of
covers — as I to

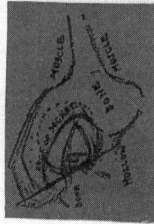

A USEFUL TENSION

Susan Bee and Charles Bernstein, *Fool's Gold* (Chax Press, 1991)

Annabel Lee
Vehicle Editions

Vehicle Editions was founded in 1976 by Annabel Levitt with a sense of responsibility toward cultivating contemporary literature and a love for book arts. She chose the name when learning about the three "yanas" of Tibetan Buddhism with Chogyam Trungpa Rinpoche. The term "vehicle" is also used in printing where it refers to the substance added to an ink that will aid its even flow over the rollers of a printing press. A printer (letterpress and offset), hand bookbinder, teacher of book crafts, bookkeeper, phototypesetter, monotype typesetter, hand typesetter, copyeditor, and writer, her poetry and prose have been published in over 50 publications, including print and online magazines and in books. As a writer herself, the publisher is particularly receptive to new directions in writing. She has worked for many other publishers (including as managing editor at Stonehill and as production manager at Aperture) and worked extensively with art book publishers on behalf of European printers. An active member of a community of poets, prose writers and publishers, she sits on the board of directors of The Poetry Project at St. Mark's Church and was formerly secretary/treasurer on the board of Center for Book Arts, New York. Thus Annabel Lee (she married the Lee in 1988) brings diverse experience to her role as publisher and has full involvement with the artistic, technical, literary and business aspects of the company.

The authors of Vehicle Editions include Jayne Anne Phillips, Ted Berrigan, Richard Hell, Christopher Knowles, Barbara Guest, Tony Towle, Clark Coolidge, and Carter Ratcliff. The artists the publisher has collaborated with in the making of Vehicle Editions include Alex Katz, Yvonne Jacquette, Joe Brainard, and Rudy Burckhardt. Editions range from 100 to 5,000 copies depending on production methods and intent. Vehicle Editions has employed commercial printers and binders for some titles, and for others all work has been done entirely by hand. Authors, artists, craftspeople, apprentices, and the publisher work in close association, collaborating on format, production, and editorial decisions, to ensure that the format of each book reflects its contents. The attempt has always been made that the book's exterior be an expression of its interior. For this reason, Vehicle Editions do not often resemble each other.

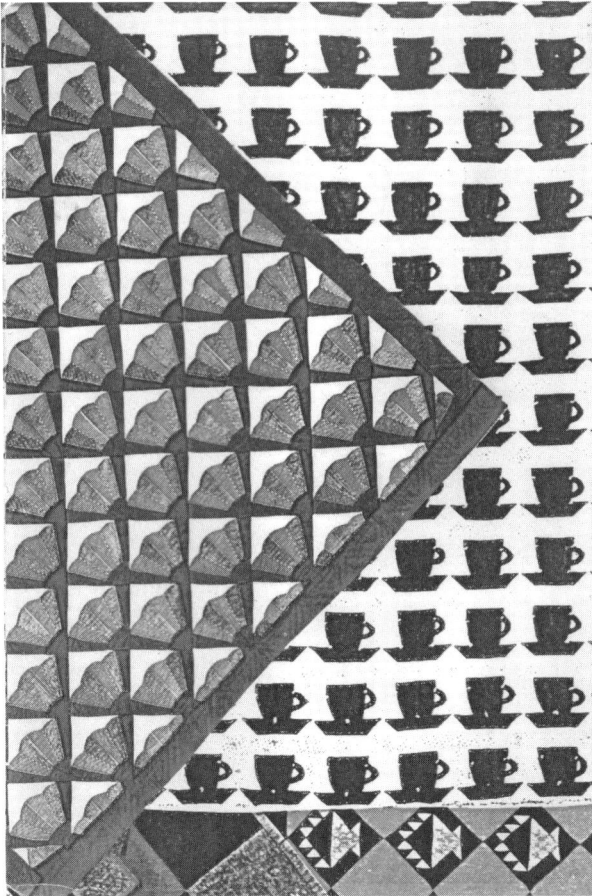

Barbara Guest, *Quilts* (Vehicle Editions, 1980)

KS: Was Vehicle Editions your first experience in publishing?

AL: The first publication on which I worked was *The Great Speckled Bird* newspaper in Atlanta, Georgia. This was my first experience in publishing.

I had dropped out of Sarah Lawrence College and spent a year living on a Tahiti Ketch in the Caribbean. While there I was seduced by the smell of printing ink in offset printing shops I visited on various islands because my boyfriend was an old-fashioned journeyman printer as well as a sailor. Then I was living in the Little Five Points neighborhood in Atlanta and working at Sojourner Truth Printing Cooperative on Euclid Avenue N.E. This part of town was diverse, eclectic, and what's popularly referred to as bohemian. Weekly we shot the artwork and laid out the film for *The Great Speckled Bird*. We were a small offset shop with only an AB Dick 360 press. I learned to work those machines, however the actual printing of this particular newsprint publication was done at a web shop where the management was accepting of the content. Notice that I refrain from saying that they were sympathetic with the contents of the newspaper. I don't think the sensibilities of these Georgia middle class men were actually sympathetic with the anti-Vietnam, pro-SDS, pro-Weatherpeople, pro–Black Panther, pro–gay/lesbian/transgender, pro–women's liberation, pre–new age new age content of *The Great Speckled Bird*. It was one of the important newspapers in the US at that time, right up there with the other left-leaning papers such as the *Village Voice* in New York, the Boston *Phoenix*, and some others.

After we turned in the camera-ready film and the web printing was completed overnight, we'd go to Underground Atlanta, a downtown scene in its heyday then that had started in 1969 with clubs featuring bands like Wet Willie and Little Feat, and head-shops and cafés. Think Bourbon Street in New Orleans. We'd hawk the papers in the street for a little pocket money. The job working at Sojourner Truth paid room and board but not much cash, so any little side jobs were welcome. It was a dangerous business, though, selling *The Great Speckled Bird*, because the majority of the population in Atlanta was anti-everything we stood for and we were harassed by well-meaning Southern citizens who were protecting their values. And sometimes we were harassed by the police as well.

After leaving Atlanta because I didn't quite fit in, I found another job at a printing shop north of Boston. I'd gone up there hoping to work with the cooperative who'd printed *Our Bodies Ourselves* on newsprint but they weren't taking on any new people. At the offset shop where I was employed, we printed pro-union pamphlets about health and safety issues for the workers at the GE plant in Lynn, Massachusetts. However, I developed some back problems due to heavy lifting on that job and decided to return to Sarah Lawrence. Grace Paley was my don and I spent another couple of semesters studying with most of the writers on the faculty there. I also took occasional writing workshops at the St. Mark's Church Poetry Project and attended many readings there. I was living down the block on 10th Street. For my two-day-a-week commute I took my bicycle on the subway to the top of the Lexington Avenue line and rode the last five miles to the Sarah Lawrence campus in Bronxville, just over the Westchester line, except for the times when I'd get rides with Galway Kinnell in his Saab. While a student I got a part-time ghost-writing job working for a woman who was writing a book about her late ex-husband Frank Loesser. Her publisher was impressed by my talents at writing and my printing background so he asked me if I'd prefer working at the publishing house to working for her.

My favorite thing about my job with her had been the iced coffee she made, and working for a publishing company was a thrilling opportunity, so I leapt at the chance.

Chelsea House Publishing Company wasn't the large successful operation it is now. They published mostly academic books and my duties were fairly scattered. They hadn't been looking to fill any vacancies when I showed up so they gave me any work that came up. I did fine. After I'd been working there for a while the partner in the firm who'd brought me in said he thought I'd have more fun and make myself more useful working at his son's new publishing house, Stonehill. In the meantime a woman at Chelsea House was just giving up her apartment to go back to France so I inherited her six-flight walkup. I moved to East 17th Street between Third and Irving, down the street from Max's Kansas City, which became my second home.

Stonehill Publishing Company was run by Jeffrey Steinberg, a brilliant, drug-crazed maniac who had been at Straight Arrow, the book publishing arm of *Rolling Stone* magazine, before he went out on his own. Our offices were on 57th Street between Park and Madison. The apartment on 17th Street was part of the deal and the rent was paid as part of my meager salary. I walked to work up Park Avenue South, 40 blocks. I needed the exercise. And when we had meetings after work they were always at Max's.

We were a small staff. Jeffrey, the publisher, had a room of his own as his office. His wife Dee sat in the anteroom you entered from the hallway. That is, Dee was secretary until Jeffrey hired another secretary who was also his lover and whom he installed at the Park Lane Hotel as part of her salary. David Dalton worked with the business but didn't maintain a desk there. The highly acclaimed author and journalist Jonathan Cott, who like David was a *Rolling Stone* writer, had a desk in the interior room along with Peter Swales who would later become known for the work he began at Stonehill on Sigmund Freud, which is chronicled in

Janet Malcolm's book *In the Freud Archives*. Jonathan and Peter and David were the chief editorial staff. There were also a couple of people handling production work and what served as business management in that same room, in this highly illicit operation. We had the City Marshalls shut us down during my time there and we had regular visits from a major drug dealer and from a pimp who wore the most fabulous suits. And we made books. Philip Agee's *CIA Diary* (1975) was one of our biggest sellers and had caused a lawsuit with the printer over content.

I was given the title of Managing Editor after working there for a while since there was no other managing editor and I had become a sort of jack-of-all-trades around the office. I worked on permissions, on production (especially after the woman handling production walked out), editing, proofreading, cleaning up artwork for an illustrated book of children's literature, and whatever came up. One of my favorite aspects of the job was the occasional visit to a printing shop where I'd get a whiff of that smell of printing ink. I had the opportunity to bring in an author so I suggested Anne Waldman. Jonathan Cott also knew her because they'd both grown up in Manhattan and they both attended Friends Seminary. I suggested that it should be a book that was not her poetry. I contacted her and once she was in the office with her scarves and dynamism and razzle-dazzle, my role in that book dissolved and Jeffrey handled the rest himself. Her book *Journals and Dreams* (1976) was the result.

It was a great job. I took printers out to lunch, we all spent time in the back room at Max's with the crowd from Warhol's Factory, and my long-term friendship with Mickey Ruskin began, a friendship that would be a comfort for many years to come. I learned *The Chicago Manual of Style* on the job and I'd take it home and read it cover to cover. And I was part of the creation of books: from idea to finished product, working with authors, editors, printers, graphic designers, agents, and a range of people on the downtown scene active in the worlds of writing, painting, sculpture, and drugs.

The job ended badly, but not the sort of bad you might suspect. Stress was the killer. It was a 24/7 job as you can probably tell from my brief description so far. While working in printing shops before coming to New York City, before this Stonehill job, I'd had some incidents with back pain, sciatica, and difficulties bending, sitting, and walking. In my Stonehill job, sitting at a desk most of the day, sitting at a table at Max's long hours into the night, I was not taking care of what I soon learned was a major flaw in my spine. I have a malformed disc. And during that time the only exercise I got was the walk to work and spinning Sufi style: I would go to the Byrd loft on Spring Street where Robert Wilson, the director, had open houses and people danced. We did a lot of spinning, learning techniques from the choreographer Andy de Groat who would later choreograph the opera *Einstein on the Beach* (1975). Then I'd go back to my 6th floor walkup on 17th Street and spin some more.

I ended up in the hospital in traction after numerous incidents and a string of practitioners of various persuasions: acupuncturists, osteopaths, chiropractors, orthopedists, and others. It was about a year and a half of limited movement, workmen's compensation followed by unemployment, the Alexander technique, and beginning a t'ai chi practice that allowed me to study hand bookbinding with Richard Minsky at the Center for Book Arts. There I was in a shop with that intoxicating smell of printing ink and I began printing on the letterpress machines there. Jonathan Cott asked me if I'd print and bind a small edition of a manuscript of poems of his called *Charms* so he could give them to friends as gifts. We never did that project. But I realized I was on the road to being a publisher myself.

KS: "On the road" is the right phrase, both for its Beat-era connotations and for what was to become Vehicle Editions. Many independent publishers of poetry and literature don't have a professional background in the day-to-day activities of the printing and publishing industries, but you did. How did you become interested in hand bookbinding—and

what was the Center like in those days? If I recall correctly, the Center wasn't at its current location on West 27th Street.

AL: Center for Book Arts was located at 15 Bleecker Street. Richard Minsky lived there, downstairs, and it was a storefront with lots of windows on the street. I have memories of the place over a lot of years so it's hard to place what was where when, who was doing what. For the moment, and to keep my reminiscences somewhat limited, I'll try to keep most of this information pre-1978. Minsky founded the Center in 1974 so when I got there in 1975 it was "established" in my mind and I didn't feel like an "old-timer" for many years. There was a Washington handpress sitting in the window and I always think of 15 Bleecker Street that way. And there was a Jeffrey Lew painting on the wall to your right as you walked in the door. When I worked late at night, which was often, I had to roll those big security gates into place and lock them up if Minsky wasn't around. There were a few reasons why I had no reason to be nervous very late at night. For one thing the Bowery bums were harmless, and they were the ones most likely to be loitering on the street late at night. For another thing, CBGB was right down the block on the Bowery on the far side of that T-intersection with Bleecker Street, so often there was a scene on the streets late at night and that crowd was neither affluent, which would invite crime, nor were they criminals themselves— they were a bunch of harmless, tough-looking punks. Beginning in December 1976, I lived on Mott Street so once I walked south and passed the Volunteers of America donation on the far side of Houston Street and was in Little Italy, the Gambino "family" was watching out for me. However, when I was first going over to the Center I lived on the top floor of Kenward Elmslie's townhouse on Greenwich Avenue across from the top of Jane Street where John Lennon and Yoko Ono had their pad and I'd walk across Bleecker and a few blocks north on Seventh Avenue to get home.

The Center was a congenial place, a beehive of activity, with lots of projects going on. In order to jog my memory I went back through some old files and through old journals and did some emailing with Minsky. Unfortunately I had heaps of paperwork about the Center that I tossed about two years ago that related mostly to activities of the Board of Directors when I was secretary, secretary/treasurer, and simply member of the Board during some of the years between 1975 and 1989 when I left New York.

The first mention I find of the Center in my journals is in September of 1975 when I must have started taking a bookbinding class with Minsky. I will be forever grateful to Minsky for teaching me how to fold a piece of paper—and more of course. I'm never without a bone folder and the entire class that was devoted to that skill was well worth it. Another skill he tried to teach me in that class was how to sharpen a blade for paring leather so the leather lies flat when you glue it down on the binder's board. The knife is sharpened on hard Arkansas stone in a circular motion, then you draw the knife across the strop. You have to move the paring knife across each of these devices without breaking the straightness of wrist. My problem with doing this had to do with an imbalance between strength (firmness) and tension. I never got that skill down and, who knows, if I had I might be a fine bookbinder today. But I failed to learn that refined and subtle skill. I still do, however, put handmade books together fairly frequently.

The main source for paper that we used at the Center in those days was Gem Paper located six stores south of Houston Street on Broadway. It was a virtual warehouse of job lot paper: cartons and sometimes skids full of a broad variety of paper left over from who knew what sources. It was a treasure house and it didn't matter if you were looking for some quirky 100% nylon fiber paper (which I found there and used as endsheets once) or you were looking for 100% cotton fiber paper or paper made from chipboard or anything—you'd have a great selection, rock bottom pricing, and you couldn't know in advance the color, weight, or quantity that they'd have on hand until you walked in and perused the stacks upon stacks of papers. Of course you could pay top dollar and buy handmade sheets or other good paper products at New York Central Supply or you could go to Pearl Paint, but I almost always shopped at Gem unless I was buying a huge quantity directly from a paper dealer like Lindenmeyr.

The Center was well fitted out. There was the guillotine, the board shears, the paper cutter, type, presses. My first printing project there was a card announcing an event Rhys Chatham and I did at St. Mark's Church. Rhys presented music and I presented poetry. The card was printed on cardstock from Gem that was preprinted flat turquoise with a thick glossy coating. I set up Goudy handset type in a chase and printed probably about 100 to send to my friends. Then I printed a broadside of a poem I'd written that people liked when I read it at readings: the Erie-Lackawanna Railroad Train Poem. That was handset Goudy Old Style and I went up to the New York Public Library on 42nd Street and found a couple of nice illustrations: train tracks and an image of a train, that I had made into blocks at an engraver's shop. The type was set in a 10˝ by 15˝ chase. It was printed in three colors: silver and white lake for the tracks, silver and cadet blue for the type and silver for the train. Although I would print in silver again for the Vehicle Edition *Airmail Postcards* (1979) by Franco Beltrametti, I only did so for the covers because silver ink is terribly gummy and doesn't flow over the rollers very well.

I don't remember when I learned paper marbling techniques but I did that at the Center also. The first bookmaking workshop I gave on my own I did in the summer in Boulder, Colorado ($11 per student per day). I'm not sure on the year for that but it was before 1977. After having worked only with "cold type" previously, the Center introduced me to hot metal type. I used type at the shop, on occasion I had type set Linotype, and fortunately I had the opportunity to work with Pat Taylor (an insurance executive who had a Monotype shop at home for a hobby) at his Odd Sorts Letter Foundry in Larchmont, New York making monotype using the classic old machines with a vat of bubbling, boiling lead by your knee that was squirted into the letter molds as you punched the keys and then cooled with water to set the type.

I also have a journal note about visiting George and Susan Quasha in Barrytown at their Station Hill Press in those years. I printed on a Chandler & Price platen press that belonged to the Center but that somehow ended up with Trish Nedds. She moved up to Barrytown and took that press with her when she became the production manager for Station Hill. That particular Chandler & Price had been at the Center first and it's the press I printed two Vehicle Editions on: *Continental 34s* (1977), a selection of my 34-syllable poems, and *Counting* (1978), the first prose work by Jayne Anne Phillips.

Here are some of the people at the Center in those early days, before 1978, as best as I can recall (with a little help from Minsky). There was Kathy Weldon, the director and then-girlfriend of Minsky. She was a hard-worker and had her hands full and tried her best to be business-like while managing an organization that didn't quite fit the business mold. Things got screwed up at times. Nick Caraccio was a friend of Richard's who was one of the three original members of the Board of Directors: Nick, Richard, and Rick Wall, the Volunteer Lawyers for the Arts lawyer who incorporated the Center. Toni Weil was an apprentice at the shop, a printer who many years later would marry Michael Uytenbogaart, the excellent printer who printed *Train Ride* by Ted Berrigan and who'd worked previously with Coach House Press in Canada. Randy Hunt was an apprentice in those early years, an expert bookbinder, and his then girlfriend Mary Jane Etherington was also an apprentice. Randy was a superb true craftsman, not only in book crafts but also in fine woodworking. It was through Randy and his friendships with David Hockney and Henry Geldzahler that I was privileged to visit Geldzahler's 9th Street place and enjoy the garden and the fabulous collection of art including heaps upon heaps of Basquiats and Hockneys.

Years later Randy bound hardovers for me improvising an ingenious method using the offset printed (at Meriden Gravure) sheets of Vehicle Edition *Fast Lanes* by Jayne Anne Phillips with two-part drawings by Yvonne Jacquette. Two of the other apprentices whom I remember well are Peter Seidler who is a genius that went on to real-world success, Reggie Walker, and Susan Rabinowitz. The very talented and inspiring bookbinders who I remember were working and teaching there in the early days were Hedi Kyle and Mindell Dubansky. Mindy later married John Cliett, a neighbor on Bleecker Street who was a friend of Minsky's and who visited the Center frequently. Mindy went on to work at the Metropolitan Museum of Art. Barbara Mauriello arrived at the Center after 1978. She is also a great teacher of bookbinding and I took classes with her after the Center moved to 626 Broadway. Dikko Faust came to New York City from Wisconsin, met Esther Smith and their Purgatory Pie Press got involved with the Center in the late '70s. I got to know them well because I found them an apartment in my building on Mott Street so we became neighbors. The people who loved the Center and supported its efforts whom I remember from the early days are August (Augie) Heckscher, Rose Slivka, Fabio Coen, and Polly Lada-Mocarski. Fabio Coen, a very elegant northern Italian gentleman, was in that first bookbinding class I took and later was on the Board. Rose Slivka would be a very important person in my life because she hired me as a typesetter and for other tasks on her publications *Craft International* and *New Work*, a magazine about the craft of making hand-blown glass. The very dear Ken Milford who served on the Board later actually showed up after 1978. Joan Davidson also likely showed up later but I had known her since 1973 because my father (an architect) worked for Urban Development Corporation (UDC) and I met her through him. UDC was a Rockefeller project and Joan was involved with it. Joan may have been around earlier than 1978 though because of her role as Chairman of NYSCA. Other people I knew who were around before 1978 were Douglass Morse Howell who was working for Tatyana Grosman's Universal

Limited Art Editions out in West Islip; and Dick Higgins, the great Fluxus artist and founder of Something Else Press; and Alison Knowles, another great Fluxus artist who incorporated papermaking in her artworks and performance pieces; and Albert M. Fine, poet, composer, musician and Fluxus artist; and Ray Johnson, famed for his mail art, his collages, and his performances; and Rick Fields whom I worked for out at Naropa in Boulder on the publication he edited, *Loka*.

Besides taking hand bookbinding classes and printing letterpress, I became more involved with the Center as time went by. In 1976 when I took the apartment on Mott Street at the corner of Prince, which I kept for the next 17 years, the location was perfect because it was halfway between my boyfriend's place on Broadway below Spring Street and the Center at 15 Bleecker at the top of Elizabeth Street. This location facilitated my use of the shop at odd hours or in between other jobs with the possibility of running home and getting a little more cleaned up (in my tub in the kitchen of that railroad flat) and changing clothes for other destinations.

In 1977 a very bonding experience happened for me and the Center. I was asked by Kathy Weldon, the director of the Center, to be co-coordinator of the Hand Papermakers' Conference. It was very engrossing and I was extremely pleased to be valued so much as to be hired by the Center to work with such an esteemed group of artisans. We used the church across the street for some of our activities because our space was limited. The only other use I knew of for that community center was it was the place where the Bowery bums went to be fumigated: not just showers, but delousing and whatever other chemical treatments were in general usage in 1977 for the removal of parasitic bugs that were making their homes on these drunkards' bodies. We had asked Robert Rauschenberg, who lived a couple of blocks away on Lafayette Street, whether we could use his chapel for some of our conference activities, but the space just wasn't right, however the visit there to check it out was a big thrill. Walter Hamady of Mount Horeb, Wisconsin (works of the Perishable Press); Elaine Koretsky of Brookline, Massachusetts (hemp paper); Tim Barrett of Kalamazoo, Michigan (papermaking in Japan); Kathryn and Howard Clark of Twinrockers in Indiana (European tradition of hand papermaking); and Helmut Becker of the University of Western Ontario (growing and processing flax for handmade paper) were just some of the many gifted experts who participated in this conference.

During those years, from 1975 until 1978 when I received my first grant, a National Endowment for the Arts Assistance to Small Presses grant in the astoundingly huge amount of $8,000, Center for Book Arts was just part of a very diverse active life. In 1975, while living on workmen's compensation and recovering from a hospitalization due to back trouble suffered as a result of too much heavy lifting in offset printing shops, I applied for grants to set up a series of poetry readings in Philadelphia called "Living American Poetry." 1976 was the bicentennial year and there was a lot of money floating around. However, with Mayor Rizzo and the political machine operating in Philadelphia at the time, it proved to be an unrewarding effort. I had hoped to create a sort of satellite series to the St. Mark's Poetry Project reading series and poets who came to New York for a Wednesday reading there could then read on Thursday night in Philadelphia, only an hour and a half away. It was a bargain for the Philadelphia crowd, but they wanted nothing to do with the roster of poets I was proposing and considered me a sort of outside agitator when their poetry scene, centered around *American Poetry Review*, run by Stephen Berg and Arthur Vogelsang with friendly camaraderie of C.K. Williams, was a known quantity.

The process introduced me to the grant game, though. And this proved very valuable once I was a regular at the Center. Besides taking bookbinding classes and then bartering time on the letterpress machines for my projects in exchange for printing ephemera for the Center, I also began assisting with grant writing and budgets pretty early on when Kathy Weldon and I got friendly (she lived around the block from me on Elizabeth Street) and she realized that I didn't mind doing tedious math chores.

Since writing about Center for Book Arts led me to look back at my "Book Book," I found the epigraph I chose for it and it somehow seems every more apt now than it did then. It's a quote from Nicolas Barker from the December 7, 1973 issue of the *Times Literary Supplement*, an issue devoted to printing and book production. He wrote, "Flexibility is the key to the future... The division between author and book-manufacturer will become fluid, rather than a watertight bulkhead. The division between professional and amateur printer will also become more fluid... If the lines between author and reader are less rigidly drawn with each party ready to accept a different division of work if the project demands it, then all will be well. It will also be, in theory if not in practice, a return to pre-Gutenbergian methods of work."

KS: And why did you call your press Vehicle Editions?

AL: When I was an apprentice in an offset printing shop, I learned that the "vehicle" in the printing process is the solvent of an ink into which a pigment is added. In other words, this is the substance added to ink to make it possible for the ink to flow evenly over the rollers of the press and adhere to the plate with no bubbles or gumming or other inconsistencies. As a result the impression on the final page is flat, smooth, and even. The term, vehicle, applies to letterpress printing, stone lithography, to all methods of printing.

This is a delightful fact for me since I am a big fan of many types of vehicles. Among trains the Wuppertal Schwebebahn is one of my favorites—a suspended monorail train in the Ruhrgebiet in Germany featured in Wim Wenders' movie *Alice in the Cities*. Among cars I favor Maserati four-door sedans and I drive a heavy steel Volvo that I love. My bicycle is a Dune Commander with no gears, big fat tires and a wide seat. Among airplanes I'm thrilled that "Like a G6" is the name of a current pop song by Far East Movement featuring The Cataracs and Dev—a G6 is a Gulfstream G650, a twin-engine jet airplane. Then there are sport utility vehicles like skateboards and canoes. The most important boat in my life was my home, a 30-foot Tahiti Ketch where I lived for a year in the Caribbean. Then there are all the rest of the vehicles on land, air, and water. And I've got a nice little collection of toy vehicles that are kept in active service.

Most importantly, in 1975 I first heard the Buddhist Kagyu lineage teachings of Chogyam Trungpa Rinpoche at Naropa and began to grasp the roles of the Mahayana Greater Vehicle, the Hinayana Lesser Vehicle and the third Vehicle called Vajrayana, a form of Tantric Buddhism also known as the Vehicle of the Text. These are means toward awakening compassion along the path toward enlightenment, or, as many Westerners like to call it, the quest for Nirvana. That summer, coincidentally, or karmically, and in the Dharma, I realized that I had enough of the necessary skills and access to excellent facilities to make it possible for me to begin publishing independently. I was moving from offset printing to letterpress printing and I was teaching and practicing various styles of hand bookbinding. I had already had a job as Managing Editor in a New York publishing house and I had worked on editing, proofreading, ghostwriting, and other book projects for other employers. I was also practicing sitting meditation and t'ai chi. While at Naropa I was introduced to the writings of the dancer Douglas Dunn. I was also getting to know Jayne Anne Phillips who was moving from the writing of poetry to fiction. There were grants to be applied for and I was inspired to leap into the role of publisher.

More recently I have learned that the term "vehicle" is used in the landmark 1938 case Lovell v. City of Griffin where the then-Chief Justice of the Supreme Court defined "the press" as "every sort of publication which affords a vehicle of information and opinion." The term "vehicle" as defined in this decision takes on new relevance today as the internet provides new opportunities for the flow of information and artistic expression to push new boundaries.

This significance of "freedom of the press" which now includes everything a printing press produces as well as everything a home printer can print had played a key role for Vehicle Editions. When I published *Train Ride* by Ted Berrigan, the book had already been turned down by four other publishers because of the proliferation of the word "fuck." And when I published *Hot and Cold* (1998) by Richard Hell, the cover we chose, his delicate drawing of a limp cock held deftly between thumb and forefinger, makes a clear statement about the implied freedoms in the expression of opinions and in broadening the range of writing and visual imagery made available to the general public through the various publishing modes.

Of course, the idea of a vehicle in Vehicle Editions is also that the art and literature included in each book are intended to transport the reader.

KS: I know you took an active part in the making of the Vehicle Editions titles. Could you summarize for me what sort of tasks you did?

AL: I guess the editorial work would be as good a place as any to start to answer that question. As editor, I solicited every title except two. *The Traveling Woman* (1986) came in "over the transom," recommended by a couple of gallery owners who knew Roberta's artwork and she had never written anything except captions for her paintings before. The other that was recommended was *The Day Before Yesterday*, a collection of short stories by Leon de Winter. I was interested in publishing his novel *Place de la Bastille*, however the Dutch publisher suggested we produced several books together and begin with the collection of stories instead of the novel. As it happened, we never found the money to co-publish the other books on our list.

Collaboration was the key to making all the books. I worked with all the artists and authors closely to create a book that we would all be happy with. *Typings* (1979) by Christopher Knowles was the most collaborative in the sense that it had many people involved with the collaboration on design and I did only the final layout on my own. I worked out co-publishing venture arrangements with Uitgeverij in de Knipscheer for *Counting* and *The Day Before Yesterday* (1977) and with Brooke Alexander Gallery for *Fast Lanes* (1984). I also negotiated an arrangement to share film for the images by Alex Katz for *Give Me Tomorrow* (1983) with Alpine Fine Arts and the arrangements for using Christopher Knowles' artwork for *Typings* with Holly Solomon Gallery.

Score (1977) was completely edited by me in the sense that Douglas Dunn gave me a heap of notes and drawings for his dance piece Lazy Madge and I sorted them, categorized them and arranged them. Some authors, Simon Pettet and Michael Lally, for example, collaborated with me in deciding what writing would be included in the Vehicle Edition and what would be left out. And I collaborated with Scott Rollins on the translation from the Dutch of Leon de Winter's stories in *The Day Before Yesterday.*

The greatest innovation I made in my work on Vehicle Editions is the cover for *Airmail Postcards*. I bound those books in my kitchen—this was usual for me, and I had many helpers and apprentices on these binding projects. However I designed the binding for *Airmail Postcards* because of the way Franco Beltrametti sent me his original artwork from Switzerland. Everything came over in standard issue European-sized airmail envelopes. The work fit so nicely inside these envelopes I decided to make the book that size. Then, when I realized that I had lots of extra cover stock from *Train Ride* (1971), a luxurious high-cotton-content bright white paper, I decided to use that for

the interior of the book. This meant that the cover did not have to be a heavy stock to hold the books together. I experimented with envelopes and knew that, since envelopes are made to resist wear on their folded edges as they pass through the postal system, they could be strong enough to serve as the cover. The challenge was to create a spine. After lots of experimenting I decided that the stiffness that homemade flour paste, when dry, gave just the right structure to the spine of the book and thus the book was designed to be handsewn as signatures of cover stock that was then slipped into a cover composed of two envelopes. It seemed so perfect, so simple, so cheap, so practical, I thought it might bring me my first million. I'm terrifically proud of the design.

The other softcover books I bound on my kitchen table were *Continental 34s, Light & Shadow* (1977), *Train Ride* (about a third of the run), *Counting* (first printing) which were all flexbound using polyvinyl acetate and a binding device designed by Richard Minsky and *Hot and Cold* which was handsewn in signatures like *Airmail Postcards*. I bound *Quilts* in a kitchen-table situation, handsewn as just one signature, at Écart in Geneva, Switzerland. And I made limited edition hardcovers for *Train Ride, just let me do it* (1978), *Light & Shadow, Continental 34s, Counting,* and *Hot and Cold.*

The fundraising was always a challenge and took up a lot of my time. There were grant applications to write and I went around to galleries to try to drum up support for co-publications with their artists. There were fundraising events to organize as well from time to time, including a Vehicle Editions benefit reading at Giorgio Gomelsky's Zu Club in Chelsea. (Among his many claims to fame in the rock and roll business was that The Rolling Stones were the house band at a club Giorgio Gomelsky owned in the early '60s.) The first three books I made before I got any grants. But they were done totally on the cheap. *Continental 34s* was typeset by me, printed by me, paper was job lot from Gem Paper, and all binding was done by me and helpers. *Light & Shadow* by Simon Schuchat was inexpensive, typeset by me, printed at The Print Center in Brooklyn, bound on my kitchen table.

The most exciting work I did was the letterpress printing. I used a Chandler & Price platen press for *Continental 34s* and for the first edition of *Counting*. I also trained Liz Phillips to print *Airmail Postcards* on Chandler & Price and printed the covers using a very sticky silver ink. I learned a lot from Michael Uytenbogaart who printed *Train Ride*, and served as his assistant.

I printed *Smithsonian Depositions* (1986) on a Xerox copier in the office of an architectural practice. The money I spent on that book was on the paper: Strathmore Writing, a high cotton content stationery paper, not a book paper at all. And I collaborated with the cover artist for *Quilts*, Deborah Freedman, on that cover. We cut up images of quilts and photocopied them in spontaneous collage arrangements on the bed of a color Xerox machine at Jamie Canvas on Spring Street in Soho. This particular color Xerox machine was influencing the work of many New York artists in those days because color copying was an entirely new thing and by moving the image while the machine was scanning the image it was possible to create wild color separations, which we did.

When I did not print the books myself or work closely with the letterpress printer, I did print supervision in most cases. I went on press with *just let me do it* in Montreal, with *When I Was Alive* (1980) in Brooklyn, with the second printing of *Counting* near

Detroit, with *Give Me Tomorrow* in Zaandam, Holland, with *Fast Lanes* in Meriden, Connecticut, with *The Traveling Woman* in Zwolle, Holland, with *Conversations with Rudy Burckhardt* (1987) in Dalton, Massachusetts, and with *Hot and Cold* at a digital shop in Great Barrington, Massachusetts.

Typesetting has always been one of my favorite activities. I used an ancient monotype machine up at Pat Taylor's Odd Sorts Letter Foundry to set *Train Ride* and *When I Was Alive*. I chose Gill Sans for *Train Ride* because it is the face used in the London Underground and I chose Bell for *When I Was Alive*. I did the typesetting for *Score* and *Smithsonian Depositions* on my IBM Executive typewriter which allowed for variable letter-spacing in increments of six. In other words, the capital M was six units wide and a comma was one unit wide and all the letters, numbers and punctuation fell within that range. I typeset *Light & Shadow* in Patina and *just let me do it* on the IBM mag card composing machine where I worked for Rose Slivka typesetting at *Craft International* magazine. I typeset *Quilts* on an IBM 82 magnetic card composing machine at Matthias Jenny's Nachtmaschine press in Basel and printed out the pages there, four-up, in a quantity of 50 copies because half of the edition of 100 was the signed edition with custom covers. Thus every page of those 50 signed copies was an original typeset specimen and the pages of the unsigned 50 copies were photocopies. *Fast Lanes* was set in Palatino and I found Serpentine for the cover. I typeset *The Traveling Woman* in Journal Roman. I chose Frutiger for the text and Meridien for the blurb on the back, both designed by the Swiss designer Adrian Frutiger for *Conversations with Rudy Burckhardt* by Simon Pettet. Rudy was Swiss. The type was set by a type shop on Broadway in Manhattan. Even though I did not set the type for Rudy and Simon's book, I did lots of calculations when designing the type. For one thing I had them set the text line for line from the manuscript I provided. I measured Simon's longest lines (his questions) and the longest was 81 characters wide. With 2.58 characters per pica in 11 point Frutiger, this meant I would specify a 32 pica width. And given the height of the pages, determined by the photos and especially the photo chosen for the cover, the Frutiger was set 11 on 13 to balance the white space on the pages, based on shortest and longest text pages, as well as the shortest and longest question and answer sequences in their interview. And I set *Continental 34s* using Goudy Old Style handtype and exquisitely subtle kerning with slivers of copper. There was a little handsetting of type to do for *Airmail Postcards*, but most of that book was the author/artist's original work recreated using metal plates, the way Joe Brainard's cover for *Train Ride* was done. *Counting* was set in Palatino. I supervised the typesetting of *Give Me Tomorrow* by working closely with a type house in Amsterdam. Richard Hell and I put together the manuscript of *Hot and Cold* in PageMaker.

KS: You published Ted Berrigan's *Train Ride* in 1971, and almost 50 years later, printed a close facsimile. Can you tell me a little bit about what prompted the reprint?

AL: *Train Ride* was actually published in 1978. Ted thought the copyright should be the year the poem was written, rather than the year it was published. Over the years, *Train Ride* was the one Vehicle Edition for which I consistently got orders from Small Press Distribution. So, in May of 2011, when my daughter was finishing her college undergraduate program and I was setting my sights on new vistas in my life, I figured the easiest way to get the press up and running again was to reprint that title. Copies of *Train Ride* would sell, I figured.

So, I wrote to Ted's literary executor Alice Notley, who was living in Paris. Ted's sons, Anselm and Eddie liked the idea, or at least they had no objections to a reprint. Alice, however, had a different point of view. She asked me to be in contact with University of California Press because she had allowed them to include the poem in the *The Collected Poems of Ted Berrigan* (2007) and thus they "owned" the rights.

Of course, *Train Ride* in that *Collected* looks nothing like the original poem. Ted, Joe Brainard, and Michael Uytenbogaart and I had gone to great lengths to keep the type sizes and spacing and types of punctuation and rules and asterisks and everything all the same as Ted's original manuscript, which was a book in-and-of-itself.

Where the process had left off, turned out the copyright had to be cleared through Copyright Clearance Center. In order to figure out the fee for the rights, I had to count the number of words in the book: it's 1,882 words. It had to be approved as either a chapter of the University of California Press *Collected Poems of Ted Berrigan* volume or as a group of excerpts (400 words defines an "excerpt"). As excerpts the rights were a couple hundred dollars. Considered as a chapter of the book, the licensing fee would be about $2,500. The woman who worked for Copyright Clearance Center advised me to go with the excerpts since it didn't matter to them.

In both cases I had to use a print run of 999 copies, instead of a print run of 1,000, which is fine though a bit absurd, because the price goes up when the print run is over 999 copies and up to 4,999 copies. So, the forms were all filled out online and that was pretty much it for permission for the poem.

Then I had to get permission from Joe Brainard's executor, the poet Ron Padgett, for the artwork on the cover. Ron was very kind in his method of offering me a simple letter of agreement about the book. He did impose a limit that no more than 1,000 copies be printed (the original edition was 1,500), and he just wanted some copies of the book in return.

The original artwork was done in all black pieces of paper (many from a Monopoly boardgame) and Joe was very specific about the red. Joe and Ted and I called it Tareyton red, because it was the red color on a Tareyton cigarette pack. Joe smoked Tareytons and used the cigarette packs in his collages regularly.

The printer, out in North Kansas City, made proof after proof before I liked the red of one and, when I did, I showed it to Ron who agreed. Then we had to find an endsheet, however that turned out to be easier to find than the difficulty in having them match the ink color. The endsheet is an odd stock with a super-smooth machined finish on only one side, however it matched the right ink color, so Ron and I were both satisfied.

999 books were printed, shipped them to me, I opened the box and... horrors! The red was wrong: totally wrong. It was very dark and almost purplish. It had been such a long haul getting an ink to match and then it turned out that they had used a lamination on the proof and the books were not laminated. I discussed it on the phone with the printer and they agreed to accept the shipment back at their cost to evaluate the situation. When they saw the books and compared them to the proof I'd approved they agreed with me. Their error. And they printed the books all over again.

[2018]

Annabel Lee with Barbara Guest (1980), photo by Erica Lansner

Inge Bruggeman
INK-A! Press

Inge Bruggeman is currently Associate Professor and Area Head of Book & Publication Arts in the Art Department at the University of Nevada Reno. After fourteen years in Portland, teaching at the Oregon College of Art & Craft while also running a letterpress and book arts business called Textura, she decided to dive in to academia full-time. She left the business behind and began at UNR as both a Professor and as the Director of the Black Rock Press while building the new book arts curriculum. She currently works closely with the new director of the BRP, which has become a unique entity connected to the new Book & Publication Arts program which functions as a kind of publishing laboratory focusing on community outreach and student professional experience through experimentation in creative, artistic publishing.

Bruggeman's personal work concentrates on a variety of book related art that is generally text-based in nature, but not always entirely legible, from artists books and prints to more sculptural bookworks. Her work revolves around the idea of the book—the book as object, artifact, and cultural icon. She is focused on the r(evolutionary) nature of the book, in that it is: a) both a technology and an artifact in constant evolution along with the people that interact with it, and b) it is simultaneously a medium that is turned to as a means of expressing alternative and often radical ideas in the form of both the democratic multiple as well as the more singular, auratic work.

Most of her work is simply created under her name, however she also continues to publish limited edition works under the imprint INK-A! Press when she collaborates with other authors. Over the years Bruggeman has published fine press artists books by authors such as Madeline Gins & Arakawa, Michael Hannon, Hank Lazer, Alan Loney, Michael McAllister, Cissy Ross, Lynne

Tillman, Laura Wetherington, and John Edgar Wideman. She has also created broadsides using texts by authors like Charles Alexander, Kathleen Fraser, Kevin Sampsell, Manil Suri, and Steve Yarbrough. In addition, she has had the pleasure of creating works for other presses and organizations and in so doing working with authors such as David Abel (Black Rock Press), Bill Bissett (Granary Books), Bill Holm (Minnesota Center for Book Arts), John Irving (Rainmaker Editions), Lora Lafayette (Write Around Portland), Barry Lopez (Codex Foundation), J.H. Prynne (Charlie Seluzicki Rare Books), Ben Lerner, and W.S. Merwin (both for Columbia College Chicago Center for Book & Paper Arts).

INK-A! Press was created during the final year of Bruggeman's undergraduate study at UC Santa Barbara in 1991 under the mentorship of Harry and Sandra Reese of Turkey Press. INK-A! Press has functioned as an exploration of the visual, typographic, material, and structural elements that go into "reading" a book. Early on, she was influenced by Ulises Carrión's *The New Art of Making Books* (1975) and she has been exploring the potential of the book ever since. Although based in a strong sense of craft, her publications have sought to question conventions of reading and interacting with books.

Alan Loney, *Nowhere to go* (INK-A! Press, 2009)

KS: I admire your modesty, Inge. Since you generously agreed to this interview on the condition that the focus isn't entirely on "you," perhaps I could begin by asking about your immediate mentors. For example, I understand that you studied in Alabama, where you earned an MFA in book arts—was that your introduction to the art of the book?

IB: My introduction to the art of the book happened as an undergraduate student at the University of California, Santa Barbara. After high school I lived in France for almost two years, so it seemed logical to pursue a degree in French literature—it was that, or marine biology, or political science! Midway through my studies I took a class on the twentieth-century livre d'artiste in France. We met in the special collections department of the library every week where we studied these impressive and theatrical orchestrations in book form between publisher, artist, writer, and production artists. After experiencing these works of art, particularly the work of Ilia Zdanevich, and understanding how books could be expressive, artistic vehicles for ideas—I was hooked. I remember thinking to myself that it would be impossible to be bored with this field of work because of its limitless potential—text, image, structure, the history that has made the book what it is, the future of the book as object and cultural icon, the unfolding of time in a container, and on and on. It also made perfect sense as it united my existing interests in art and literature. I had been taking printmaking for several years and often found inspiration and subject matter while reading. I had definitely found what I wanted to do with my life and immediately got a job in that same special collections department of the library to have more access to the work. It was at this time that I was directed to my first mentors, Harry and Sandra Reese of Turkey Press. Taking classes from Harry Reese blew apart my perceptions of the book even further and seeing the work that he and Sandra have done together over the years was truly inspirational. Their work pays homage to the past and the history of the crafts we practice, but at the same time moves the book into uncharted territories, expressing modern ideas of what the book can be as an art form and as a cultural icon. The typographic playfulness in their book *Five Meters of Poems* (1986) is their own unique interpretation, yet it simultaneously pays homage to the expressive typography of the early avant-garde, as well as printer/artists like Ilia Zdanevich. I have always been interested in this idea of connecting to or referencing the past. It is essential in all art to be aware of what has already transpired, but it is especially fitting for artists books in particular because the book as cultural icon is so linked to the history that made it. It is compelling to see work that builds on this foundation and we see this in another work of Harry's titled *Arplines* (1990), which is an open homage to Jean Arp. In this work, Harry Reese has made the leap into the past, entered into a collaboration of sorts with Arp, and returned to the present to re-envision a project inspired by this artist and the era in which he lived. I am grateful to have found Harry and Sandra Reese when I did, otherwise my life would most likely look very different.

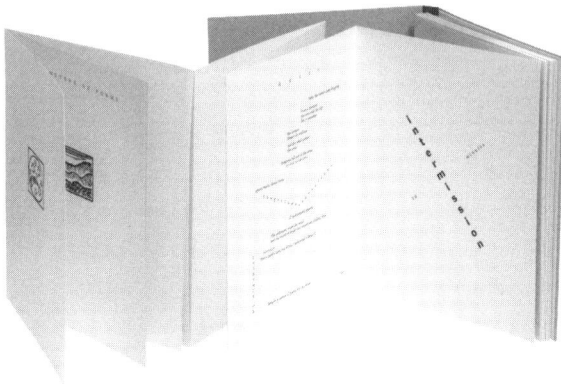

Carlos Oquendo de Amat, *Five Meters of Poems* (Turkey Press, 1986)

At this point I couldn't get enough, so during my years as an undergraduate student I was also taking continuing education courses on paper marbling, basic bookbinding, and I also took my first papermaking courses around this time during a summer on Martha's Vineyard while I was working on an organic lettuce farm and brushing angora rabbits for their fur.

After graduating, I was full of ideas and had been dabbling in all things book arts, but didn't really have much control over the craft aspect of things so I decided to attend the University of Alabama Book Arts Program. It was the perfect next step and really grounded me in the satisfactions and the realities of producing this kind of work.

My second mentor and professor, Steve Miller, was extremely supportive during my years in graduate school. He was very active in connecting his students to the national book arts community and laid a strong foundation for producing solid work. I see him as a fantastic printer, bookmaker, and an amazing people person. Describing Steve Miller as a people person might sound a bit trite, but people are what his work is all about. If I could take a leap here, I would say that the biggest thing I took away from being a student of Steve's is that the book can be much more than just a book, it can be the heart that connects us all together. Books are about people: writers, poets, artists, designers, and makers, and this collaboration is about community and creating a better, more beautiful life. I apologize for the corniness, he might not ever say anything like that, but I think it's true. I don't think of myself as a great collaborator, especially when it has to do with my own work, but in my business I collaborate with artists and designers all the time and I am inspired by Steve Miller's view of printing, and of the book being able to bring people together. I am particularly inspired by his work and collaborations with artists in Cuba. I am looking at the chapbook he produced titled *Skin* (2005) with poems by Dan Kaplan and images by Julio César Peña Peralta. It is modest in scale, and like his other work,

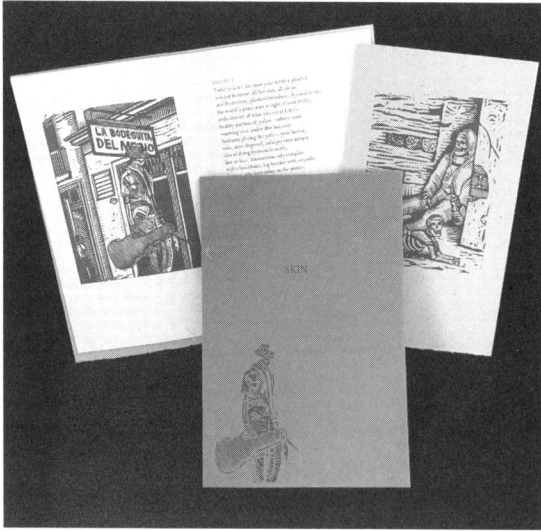

Dan Kaplan, *Skin* (Red Hydra Press, 2005)

everything about it is careful and meaningful. I am reminded that one doesn't have to yell to be heard, and it is in these quieter and humbler spaces that we, the viewer/reader, can become more intimate with the work and find ourselves more a part of the community that he is trying to connect us to.

KS: You said that you don't think of yourself as a great collaborator, especially when it has to do with your own work... you also say that in your business, you collaborate with artists and designers "all the time." Could you talk a bit about what you mean by collaboration, and how it works in your books as well as in some of the other artists you've mentioned, like Steve Miller, Harry Reese, and Ilia Zdanevich? It seems there are a number of distinct but related traditions here, and that the definition or approach to collaboration is a major part of the artists book.

IB: The subject of collaboration is a tricky one, mostly because there are different kinds of collaboration and there can be different levels or ways to collaborate, both in a project and outside of a project. The book form does lend itself perfectly well to collaboration because it is such a multi-faceted medium to work in, with so many different possibilities for collaboration. However, when I define myself as not being a great collaborator, I am thinking of what I believe to be a true artistic collaboration—the form of collaboration where two or more people are working simultaneously on a project, influencing each others' ideas, pushing each others' boundaries, and creating a project that not one of them could have made on their own, individually. Perhaps this could be called "creative collaboration." In this sense, I feel like I am too much of a process-oriented maker to have a great desire to work collaboratively. I want to experience the process myself and have that excitement of experiencing and responding not only to a technical process but the evolution of an idea coming full circle within my own brain and body. I have to admit that for me the actual art making process is perhaps a little more of a self-involved experience and an inquiry into the nature of something larger than myself, but through myself. For quite a long time I would not have been so forward or resolved about this, but now I am a proud "non-creative collaborator!"

That being said, I will now proclaim that I am an avid "technical collaborator" (as opposed to "creative collaborator") and someone who actively seeks the exchange of ideas and information—just not so much in the direct process of making a work of art. Teaching in the Book Arts program at the Oregon College of Art and Craft is a vital part of my life as an artist and something I see as a collaboration of sorts. It is a critical part of developing, sharing, and expanding as an artist—to remain in conversation. It is for this same reason, too, that I enjoy traveling to teach workshops, give lectures, attend conferences and book art fairs, etc.—to continue to open up the dialog and ways of thinking that will hopefully affect my work and advance the field of artists books in general. Maybe we should change this form of collaboration to "techno-socio-collaborator!"

My business life is also very "techno-socio-collaborative." In my business of working with artists and designers I facilitate the translation of another artist's work into book form (or other re-lated sequential formats) and/or designing work for letterpress printing. I advise people on how their work can be engaged with differently when seen through the special lens, or format, of the letterpress printed or mixed media book form. For me, this type of collaboration does not necessarily focus on experimentation or a high level of risk-taking that is so crucial to my own artistic practice. This kind of collaboration is more about applied knowl-edge and technically figuring out how to make a given concept function well in its new housing. The types of collaboration that happen at school and in my business definitely feed what's hap-pening in my own work, and vice versa.

In some of my own projects, particularly those for INK-A! Press, I enjoy responding to someone else's text and representing the work in a new context. The making of these works is not a col-laborative process really; the authors have to be interested in giving me permission to visually and structurally translate their texts and imply a very particular response to the reading of their texts. It is, however, a literary work and I generally try not to interfere or alter the writing beyond anything the author is com-fortable with. Although not a back and forth collaboration, I am definitely responding to someone else's literary creation and re-sponding to certain ideas in their writing, and this does make a big difference compared to the other prints and artists books that I make that are all of my own making, responding to a gen-eral idea of my own, as opposed to a given text. Over the years there has been a lot of pressure to abandon the literary-based books in favor of work that is solely my own. It is easier, with this kind of work, to get exhibitions and show your own work in the contemporary art world, instead of continuing to work in a more marginalized zone, however I am still very compelled and inspired by the traditions of the fine press book. I really admire, for example, the collaborations that Steve Miller is involved in. Everything in his work is a tribute to the people involved and to the craft itself, not necessarily the individual artistic voice, although that is certainly present in a quieter way.

I'm not sure I can speak to the collaborative processes of other artists, but I can say that there is nothing that I would like better than to go back in time and be a fly on the wall in Iliazd's printshop! I think during that time of the French Livre d'Artiste, Iliazd had a particular vision and brought cohesiveness to the collaborations he was involved with—he began the exciting progression from livre d'artiste to artists book.

It is interesting to me how this conversation about defining kinds of collaborations is leading back to conversations defining art, craft, and design. They are each different focuses, but at the same time, there is a great deal of influential overlap. That is the really enticing thing about the field of artists books, though—it is rich, layered, and complex, not only the work we make, but in the process involved in getting there.

KS: Could you elaborate on the relationship between what we might call the art of business and the business of art?

IB: This has actually been on my mind recently and I might take it on a bit of a tangent here, but I hope it addresses your question. There is a definite push and pull between the frame of mind needed to approach art making and the one needed for the business surrounding art making. I have learned a lot while attempting to balance these two worlds, and I have become a good businessperson, but in all honesty my strong suit has not been with the business end of things. Generally, I want to spend and do whatever it takes to make an interesting project, and follow the project wherever it wants to take me—by the time I finish a project I probably make 50 cents an hour! The artist and the businessperson always seem to be a bit at odds, but it is usually a necessary relationship worth fostering. Although the business side of things has probably taken away from time spent on creative endeavors, I feel lucky that INK-A! Press and Textura have allowed me to do what I love doing and each has informed the other. It is very empowering to develop the business-minded side of oneself—a certain amount of this is important for artists, however there is no question that it not only takes time away from making art, but it requires shifting gears, which can be difficult. People who are better at business tend to think of what will sell before they begin a project and select themes based on marketability. I've never been interested in figuring out what the market wants and then making that thing; it's always been more about an exploratory process of an idea I am interested in pursuing and that I hope others might be interested in as well. This exploratory process can be hazardous, I will admit. Sometimes (if you look very, very, very closely!) you can find mistakes in my work, because I always have an urge to try new things, probably not the best approach for my work with Textura in particular, where the work is for other clients, so I do have to watch out there, but in my own work I enjoy taking risks. I really admire Gunnar Kaldewey's fine press artists books. He does all of this incredibly innovative work within his field (and I hope he doesn't mind me saying) but I have found the very rare typo or craft glitch in an otherwise immaculately made work, however this doesn't deter me or detract from the overall concept and integrity of the work. On the contrary, it is like finding the person or the maker in the work. Although I appreciate fine craftsmanship, I prefer seeing slight imperfections in an inventive work than a perfect fine press work that does not take any risks. In a perfect world one strives to achieve control over both, and on occasion we succeed in making an innovative work that is flawless, but it is also rewarding to see an original idea being explored honestly.

I was a visiting artist at the Columbia College Center for Book and Paper Arts recently and two of the graduate students had been looking at a book I made about 10 years ago. I had my books out as part of a lecture and they came up afterwards and pointed out a teeny tiny typo, like an "e" was ever so slightly the wrong size or font. I was glad that they cared enough to notice and to bring it up. I really didn't mind that the mistake was there, I don't think it changed the perception of the book as a whole. I suppose it is a fine line, though, between sloppiness or inattention to precedence that just makes for distracting and unsuccessful work. That's another conversation perhaps.

To get back on topic, James Rosenquist said, "Being an artist, whatever that is, involves constant questioning of everything. It is very difficult to set out a plan in a businesslike manner because a happy accident could happen and someone might like your worst work... Artists work in unknown territory. If it were known, they probably wouldn't be artists. This is difficult for an artist to realize, but it's also more difficult for an audience to understand. However, when an artist is through with a work, then strange things can happen, like people wanting to be near it, people talking about it, and people wanting to own it. When this happens, artists usually don't know what to do."

This ungraspable description of what makes a successful work of art points to this discrepancy between business and art. It is largely an organic process that grows out of us, part controlled and part unknown, and if we succeed it is something that people are magnetically attracted to. It is actually this same difficulty in quantifying our attraction to a work of art that makes it so powerful—it holds us spellbound in a complex dialog between it and us. I believe we are more able to quantify what makes a good work of art now, but there is still a large part of it that is not mathematically decipherable or predictable. All this is to illustrate how I think business and art will inevitably be a bit at odds with one another.

KS: I'm interested in where ideas begin, how they evolve, and how materials and labor complicate a book's final form. Could you describe the origin of a particular book? Does it begin with sound, text, images, color, concept, or all of the above? Which one was *really* fun and/or challenging to conceive?

IB: The evolution of a piece of work is different for a fine press artists book, as opposed to an artists book or print multiple. I'll focus on an artists book that is in a strange middle ground between fine press and artists book here, specifically a project that I finished in 2003 called *A Crisis Ethicist's Directions for Use: Or How to be at Home in a Residence-Cum-Laboratory*. This book was incredibly fun and challenging to make, but I wonder if in the end, it comes across like how I feel about free jazz—fun for the musician, but not as fun for the audience. It is an obtuse book, one that is very demanding of its reader/viewer and because of this I think its audience is limited for better or worse. With a fine press artists book, it always starts with the text for me, in this case a set of directions that is excerpted from Madeline Gins and Arakawa's *Architectural Body*. I was very taken by the demanding and contradictory nature of this text. In some of my own artwork I like to investigate the visual nature of text and play with our expectations of it. Generally text is supposed to clarify, define, or describe something in a way that will enlighten us, however this set of directions does not direct us at all. It either immediately confuses and frustrates the reader, or if the reader is receptive, it demands more questions than it answers.

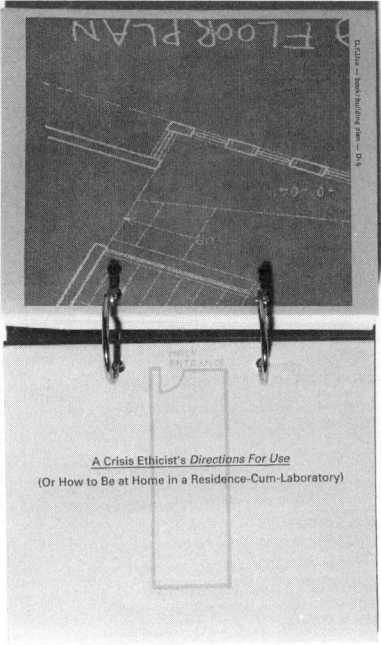

I suppose poetry and other forms of writing do this as well, but normally not in such an obstinate way. Here are three examples:

> *1. Play off of your tactically posed surround like crazy until you have constructed a precise tentativeness for yourself.*

> *3. Attempt to assign more than one size and shape at a time to the body you take to be yours for the nonce.*

> *17. Avail yourself of your tactically posed surround to disperse your landing sites of the moment in such a way as to prevent the coming into existence of a world for you.*

The text is even odder when taken out of context of the book, but I found this text to be both highly philosophical and humorous at the same time, and that mix is what attracted me to it. So the whole book project grew out of that response to the text, as well as wanting to investigate the connection between architectural structures and book structures, but not in an overt way. The most basic point of *Architectural Body* is the realization that we, as individuals, are deeply influenced by the structures that we inhabit. I was interested in thinking about how we are equally influenced by the book structures that we engage with. The idea behind both—architecture and book—being that it is not a good idea to dumb down a culture, so if we make more demanding structures, then it follows that the people that interact with them would be more engaged in creative problem solving. In the end, though, I wonder about the "free jazz factor" and wonder how many people really want to seek out this kind of engagement? I think it may be a good audience, but a more limited one.

Other decisions follow this investigation of the text and become related investigations of material, structure, image, and color. The form of the book took on a Fluxus-like box form. It is reminiscent of some kind of field manual/kit, the kind of thing that is slightly mysterious to the average person. Connecting to the Fluxus movement also felt like an acknowledgment of a similar spirit, one that presents a philosophy but in a playful way. Inside of the box is a booklet and another smaller plastic box of thumb-tacks, but no instructions on exactly what to do with them, so the person interacting with the piece has to bravely dive into the booklet for clues. Immediately one notices the impermanent metal ring binding of the booklet and on flipping the pages one sees that on the back of each folio there is a piece of an architec-tural plan. Then looking back to the thumbtacks, one can realize that the architectural plan can be reconfigured on a wall with the thumbtacks. Another direction that the reader can go in is un-folding each folio, where the text itself transforms into building block shapes, losing its readability and turning into an elemental form that interacts with other abstracted imagery pulled out of the architectural plan. Lastly, one can notice a deeply embossed, braille-like alphabet next to each direction or piece of text. This alphabet is made by envisioning the architectural plan on the wall, but a specific pathway of engagement with the building that one might take at any given moment. This pathway creates the shape of each fictional letter in this alphabet.

This was really an interesting project with lots of layers of dis-covery to it—for me in the making of it and hopefully for a small audience of engaged readers/viewers too.

KS: Do you feel that monetary value and scarcity influence the way people read and interact with books?

IB: Yes, absolutely, but not necessarily in a bad way. We read with all of our senses and with our surroundings too. We cannot help but be affected by the book object, the design of the page, and even the environment we are in while reading a book. The experience (or the idea) of a chapbook in your hands is different from how we experience a paperback book, a hardbound signed edition, a fine press book, etc. It already gives us information that we put into context of the reading. This is why book art-ists are attracted to working with the book, they are interested in the power of an intentionally presented idea or literary work.

Whether it is a zine or designer leather bound book, you set the stage for the reading.

One thing that really needs to be embraced about the field of artists books is that they require a certain kind of handling and interaction that is different from the traditional utilitarian book. The field of artists books has many approaches and areas to work within. If an artist wants to approach working with the book as a democratic multiple, they will consider the value and accessibility as pivotal to the success of the work. Perhaps this artist might be drawn to the offset printed book (like Ed Ruscha's early work), on-demand publishing, or the photocopy machine—even letterpress printed work does not need to be precious, although it frequently is related to that now. Letterpress printing has been used for self-publishing less expensive multiples, as seen by many amazing writers and artists such as Wallace Berman and his *Semina* publications. On the other hand if an artist is less concerned with the book as a democratic multiple and more concerned with other artistic ideas, say the exploration of a visual narrative throughout a sequence of pages—this artist may produce an edition of 20 artists books that require being shown under glass and are significantly less accessible. This book may be more like a three-dimensional, editioned painting and it will certainly be read differently when brought out from a special collections vault for viewing than a chapbook made in an edition of 500 and given to you by a friend. They both are artistic endeavors, made to be experienced in different ways depending on the intention of the maker. Although certain media do lend themselves to being more or less accessible, it is certainly not media-defined; offset printed books can be expensive and rare just as letterpress printed books can be inexpensive and accessible—it totally depends on the maker's intention, how and why they are working with the idea, and the structure of the book.

KS: When I was in Portland a few weeks ago I had the chance to see your recent edition of Alan Loney's poetry. Loney is a great poet and printer, and one of the few people I know who can discuss Charles Olson and Stanley Morison seamlessly—could you talk about how you conceived this elegant book?

IB: When I read the collection of poems that Alan Loney sent me—*Nowhere to go* (2009)—I was struck by their dark beauty. It seemed to me like the poems were questioning their own relevance when faced with the immensity of death and the fragile nature of our existence. How do we find the words? What use are they to anyone? For me, the poems answer their own questions with beautiful resolve. They are relevant, because they are fundamental. I could really feel the connection between the word, the body, and the book, each one essential to the other—the poems are life, our impermanent bodies are not. In the face of intense tragedy it is sometimes difficult to find relevance in the seemingly small act of writing a poem or making a work of art, but in actuality it is the most fundamental to who we are. The poems made me think about faith, not a religious faith necessarily, but a belief in our own simultaneous smallness and brilliance. The book envisions the dedicated act of writing poetry and the fact that it can sustain and suspend someone's faith in life and death. The question of relevance is clearly resolved in the very permanence of the kind of art that strikes a chord in us, the beauty of the life we do get to live, and this shared experience across time.

I am honored to have had the opportunity to work with Alan Loney's poetry, and to join the best of company in this regard. Many small, independent, and artistic printers and publishers are working with his poems precisely because he is so interested in having others envision the space of the book that his words can live in. He is a printer and publisher himself who thinks about the significance of reading the entire book, not just the words—and he writes with this in mind. I just serendipitously came into possession of a beautiful book that Claire Van Vliet published through her Janus Press in 2003 with a poem by Alan Loney titled *Rise*. I am somehow reminded of everything that is important when I look at this book. The materials, structure, typography, text, and image are so beautifully married in this piece that it makes me feel like I am at the very beginning again.

KS: In the mid-'90s there were a number of important books published that attempted to chart the history of artists books and help define the field of scholarship and creative practices (Drucker's *The Century of Artists' Books,* Castleman's *A Century of Artists Books*, Brad Freeman's influential *Journal of Artists' Books*, etc.). This was all happening just around the time that you were finishing your MFA in Alabama. This was also a time where there were many compelling (even heated) debates about what constitutes an artists book, where concept meets object, where craft meets art. It seems to me that although the nature of the book will never be fixed, we now have a set of terms and common points of reference that offer continuity to the field. Where do you see artists books, as a field of discourse, going in the immediate future?

IB: I appreciate this forward-thinking question. It is an exciting one. Now that the parameters have been loosely charted (at least for such a fluid field of study), I am looking forward to in-depth conversations focusing on the different branches of the larger whole. Another overarching survey in the field of artists books is never a problem, seeing as how there are only a handful, but I feel like now there is great potential for more focused studies within the specific branches of the field. For example, Betty Bright is currently focusing on fine press books and the area where they seem to be merging with artists books. I'm not privy to unpublished info, but I believe she is discussing the tradition and the strong craft foundation that built the fine press movement and then she is evaluating modern trends and translations of the fine press artists book by contemporary artists. This is the kind of more specific discourse that I expect we will be seeing more of. I think we are all ready to move beyond the question of what is a book.

I have been interested myself in contemporary letterpress printing and evaluating why, when, and how it can be used effectively in contemporary art. An artists book today can be digitally printed, offset-printed, and rubber-stamped, and we as artists should realize that every medium brings its own baggage along with it. By "baggage" I mean that it signifies something specific in choosing letterpress printing over another medium because it has inherent meaning in the medium itself. A work of art is always stronger when it successfully acknowledges what it is made of. I organized and co-curated a small exhibition in 2008 called *Fresh Impressions: Letterpress Printing in Contemporary Art* at OCAC—its goal was to highlight work that used letterpress printing to help convey an idea. We were looking for work that we couldn't imagine existing in any other media and we sought to define why that was. What was signified by the use of this specific medium and how did it fit in with the greater concept of the work of art? We wanted to establish the value of the letterpress quotient.

I think we will begin to see more and more interesting investigations into particular areas of the field of artists books that will in turn push the field to even broader conversations. I am currently focusing on letterpress printing and the multiple and how multi-sheet or multi-page works can move into the arena of installation. My own field of study is definitely expanding from the world of artists books to the world of prints, multiples, editions, and related works on paper—as if artists books wasn't already enough! But in actuality it isn't enough. It isn't a broad enough term to encapsulate the dynamic conversations that are ready to happen next.

[2016]

Anna Moschovakis
& Matvei Yankelevich
Ugly Duckling Presse

Ugly Duckling Presse is the publisher of the book you are holding, and hundreds of others. No two books are designed alike (aside from those that are part of a series), form following content, as we see in the works of The Jargon Society, Coracle, and so many other legendary small presses. All books are made in collaboration by UDP's volunteer editorial collective. Its studio and print-shop has been located in the Old American Can Factory in the Gowanus neighborhood of Brooklyn, New York since 2007. A nonprofit organization, UDP fosters education in the art of printing, design, editing, translation, and literature from all over the world through events, publications, and public outreach.

Founded in 1993 as a zine before expanding to other genres and formats in 1995 and taking shape as a collective in the late 1990s, UDP focuses on younger and lesser known authors and has revitalized works of the past swept into the dustbins of history. Because their books are not designed or printed by one individual or partners, which is common in small press publishing, nor constrained by industry standards, the aesthetic of UDP's books are too eclectic to describe: there are few approaches to publishing that they have not explored, other than the most banal and conventional.

Though focused on poetry, UDP has published experimental nonfiction (see their Dossier series), performance texts and documentation, and books by artists. Their list includes Dodie Bellamy, Aase Berg, Jen Bervin, Anne Boyer, Simon Cutts, Constance de Jong, Mónica de la Torre, Christian Hawkey, Tatsumi Hijikata, Pablo Katchadjian, Tinashe Mushakavanhu, Tammy Nguyen, Cecilia Vicuña, Lewis Warsh, Simone White, and hundreds of others, not to mention those who contributed to UDP's magazine 6×6 (2000–2017). Their forty-odd titles in the Eastern European Poets Series include Elena Fanailova, Mariana Marin, Dmitri Prigov, Lev Rubinstein, and Tomaž Šalamun. Their Lost Literature Series has brought back into print some noteworthy avant-garde projects (e.g. Vito Acconci and Bernadette Mayer's magazine *0 to 9*), overlooked U.S. writers (Bobbie Louise Hawkins, Laura Riding), and many twentieth-century works appearing for the first time in English translation, including many from Latin America like Carlos Oquendo de Amat, Amanda Berenguer, Marosa di Giorgio, Alejandra Pizarnik, and so on.

I once had a dream that UDP partnered with the local farmers' market, where people could pick up produce and books together. We are what we eat, and we are what we read. UDP's emphasis on direct distribution is similar to the community-supported agriculture model, bringing readers the freshest, most organic books direct from the publisher to the reader.

I conducted this interview with two of the collective members at the Can Factory, just a few years after the press had expanded from its chapbook-and-zine endeavors into trade books and more ambitious editorial projects.

KS: Are the qualities that make bad printing good the same as the qualities that make good printing bad?

AM: I had a great film professor at Berkeley in 1989, just as domestic video cameras were becoming more popular, who said every bad movie is good.

MY: Are you asking if something like a smudge could be desirable?

KS: In other words, there's nothing precious about UDP books. They're quite beautiful, but I wouldn't hesitate to read one on the subway—they're portable, utilitarian, legible. The "beautiful book" is usually associated with the private press tradition, something very different from what I think you're doing, and yet you're making books that are very much aware of their bookishness.

AM: We are not interested in making those types of books, it's true. It opens up the question of craft versus art. It seems to me as if the well-crafted object is often more important than the content in those "beautiful books"—as if the words simply served the form or the visual art. They seem to have been constructed from the idea of the beautiful object backward, where we, generally, begin by designing a book based on the text's requirements. Speaking as an amateur printer, I can appreciate the work that goes into a fine letterpress edition, so it's sad to see so much time and energy go into producing a perfectly printed book where the writing seems to be an afterthought. I rarely see books where the writer, artist, and artisan seem to be engaged in an exciting conversation.

MY: That's part of it, but for us it's also about summation, expedience, economy of means, and the fact that we have very limited resources. The decision to use commercial, rather than handmade papers for example, is one part of our aesthetic, but that's dictated by finances. That said, I don't think that if we had a lot of money to throw at each book we would necessarily do anything different. Limitations have shaped our thinking from the very beginning, so we've become accustomed to doing things with whatever scraps of paper we can get. This was especially true in the beginning when we were going to paper companies that had discontinued items, trying to determine if there was enough to print an edition.

AM: That's another way of designing backwards.

MY: But it's a better way of putting the cart before the horse.

AM: Using found and available materials to nurture the design makes more sense to me than seeking out exotic materials—gold leaf and vellum, for example. The concept of value has always been important to us as a collective, because what we value and find valuable is inherently more diverse than that of the private press operated by an individual or couple. What we do is entirely informed by the thinking of all the people involved.

MY: When UDP started, most of us, Ellie Ga, Julien Poirier, Anna, were just getting interested in books and looking at very different things. Julien, for instance, was inspired by things from the '60s like the *East Village Other*—he found that acid newsprint really alluring. For me, it was Russian Futurist books printed on found, non-archival materials. What could be further from the *livre d'artiste* tradition? There was no distinction between an artists book and a book for the Futurists, and collaboration was almost a given—very rarely was it the work of one author, which is something that continues to influence me in terms of my thinking about UDP as a collective project. That doesn't mean that I only want to make collaborative books, but in a sense, all books are.

AM: They're all collaborative.

MY: Collaborative, yes, but not always collaborations, like painter and poet collaborations. We're asked to speak at small press and artists book conferences from time to time, which is great, but I was once on an artists book panel at MoMA and felt really out of place. We were also invited to Yale to speak about book arts at the Beinecke. The association is still sort of unclear to us, but people tend to think of our books as somehow fitting into the tradition of the democratic multiple, but our books aren't really about being books—they're a way to distribute poetry. The appearance of a book is important because it says something about the content, but the appearance isn't the content. That said, when it comes to distribution and editorial decisions, some of our ideas coincide with Fluxus, and the publishers and bookmakers that came out of that particular period. Many of the poetry books from endowed academic presses are expensive; they bore the hands and eyes because they don't have the luxury of using discontinued or recycled paper. In that sense, the fact that our editions are relatively small essentially alleviates us from the problem of aesthetic homogeneity.

AM: In other words, a sleight of hand.

MY: Exactly. What's the difference between a book object and a fetish object? We're starting to see that our affordable little books, like John Surowiecki's *Further Adventures of My Nose* (2008), are being sold for ridiculous prices by rare book dealers. The book has some color plates that we tipped in by hand, but there's nothing special about it in terms of materials.

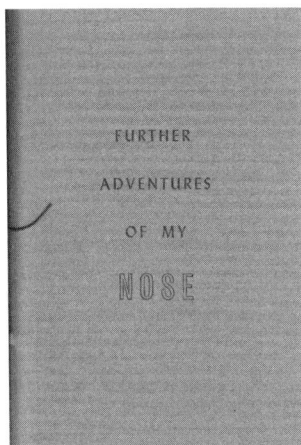

AM: The guts were printed on our laser printer.

MY: And a pretty sloppy cover printed on our letterpress. It was bound by hand, so I can see why it could catch on as a rare book selling for 50 dollars, but it strikes me as ironic that they were originally only five dollars—and that was just a few years ago.

AM: James Hoff's book was literally just a quick Kinko's thing that we did about ten years ago and it is now selling for 25 to 35 dollars by rare book dealers on the internet.

KS: It isn't uncommon—think of *Semina* or Zephyrus Image. These people were interested in making books that were strictly non-commercial, and now cost a pretty penny, at least in part, because of their fugitive nature.

MY: Yes, but what happens to a book when it becomes a fetish object?

KS: Well, that's one of the reasons UDP's Lost Literature Series is so compelling. For example, Vito Acconci and Bernadette Mayer's *0-9* was an extremely scarce magazine until your facsimile appeared.

AM: That's ironic, given that there's only so much we can do to keep our own books in print. We publish about 30 books a year, and we do keep the paperback books in print for the most part, but keeping all of the chapbooks in print would be impossible.

MY: And there's something important about allowing ephemera to remain ephemeral. Now that everything exists in an always-available digital condition, ephemera has come to mean something else.

AM: And many presses are using print-on-demand technologies to keep everything in print, so the edition doesn't really exist to begin with—the book exists in a state of eternal youth.

MY: They're thin, like chapbooks, but they're perfect-bound with glossy covers, ISBN numbers, bar codes, etc. I don't think that approach respects the idea of the chapbook at all. The wonderful thing about ephemera is that it's made for a particular occasion, or it becomes an occasion. The artists and writers have a thing that they can trade or give away.

KS: So the ephemeral, handmade chapbook is always in danger of becoming a fetish object, while the clean, print-on-demand, commercially produced and distributed book faces different dangers?

AM: Fetish objects are funny because they get out of hand—but only because they are, to some degree, handmade. We have always tried to not *just* keep prices low, but to sometimes keep them ridiculously low. Because we wanted UDP to have a future, our books are now priced kind of normal. We had a joke in the beginning that the books should cost either one dollar or one million dollars, just to insist that the value of the literature, poetry, and translation that we publish isn't really determined by market forces.

MY: How can you put a price on a poem?

AM: What price could you put on it? The authors usually aren't getting paid anything for their work, and most small press editions are produced at a loss. We've never done any calculations to determine our sustainability, which is stupid and willfully so, but I remember talking to somebody who really knew the business of publishing, about how you're supposed to calculate your sales price based on the cost of goods sold and the percentage of this and that, and how you come up with your list price, etc. I was kind of dumbfounded because we just kind of ask: what do you think this book should cost?

MY: We should just sell by the pound from now on!

AM: We've made chapbooks entirely out of material that's lying around where we literally haven't paid a cent for anything and we'll sell that for five dollars, then there will be another book that's way over budget and that will sell for five dollars as well. I guess it kind of...

MY: It kind of evens out. We sometimes price them at fourteen or fifteen dollars, which I think is still a little cheaper than a lot of editions coming out. If someone orders directly from us, we can give a discount to make the price cheaper—ten dollars or so. A book should be affordable if you look in the right places. We under-price amazon.com because we don't charge shipping and I think that's good because we want to discourage people from thinking that amazon.com is the best place to shop. Pricing is part of the value of these things, and value has been part of our experiment from the outset—an attempt to prove the lack of value that culture attaches to the kind of poetry that we publish. I like saying "poetry," but I'm not talking about a genre, rather something to do with where it exists in the culture.

AM: Or just outside of mainstream culture.

MY: Right. I think poetry is sort of a nice term to identify something that is noncommercial. It is invaluable in a sense, and I find it ironic that nobody wants bookstores to shut down their poetry sections and so forth, and yet it's the least profitable section. We went on the poetry bus with the Wave Books people, and stopped at McDonald's where we were doing this very problematic thing where one of the poets would read a poem to some sort of "regular guy" and solicit a response.

AM: At a gas station on the highway.

MY: Of course everybody says, "Uh, I kinda don't get that but I love poetry," or "I liked that, I love poetry." Everyone loves poetry because it's supposed to be self-expressive, people admire the idea of its purity.

AM: It's the human soul.

MY: Exactly. It's priceless because people don't want to buy it because it's the deepest form of spiritual expression. It's a strange conundrum. I wasn't necessarily interested in poetry solely or primarily when starting this press though it has become more central as we went along because I met more poets and read more poetry, but in the beginning I thought we would do it sort of as an experiment in publishing noncommercial work, which means you have to fail in a commercial model first, but since we couldn't do that we just keep failing at the same level!

I'm still trying to get back to your question. We obviously like aesthetically pleasing things, and we like the smudges and the imperfections and so forth, and that's why we never trained as letterpress printers. We have these dumb questions that you answer for us sometimes, like the time you noticed that an important part of our printing press was missing!

AM: Pretty much everybody at the press is interested in doing everything, so none of us are specialists. There's not one master printer and one master bookbinder and one master of publicity. I think everybody is fascinated with the organization of it all and we all have different amounts of time to donate at different periods in our lives. We're all interested in the conceptual development of the press as much as the physical creation of the books, so we don't have time to become really good printers or really good at anything. It's fairly non-compartmentalized.

MY: It's like being in a band where nobody really knows how to play their instruments.

AM: It's a punk band where we switch instruments a lot too.

KS: But the books always look good.

MY: *Always?*

AM: I'm not so sure.

MY: We've just gotten good at hiding our mistakes.

AM: I think the overall effect is really more than the sum of its parts—if you took any one of our books and scrutinized it you'll find a mess. Every one of them has at least one major flaw or typo.

MY: I think Anna meant "flaw" in terms of the conception of the design or the execution of the design.

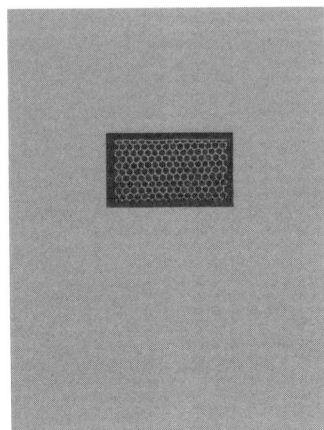

Jen Bervin, *Nets* (UDP, 2004)

AM: I could look at any one and say "I wish I had done this differently" but whenever we have the opportunity to bring them all out together at a book fair or something, that's when people start to say, "You make beautiful books." I hear that more often than, "Oh, this is a beautiful book." So there's something about nonconformity of the whole that's beautiful, none of the books resemble one another.

MY: The eclecticism of our editorial taste is reflected in the eclecticism of design.

AM: It's probably got something to do with the mind's appreciation of variety, the variety of colors and textures. In turn, I love to look at series of books that have a really distinct design like Futurepoem Books or Melville House—but that uniformity is satisfying in a different way. Uniformity with variations in color creates a certain sense of happiness.

MY: Could we call it an Apollonian versus Dionysian aesthetic experience?

AM: We somehow decided to be odd and irregular.

KS: Is that why you named the press after the ugly duckling?

MY: I think the name came out of a zine that I edited. It had an ugly Dadaesque aesthetic. I saw a Dada exhibit recently and there was this one magazine that Ryan Haley and I loved. It's just called "stupid" with an exclamation mark upside down or something. My zine was distributed by sticking it into other people's publications or just giving it to people who looked like they would either be outraged by or enjoy the content. Ellie Ga started working on the zine with me when we met in 1998. She helped me make a few of the last issues and brought in more visual complexity, but it was still interesting for me to make something so ugly that it looks really great. I guess that is one answer to your question, but it also raises the question of boundaries—Dada's ugly, and then there's *ugly*.

KS: So what's the difference between ugly and ugly-ugly?

MY: Right.

KS: You said Dada is ugly, but you mean beautiful, right?

MY: Which one is which?

KS: That's what I want to know.

MY: What does ugly-ugly mean?

AM: Print-on-demand books with horrible covers are ugly-ugly.

MY: Gross.

AM: Painful.

MY: Disgusting. But sometimes we would use the word "disgusting" to describe something that we like.

AM: Right.

MY: As if to say, "That's so disgusting, it's…"

AM: "… it's beautiful!"

MY: The cover Filip Marinovich drew for his *Zero Readership* I really loved because it was just this black and white thing where I asked him to draw a notebook and he just smudged it so much that it looks like it's going to come off on your hands. I think he used Cray-Pas and I thought it was beautiful and kind of disgusting, that black smudginess that maybe otherwise, on its own, without this sort of placement in the book context, would not be anything remarkable.

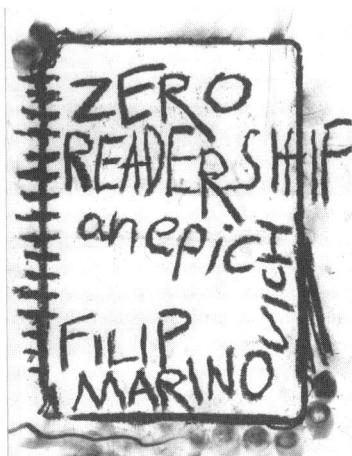

AM: We're not making any statements about aesthetics—we're really talking about nonconformity. We don't make anything that we really think is ugly.

MY: Or ugly-ugly? There are a *few* things that some of the other people have made that I think are pretty ugly.

AM: Between ourselves, we may disagree. We want to make mistakes, even deliberate mistakes, in a useful way. If expedience was all that really mattered, we would make everything look identical.

MY: I think you were right when you said it's actually a big cover-up.

AM: It's a big cover-up.

MY: The eclecticism and oddness makes it easy to make mistakes that don't look like mistakes.

AM: Happens all the time. But I should clarify and say that Ugly Duckling is not committed to making ugly books, but we do want to make books that are different. Isn't that the supposed moral of the children's story?

MY: The other moral of the story is that it doesn't want to grow up, and that's what we're trying not to do too. Not that there's been many conflicts within the collective, but it is difficult for any organization to sustain itself while avoiding the limitations that often come with maturity.

AM: When you're in your 20s and early 30s you have one kind of energy and you can't always sustain that forever, and that brings up the question of growth.

MY: In the late '90s I met a bunch of the people that started the press and they were interested in the idea of a "junior artist."

That infantile, unprofessional approach to the books was there from the very beginning, and it seemed it would be fine to try to continue being junior artists or Ugly Ducklings or whatever prevailing metaphor worked in order to keep ourselves from becoming stagnant. I think that has to do with the question you asked, at least about the difference between fine printing and what we're doing.

AM: If we get the idea to do something new, we have to feel like we can just do it, and if we don't do it perfectly it's okay, we can still put the book out.

KS: That brings me to my second question, which concerns the writing itself. Do you think that Ugly Duckling is committed to publishing minor literature? I'm not using the term technically, in Deleuze and Guattari's sense, but is there a general devotion to authors who are less likely to be picked up by a more mainstream publisher?

AM: No, not as a strict rule, although it's funny because we do get more and more fiction and poetry manuscripts by well-known writers. We do get submissions for titles that seem like more than we can or want to handle. People seem to think that we could or would become a press with a larger readership but we don't know how to do that, and we're not really interested in doing that. I think our readership is growing, but our authors aren't going to appear on the Oprah Winfrey show anytime soon.

MY: Some of our editors who aren't necessarily so much a part of the poetry scene can recognize a résumé disguised as a cover letter and their reaction is usually "they don't need us." We're getting more manuscripts from highly accomplished poets, and maybe their poetry is good, well-crafted, you know, all the criteria that would typically work in someone's favor. When we're looking at manuscripts for the magazine especially, I find that whenever there's a comment from one of the editors like "well-made" or "well-crafted," those are the things that get shuffled to the stack of less exciting things.

AM: Which means a lot of manuscripts we've said no to end up coming out with other presses, which is great.

MY: We find quality in them and yet that's not what we seem to be drawn towards. The rejected manuscripts often have cover letters that say, "I've published ten books and blah, blah, blah."

AM: It's true, that seems to put off our editors more than a wacky manuscript with some kind of unprofessional handwritten note thrown in the envelope.

KS: So you're interested in people who aren't very professional?

AM: We want people who aren't very accomplished.

MY: Yes, people who are doing something but aren't very good at what they do is a nice way of putting it.

AM: People who are doing something—I think that is a nice way to put it. Writers who are just trying something new and they're not good at it yet because it's so new nobody knows if it's good.

KS: But many people feel that way about Modernism and everything thereafter—*how do you know it's good? It's all so new!*

AM: I know something's good (for me) if my mind doesn't wander when I'm reading it. I'm reading all the time and there are very few things that I read where my mind doesn't start to wander.

KS: But isn't wandering part of the magic? I dig Ashbery because he makes my mind wander.

AM: That's a different kind of wandering. You're talking about the imagination, and the imagination is affected by what you're reading. I'll come to the studio and sit down to read 30 manuscripts and my concentration, well, it's a very physical response when I know something is engaging me. I think that's what I mean by engagement. When I read a manuscript and somewhere in the process I stop reading as an editor and start reading like a poet I know that I've found something I'm interested in publishing.

KS: Do you do all of your UDP reading at the studio?

AM: Sometimes I'll be trying to read through manuscripts and there's music on or people using the letterpress, so I'll bring stuff home and do it in the peace and quiet of my own space.

KS: How many manuscripts do you get in a year?

AM: We've never thought to count.

MY: We're not accepting any more submissions for the time being, and yet we have at least somewhere between 100 and 300 full-length manuscripts to look at, and for 6x6 it varies, but there are probably ten things every week or so. It doesn't sound like much, but it adds up. Fortunately, we do get a lot of decent work because we don't ever advertise. We've never listed in any kind of *Writer's Market* directory or anything like that, so we don't get too much random stuff.

AM: I think we've been getting more and more submissions the longer we're around. I don't know how to put this, but we're starting to get a lot of submissions by students of our peers, and it's good that young writers are sending their work out, but there's a lot that's just fine, poems that do interesting things that just aren't for us.

MY: I think maybe the problem is that we decided not
to publish anything good. I
think that's a good policy.

KS: That's an ugly policy.

AM: People should feel good
if we reject their manuscript.
Lev Rubinstein is good.

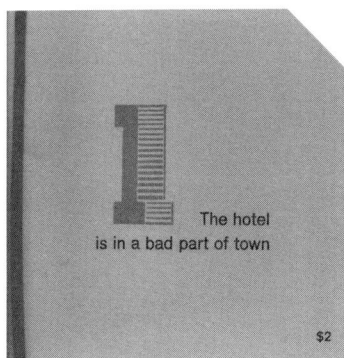

The hotel
is in a bad part of town

$2

MY: Good or great?

AM: We only publish great stuff—great is the opposite of good.

MY: The good-good quality makes me a little antsy. I think of
all the good stuff that we don't publish. There's usually just
something else that we're looking for and I don't think it has a
qualitative value, I don't think it's something that we can really
describe, there are just a lot of manuscripts that are not for us,
and that's exactly what we tell to people: "This is good, but it's
not for us."

KS: "Not for us." You should print that on the back of your UDP soft-
ball jerseys.

AM: "Not for us," now that's ugly!

MY: And we could print "not for you" backwards on the front,
like an ambulance.

AM: We still haven't accepted anything sent by an agent.

KS: So who really decides what to publish? Is it a democratic process?

AM: No. No, it's totally not democratic.

KS: Does everyone select one manuscript a year, or…

AM: No, there are no rules.

KS: Is Matvei the decider?

AM: He's the decider!

MY: We tried the consensus thing for one reading period and the result was Brent Cunningham's book. That was back in 2002.

AM: But people kept calling it a "contest" and so we never did it again.

MY: Everyone used the word "contest" in their cover letters and we wrote back to them saying, "This is not a contest."

KS: Poetry isn't a beauty contest, but if it were, only the ugly could win.

AM: Consensus was really hard because we were waiting for the one thing that everybody could feel good about, and we were fortunate that Brent's book was the one that we could all stand behind. We were very happy about the book but it's also true that the experience of getting there was frustrating.

MY: Consensus doesn't really work, so we opted for anarchy.

AM: An anarchy that's fairly organized, to the extent that it's the personal responsibility of an editor to produce a book and find the money to make it happen. We want a coherent schedule so we can get review copies out on time and tend to other basic responsibilities. Because we don't have a hierarchical organization we don't have a managing editor, so it's really survival of the fittest. It's not an ideal system because some of those books end up costing the press a lot of money, and some end up making money, and the editors and authors—they aren't all equal in their ability to sell things or raise money. It feels very natural because, basically, we all respect each other and want to see what the other people come up with, and we certainly don't want to read hundreds and hundreds of manuscripts to come to consensus. Of course, we do seek the informal approval of one another, because we're here to talk about poetry, but it's more interesting for me to see someone publish something that I don't necessarily like and vice versa than to settle for happy mediocrity. Even when we disagree, there's a conversation happening and that's much more dynamic than consensus.

MY: We're getting closer to realizing an infrastructure that supports the publication of books selected by an editor. In other words, the editor has autonomy so long as he or she is working to benefit the collective as a whole.

AM: One of the compromises of growing up is that spontaneity has always been an important part of this Presse. I just love the idea that you could watch a manuscript evolve into a book in a month, on the fly. We got into some financial trouble this year and realized that we can't really sustain that activity with so many people involved because it's exponential. Everyone was constantly taking on spontaneous projects, which is great, but we found ourselves unable to distribute so many books at a time, so this is the first year that we're a year ahead of ourselves in terms of a schedule. It's a little more institutional in that sense, but we feel a responsibility to ensure that our authors' books are being handled with care, so we make certain concessions.

MY: We have a couple slots reserved for spontaneous projects. The best situation would be if the studio worked something like a communal photo lab where someone is responsible for making sure that all the chemicals are stocked, then there's someone else who makes sure that all the light bulbs are working, another person to make sure everything is clean, so that someone can basically come in with photo paper and negatives and they have everything they need to make their prints. Maybe there's a couple other people doing prints that day, or maybe you're alone, but everybody has the support of each other.

AM: There's some administrative stuff that has to remain central; you can't give everybody access to the bank account, for example, but everyone should know how to organize the budget for a book. The strange thing about UDP is that we're an organization that handles more and more money. It's a business but nobody likes to admit that because none of the volunteers wanted to learn how to run a business—they just want to learn how to make books. We're not running it like a business, but the fact of the matter is that it makes more money than any of us individually.

MY: And UDP spends more money than any of us as well. We spend everything we make. We see the statements from the bank and we're astonished. Then, a moment later, it's all gone again.

AM: It's kind of hilarious that we're still bumbling and fumbling around, and a little unbelievable that we've come this far, given that no one really knows what they're doing.

[2008]

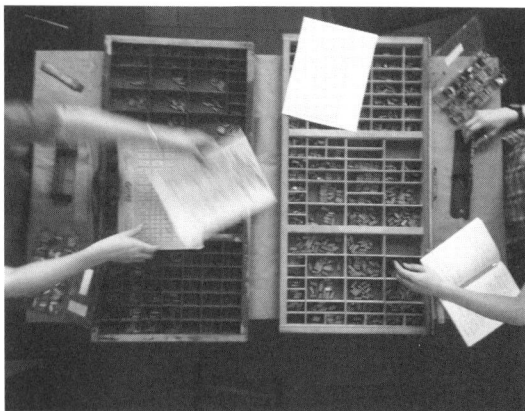

Aaron Cohick
NewLights Press

I've never met anyone who likes to print more than Aaron Cohick. When we were first introduced, Aaron was printing greeting cards for a living in San Francisco, and when he had time off, he would print his own work under the NewLights Press imprint. In addition to being the founder of NewLights Press, Cohick is also the Printer of The Press at Colorado College. Currently, after a long day of teaching students with various backgrounds and interests how to make books at Colorado College, he goes home to his personal letterpress studio, to work on NewLights Press books. His work is labor intensive by design. A creature of discipline and routine, his work is constantly evolving. He quietly chronicles his process in his brilliant journals, reflecting on philosophy, typography, design, process, and aesthetic experience.

Cohick grew up in Pennsylvania, studied the art of the book in Arizona and Maryland, reads and writes with an unbridled imagination. His work merges tradition and innovation, technical mastery and chance, the legible and illegible, inviting readers to see in new ways. A champion of innovative poets, and process as a pleasure in bringing content to form, Cohick is as much a publisher as he is an artist, or vice versa. Or a bridge between the two, like so many of his predecessors he admires. Cohick's work, under both imprints, are held in many public and private collections, including the Library of Congress, the Thomas J. Watson Library at the Metropolitan Museum of Art, the British Library, the National Library of Australia, the Letterform Archive, the SFMOMA Library, the Newberry Library, and the Tate Britain Library.

The book is a dangerously unstable object, *always between,* continuously opening. It is interstitial, occupying many planes at once.

(2) The book is a dangerously unstable object. It is shot through with sunlight, hooks, teeth. It blinds, catches, gnaws. It consumes us, overwhelms us, undermines us, empowers us. From the book we gather the scraps of ourselves—the shabby, mortal, sagging, staggering things that we are. We are within the book and we are immeasurably kind. We will continue to fail. The book will continue to fail. But there is always the next thing, the next page, the next day.

The New Manifesto of the NewLights Press:
first iteration, 2009; second iteration, 2013; third iteration, 2017

KS: Aaron, one of the first books of yours I read was *The Collected Books of Jack Spicer* (2005)—what do you think Jack would have thought about that?

AC: I can't say with any certainty what Spicer would have actually thought about the book, but I can talk about the aspects of his practice, and my encounter with it, that led me to *The Collected Books of Jack Spicer*. I think that the most obvious connection between that book and Spicer's work is *After Lorca* and his ideas about the "poetics of dictation," where he imagines the poet not as a person making conscious choices in order to compose a poem, but as a "radio" or "medium" that channels the poem (from some outside source, "martians" or "spooks") onto the page. When he discussed this idea of dictation he made it clear that it was not the same thing as collage, appropriation, or Surrealist, chance-based composition techniques. He was adamant that his poems came from some outside source, and were not found in the world. The NewLights version of *The Collected Books* is, however, a pretty straightforward found poem, containing the bibliographic and biographic descriptions of Spicer's books

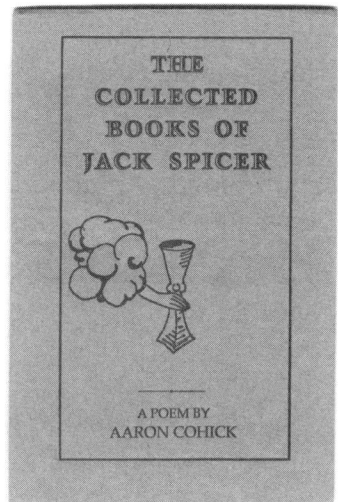

contained in Black Sparrow's *The Collected Books of Jack Spicer* (1975). I assume these descriptions were written by Robin Blaser, Jack's close friend and fellow poet, who edited that edition. I honestly think Spicer would not have been terribly interested in the text as a poem.

However, he may have responded to the book as an object. Here is the description, from both *Collected Books*, of Spicer's last book, *Book of Magazine Verse* (1966):

> 1500 copies, but number of copies not actually con-
> trolled. Cover design by Graham Mackintosh and Stan
> Persky to simulate an early issue of *Poetry* (Chicago).
> Paper for each section was chosen to simulate that of the
> magazines to which the poems were directed.

This was published after his death. But then there's also his book *Language* (1965):

> The cover design is a facsimile of the cover of *Language;*
> *Journal of the Linguistic Society of America*

and *Lament for the Makers* (1962):

> The credit information on the back of the first leaf is a
> joke and is a copy of the information given in Robert
> Duncan's *The Opening of the Field* (Grove, 1960).

And while I'm having so much fun re-typing all of these descriptions (again, almost five years later), this part of the description of *The Heads of the Town up to the Aether* (1962) led me to the physical nature of the book that I made:

> Before Jack knew there would be a large book with this
> title, he issued a ditto edition of 25 copies, brown art-
> paper covers, in 1960, of "Homage to Creeley" by itself.

The design I used came directly from the Black Sparrow *Collected*. I copied and modified the title page, and used the same typeface, Palatino, throughout. This is when my long, torrid affair with Palatino began. So the idea of the NewLights *Collected Books* grows out of those descriptions, and the book takes its shape, literally and figuratively, from them. I think Spicer would have appreciated those aspects of the book. But I don't know if he would have thought of the book as having anything to do with the reality of poetry.

But I think that movement from the text and into the object is where I find my work, where I find the "real" of the Text, so to speak. It's in that sense that *The Collected Books of Jack Spicer* is important to me. I think it's the first book that I did where the object is grounded in, and moves through, poetry, artists books, visual art, the craft/process of printing and bookmaking, and independent publishing, all at the same time.

Once I get started I can go on and on about that book and Spicer and his work, so I should probably stop after one last comment. Reading those descriptions, along with the descriptions of the various Bay Area presses in *A Secret Location on the Lower East Side* (1998), I felt very—hauntingly, almost—close to the history of what I was doing. And though my book was very much about Spicer and was a way for me to honor and deal with the profound effect that his work has had on me, I think it's important also to acknowledge the secret hero of that book, probably of the entire Bay Area scene at that time and later, the printer and bookmaker Graham Mackintosh.

KS: Mackintosh once said of Spicer, "He didn't know how a car worked, he didn't know how a refrigerator worked. He maintained that he could fix radios because one day his radio fell off his refrigerator and began playing again, and he had a firm belief he could fix radios, because a person would say his radio wouldn't work and he'd say 'give it to me, I'll fix it,' and he'd take it home and put it on his refrigerator and knock it off. That was about as well as he understood anything mechanical." Do you think there's a hint of Cartesian dualism between poet and publisher?

AC: In the texts that I have read where Spicer talked about his "poetics of dictation," he used very particular metaphors, metaphors that always held writing close to the voice, or to the mind: the poet was a "radio" receiving signals from the aether, or a scribe taking dictation from spirits. The poet was not a typesetter, looking at copy and arranging the words into a physical form. Typesetting, printing, publishing, the things that Mackintosh did, were a different activity.

Many people would still say that it is a different activity. Even most writers and artists who also run small presses would say that it is a different activity. And because writing and printing-publishing are thought of as different activities, they are. But they don't have to be. The work that I have been doing for the past few years is based on the premise that writing-designing-printing-publishing can be one (dis)continuous gesture.

I remember reading in some book of Johanna Drucker's (I can't remember which, and I don't think it's one that I own and can reference easily) where she talks about how setting lead type changed her relationship to language and to writing. How it became painfully obvious that language was a material, that even the spaces between the words and the lines were a kind of material. I think that experience is very common among writers who decide to set and print their own work by hand. I distinctly remember the first time that I tried to set my own writing in lead type—it seemed dreadfully inadequate. Each word became too much of a presence, and seemed wrong. The entire piece, once so close to me, was suddenly strange, an alien thing, heavy and glaring. That moment of defamiliarization continues to open, to yield new work. If there is a division between mind and body, I try to make the work that I do operate across that division. Or maybe the work is the interaction between the two sides. Or four sides, because we should include "spirit" and "world" in there as well.

KS: I read your work as an interaction as well as an intervention because it takes the terms familiar to writers as well as the terms familiar to printers and visual artists and splices them, creating a new context for meaning that is not decidedly visual, not decidedly poetic, but both and more than the sum of its parts. I know that you've read a lot of theory—are there any particular authors or texts that have guided you in your practice? And conversely, if you could suggest a few books about books, typography, or printing to poets, what would they be?

AC: All of the big, French structuralists and post-structuralists have been and still are important to me—Barthes, Foucault, Derrida, and Deleuze & Guattari. My introduction to that thinking actually came through looking at, thinking through, and reading about Minimal and Conceptual Art. In a way I learned that theory as a practice first, and now I am still trying to catch up on all of the texts. In some ways I am embarrassed to rattle off those four first, partly because they're so obvious, but secondly because what they represent, postmodernism generally, seems so abused, so tapped of its critical capacity these days—which is where other thinkers come in to the picture: Walter Benjamin, Frederic Jameson, and the art critic/theorist Hal Foster.

Sometimes I worry that my work-writing is a constant reiteration of postmodernist dogma. I think that it can be sometimes, and that is when it fails. Lately I've been shuffling around in early modernist art and thought—Piet Mondrian, Kazimir Malevich, and some of the other artists who developed completely non-referential painting; and early structural and deconstructionist practices, like the Russian Formalists and Bertolt Brecht. I think that there is something in that early work that can be critically and productively elaborated as a means of resistance against the model of corporate-spectacular art that is dominant today.

As far as books on books that I would recommend for poets, well, that depends on what those poets are looking for. Two of the best practical guides on typography and design that I've read are Robert Bringhurst's *The Elements of Typographic Style* (1992), a classic, and Ellen Lupton's *Thinking With Type* (2004), which is not just focused on book design, but is a good, overall, easily accessible introduction to typography in general.

The book that introduced me to the world/history of independent publishing was *A Secret Location on the Lower East Side* by Steve Clay and Rodney Phillips, another recent classic. That book continues to be important to me, because it provides me with a sense of history, a sense of community-through-time. On a good night in the studio I feel like a part of that flow, and even simple activities like folding sheets of paper in half to make them into pages, expand and connect to a larger activity.

The other books I would recommend to poets who wanted to make books would be their favorite books of poetry. But the trick is to not read only the text, but the entire object, and to see the different parts in motion.

KS: What are some of the poetry books that you admire most, not just for the writing or design or materials or illustrations, but as whole works of art?

AC: That is actually a really difficult question, because the book would have to be clearly and obviously a book of poetry, but at the same time would have to be more than that. Not a book beyond poetry, but a book that poetically activates every possible aspect of its function in a single, inscriptive gesture. A book that proliferates in the hand-eye-mind of the reader. That is, for me, the ideal Book, and I don't know if I have ever seen it, or if it could ever possibly be made. But glimpses, fragments, facets of it show up here and there. To name some primarily poetic/literary examples: Wallace Berman's assemblage magazine *Semina*

(1955–1962), because of its total attention to writing, text, image, process, and distribution. A whole way of life cobbled together and passed on to friends. I think that Emily McVarish's work, particularly the books *Flicker* (2005) and *The Square* (2009), are excellent examples of a poetry built into and activated by the temporal and spatial components of the book. And material/process too, in the case of *Flicker*. I think that Bern Porter's books of found poetry start to get there. Or some other Concrete works. Perhaps Susan Howe's books, though I have only read about her work—glaring omission in my education there. Someone whose work I would like to see more of, and to spend some serious time with, is the artist-printer Ken Campbell. I got to glimpse his book *Fire Dogs* (1991), which I believe is described as a book of poetry, but it's a book of the poetry of the studio, literally printed from materials in the studio, with a staggering amount of colors and ink on every page, heavy, humid, and gorgeous. And last but not least the 1961 Gallimard edition of Raymond Queneau's *Cent mille milliards de poemes*, where the radical structure of the writing (the combining of the lines in any order to make 1014 poems) is actualized and activated in the structure of the book, with its pages cut into individual strips to allow the reader to physically perform any of the combinations that they choose.

But again, these are all moments of the Book. It is impossible to eclipse the Book in a single, discreet object. One gets closer with a life of rigorous work. But if it were possible, we would stop trying immediately.

KS: For William Morris, the "Ideal Book" was largely inspired by the ancient and medieval eras, but also very much a response to the social and cultural conditions of his immediate present. Are you likewise inspired by particular periods of art, and what are some of the factors in our current social or political environment that you are responding to?

AC: It's interesting that you mention Morris, because his work is actually one of the "moments of the Book" that I look to. The third book in the NewLights DIY series was his essay "Useful Work Vs. Useless Toil," (2007) and the title spread of the *New Manifesto of the NewLights Press* is an homage to the title spread of the Kelmscott Chaucer. I think that Morris actually very forcefully lived out his convictions, and combined them into a total practice—not just the aesthetic of the things made, but the conditions in which they were made.

In a strange juxtaposition aesthetically, but not chronologically—I'm influenced by early Modernist painting, right after the turn of the century, Cubism, and the first entirely abstract painters like Kandinsky, Mondrian, and Malevich. All of which, interestingly, like the Arts & Crafts movement, had a utopian, philosophical-spiritual dimension to their work and thought.

Another period of art that I often look to is the work of the 1960s and '70s—Minimalism, Conceptualism, and West Coast Assemblage. This is also the time when the "artists book" first makes its appearance.

What these three periods all have in common, and what I think attracts me to them, is that they all grew out of times of great social transformation and uncertainty, and in these three periods artists and writers looked back to past models to use as guideposts into the exploration of sometimes radically new and/or completely deranged territory. The Renaissance would be another one of these times.

These were all transitional times, when meaning was highly unstable. I think that we are living through another transitional period, culturally, politically, and economically, and that meanings that we have taken for granted are once again being contested, and that there is an enormous amount at stake. Like Morris, I want to make the NewLights Press into a total practice—not just what the books look like, or even what they say (though that is still important), but how they are made and how they are distributed.

KS: What can you tell me about the relationship between new media and old?

AC: There has been a lot of discussion lately about "the death of print," a great deal of discussion now, even though people have been saying that "print is dead" for many years (one of my favorite early examples is the character of Egon Spengler in *Ghostbusters*). Despite all of this discussion very few meaningful, productive conclusions have been reached. I don't think that as a culture we are going to come to any conclusions for a good many years, but what we need to do now is ask some meaningful, productive questions.

I agree with you that "old" and "new" media are always in a more complicated relationship than the new simply succeeding and eradicating the old. The new is always an extension of the old, its basic tropes and conventions being derived from the earlier technology. And anything actually new in the "new" can be drawn in and utilized in the "old." These media grow together. They extend each other; they are each platforms for critique of other forms, of themselves. Cultural forms are extremely durable. Has any media ever really completely died?

All that being said, the roles and trajectories of print and books in culture are changing, which makes this an extremely exciting and critical time to be involved in this world. Digital distribution models are changing the power structures of publishing. It's far easier for a small press to reach a wide audience, in print and on-line, than ever before. We have access to the technology to design and print right in our homes, and we have access to the enormous amount of literature on, and actual creative precedents of, design, typography, printing, and binding.

Print is not dead. We are beginning to see it clearly for the first time, and now we can get it to ask questions about its own structures, internally and externally. This is a time to be making work, not objects—objects that are a fortress of ossified tradition—but work that does work, that sees that everything that we love and cherish about print and books is part of a *living culture*, subject to and dependent upon change for its vitality. Print is only dead if we try to freeze it in time. We can let the things we love, the things that help us draw meaning from our lives, gather dust in the museums, safe and dead, or we can take them out into the world and see what they look like in the crazy, crashing sunlight.

[2012]

Threshold Alphabet Specimen No. 2 (vertical), (NewLights Press, 2020)

Scott Pierce
Effing Press

This is the world of Effing Press. Armadillos, Willie and Waylon, cheap beer, honky-tonks, poetry, and hot Texas nights. Established around the turn of the century (the exact date is a bit blurry), Effing Press produced books, chapbooks, and broadsides using old-school letterpress equipment, offset, and digital printing technologies. Maverick poet, printer, and charismatic story-teller, Scott Pierce, founded Effing against all odds after he quit his job as a grease monkey at a can factory in Houston and moved to Austin because he fell in love with the poetry of Hoa Nguyen back in the days when many of us would receive half a dozen small press poetry magazines or chapbooks in the mail every week.

At that time, Austin was a city where one could work a minimum wage, part-time job, and still be a poet or artist. There was a lot of time and space to hang out, collaborate, and sleep in. Pierce started making books with Hoa and her husband, poet and scholar Dale Smith, publishers of Skanky Possum Press. They invited many poets to town to read on a makeshift stage they erected in their backyard on Higgins Street. It was a family-friendly event, and their kids, as well as the neighbors', would dance around in tie-dye T-shirts and superhero costumes.

Pierce moved into a building on Judge's Hill next door to the painter and poet Philip Trussell, who worked with Harvey Brown at Frontier Press in the 1960s and '70s, and ran his Chandler & Price on the first floor. It is easy to see a connection between the books Frontier published, and those of Effing, though of course Pierce had a more contemporary sensibility as editor. Some authors published by Effing include Tom Clarke, Hoa Nguyen, Dale Smith, Anne Boyer, Marcia Roberts, Farid Matuk, Tony Tost, Gloria Frym, Frank Stanford, Kent Johnson, and countless others in *Effing Magazine*.

Covers for *Effing Magazine* #8

KS: This interview is being conducted this evening, in part, because last night was the final reading in the Skanky Possum Reading Series in Austin, Texas. Scott, I understand that you got involved with Skanky Possum when your Effing Press partnered with it back in the day, but I'm a little hazy on the details. Could you tell me a bit about how you first met the Skanky Possum crew and how that coincided with Effing and the Austin poetry scene?

SP: You bet. Well, starting when I was in Albuquerque at the University of New Mexico, I was close to graduating with my useless degree in Creative Writing and was heading to New York City to go to graduate school at the end of the summer, so I had some time to kill. I had read Hoa Nguyen's poetry in *LUNGFULL! Magazine* and I loved it. Found it in the newsstand where I bought cigarettes every day. I absolutely loved her work, and it had a little bio section at the back of the magazine that said that Hoa conducts an "experimental poetry" workshop in Austin. Experimental poetry? Coming from the sheltered poetry of my undergraduate experience, that sounded perfect. My parents lived in Houston, so I was going to be going there anyway. I love Austin, so I got in touch immediately, not formally, but more like as a student, and enrolled in her course.

KS: What year was this?

SP: This was 2000, or maybe 1999. I came to Houston and I was working in a can factory as a grease monkey. I was living with my parents working a shift from four in the morning until two in the afternoon wiping down machines that were continuously running. Once a week, I think it was a Monday, I was driving to Austin to take Hoa's class and that's where I was introduced to small press, namely Skanky Possum. When I was in school there were some student zines and there were some small chapbook affairs, but mostly, I didn't know that there was any kind of trade, or any kind of publication heritage, or even a living situation of small books, of staple-bound, or less commercially-bound imprinted work—not even to mention how exciting the content was to me. But anyway, she introduced me to her press. I volunteered to help out with bindery and cover work. That's what I did for the *Skanky Possum Magazine* at the time. They were doing some books but that wasn't an event you saw much. They often farmed that out till after they met me, so that's where I was introduced to small press in general. And then of course, meeting Hoa's husband Dale Smith, and other people in Austin that were doing small press, as well as a lot of painters that were also involved in poetry, people like Philip Trussell who was a big influence on them and very much around for these events. Putting together a magazine was a community affair amongst friends. I mean, that was a party. You'd come over, they'd have the stuff printed, you'd put it together, they'd get a block made to do the cover, maybe people are hand-painting covers or adding some kind of a watercolor to the covers, and you drink and you bind. I eventually moved to Austin at the end of the summer. I moved here to Austin and started working with them regularly as a binder. I was going over there for about six to eight hours a week.

KS: To help them make books?

SP: Yes—the magazine and sometimes chapbooks. All staple-bound; saddle-stitch stuff. It was back in Dale's study in the back room. Often, nobody would be home, and I would sit there and sweat my ass off listening to jazz usually because that's the only thing they had, and you gotta be barefoot in their house, or wearing socks, and I bruised the hell out of my heel hitting their hydraulic stapler with my foot. I'd walk out of there limping after a few hours. I'd maybe or maybe not pass Dale on the way out. I didn't really know him all that well, but that's how I was introduced to them, and of course, the reading series they were doing was very regular at the time. I mean, that's not to say it was ever regular; it was always irregular. But after a while it seemed to fall into a pattern of a monthly or bimonthly event usually relying on people passing through town: poets from other cities coming through town paired up with a local poet. Having been a student of Hoa's for one session I was introduced to the series like that. I just started volunteering my time. Eventually they had children—well, not eventually. It was very soon after I got here they had Keaton. Keaton was born, and two years later Waylon was born. Of course that took a lot of time away from them putting together their work. That was about the time I was laid off from a job and it was the perfect opportunity for me to jump in and throw my hat in the ring as a publisher. Dale taught me to design books. I learned visual layout from him, from studying Skanky Possum books. They were the first things I had in my hand. I had everything they had. A very simple design, simple type, very readable, not expensive. So I just started learning the fundamentals of the software and laying out books, which later led me to my endeavors in letterpress, and then offset printing.

KS: Who are some of the poets you remember passing through town, or passing through the magazine—was there any overlap between the two?

SP: There was a lot of overlap. Of course they seemed to know everybody. In our poetry nation, Austin's out of the way, so you really relied on people coming here to visit. One of the first poets I remember coming through town was Simon Pettet. But gosh, there's been a lot. I was very much into Edward Dorn. That had a lot to do with, I think, Dale, Hoa, Philip, and a few other people in town. That might have been their initial attraction to me because Dale of course is a big champion of Dorn, a big defender of his work, and a publisher of his work, and one of the last people ever to interview him before he died. I had just been introduced to that kind of work a couple years before—Charles Olson as well. I was 23 years old. They just fed me books, you know? Dale just said, "Read this. Read this. Now read this. Now read this." And about that time, we started a salon of sorts at the studio of Philip Trussell that would happen on Thursday nights. This lasted four or five years.

KS: Who's Philip Trussell?

SP: Philip Trussell's probably the most influential person I've ever met in my life. He's a painter here in Austin. He's as much of a poet as anybody I've ever met, is qualified on the history of poetry, can speak to poetry as much or better as most quote-unquote "educated" poets and scholars, but never, never accepted the label of a poet. He's a painter but he's very much a poet's painter—as much as that's a cliché, I just don't know it to be any more true than with Philip. I became his neighbor as well. We shared a studio. I was with him all the time. And he was just like a—I don't want to say a godfather around here, but he was our sage. He was our wizard: knowledgeable in all things alchemy, and historical, and the nuances of the poets that we loved. I mean, talk about somebody who loves deeply. This man—you didn't just read something with him. He didn't just give you something to read; you studied, you know? You studied. And like with Dale, and with Hoa, Philip had done a lot of cover work. He did a lot of cover work for Skanky Possum. He designed—actually, calligrapher Sharon Roos, his partner, did the Skanky Possum block. She designed the block that went on every cover. He made a lot of the artwork for the covers of the books as well as some of their own publications.

KS: Was this his first experience with small press poetry?

SP: No, it wasn't. He's done a lot of covers. He actually cut his teeth at Frontier Press with Harvey Brown in Massachusetts in the '60s as a sort of commune pay or something where he basically bound books, or shipped books, or did artwork for food and maybe some money. I know Harvey Brown was his mentor. He was a big influence on him. I never knew the name, but since then I've come to understand that Harvey Brown was the publisher of some of the most important poetry for our generation and maybe a generation or two before us. A lot of that work, like Edward Dorn's, would not exist, and Philip designed the cover for *The Winterbook* (1972). He designed Stan Brakhage's *A Moving Picture Giving and Taking Book* (1971), which is one of the most rare and beautiful books on cinema that exists. Naturally, having stolen that book just three years earlier from my University library... and then having lost it...

Needless to say, I didn't go to New York. I never made it to graduate school. I got my education from the back rooms of painters and poets, staying up all night, reading, writing, being introduced to very simple machines like a binder or a very small press—you know, a very small proofing press, or how to cut a woodblock, how to design a stamp, how to circumvent sending manuscripts and typescripts to large printing houses, how to do it yourself: a. to save money; and b. why do you need them? What else are you gonna do with your time?

KS: Do you think your DIY ethos, or "who needs New York anyway" attitude has anything to do with the West, or with Austin in particular?

SP: Actually, I found Austin to be a large void as far as publication went. There were a few music stores in town that actually sold local small press, none of which exist anymore. That's actually where I met some of my first friends here just by finding zines; some poetry, some comics, some random anarchist literature. But there wasn't, and there hasn't been since, that I know of, any kind of small press literature scene here. There are presses around doing stuff here. I can't speak to the quality. I know they do a lot of art books. But, as far as literature, as far as words—I don't mean spoken word, I don't mean reading series, I mean books, real literature. I never found it here. So no, I don't think it was a part of Austin. As far as the West, I couldn't tell you. I don't know.

KS: What about Effing? So far you've apprenticed with Dale and Hoa, and you've met Philip Trussell. Where did Effing come from?

SP: I was laid off from a day job with a nice severance, or what I thought at the time was very nice.

KS: Can I ask about the day job? What was that?

SP: I was a training coordinator at a tech company, an English company, and I was basically going back and forth to the Bay Area, and I didn't really do anything. The economy tanked, the tech sector got all fucked up, so I got paid out to leave, which was just fine by me 'cause I'd been wanting to do a magazine for a long time. There was a girl, an artist, that I was dating. She was living in DC. I went and got her, and brought her back to Austin. We were co-habitating. By this time I was living in the same house as Philip Trussell. He was living in the back rooms. I was living in the front rooms, and, I had all this time, I had what I thought was a lot of money, so I wanted to do this magazine. I had been thinking about it for a long time. Originally, Effing was based on this idea of a magazine. I hadn't really thought far enough ahead to do books. This was gonna be a local magazine with a monthly edition, a lofty edition size, and was gonna be put everywhere all over town. It was gonna be like a social commentary magazine, another slick magazine that never lasts long, complete with sections on experimental music, correspondence on visual artwork, random bullshit on the street, maybe humor, and then, you know, literature: local. I put together a small editorial team. We would have meetings. We would go visit printers, and basically, these third party middle men that will help people like that put it together, get it printed, get it distributed. We were looking at the budgets of tens of thousands of dollars, and we were all just twenty-four and pretty fucked up actually, drunk or stoned, and going to these meetings with some of the high-rises downtown with all these print coordinators and stuff, sitting at large tables. I don't know. It was funny. We came down to earth really quick, though. We didn't do anything, and by the time I was getting around to doing anything the money ran out.

KS: You had time to think things over.

SP: Oh, too much time to think things over. Too much thinking. No things, you know? Just the thinking, dreaming, and having no clue of just how easy it is to create and trade literature; making it much more difficult than it needed to be. I took a job at a printshop as a clerk, and I was a paper runner. I was running from one of the Satellite Coffee shops. I was running paper to the plant where they would run all the offset machines, and then I'd run them. I'd drop off raw stock, and then run printed stuff back. In the meantime I was doing coffee jobs. I was cutting paper, doing basic finishing for coffee shop stuff, and that's when we put together Effing the right way by moonlighting, by getting the key, and sneaking in in the middle of the night, and running the machines.

KS: What was the first Effing book?

SP: *Effing Magazine* number 1 (2003).

KS: So the magazine came first? Who was in it?

SP: Hoa Nguyen, Dale Smith, Philip Trussell, Josh Rios, Enoch Rios, Karly Hand, myself, Dirk Michener, Travis Catsull, and Charles Potts.

KS: Did you think of it as a local magazine?

SP: No, though it was except for Charles Potts, really. Oh, there were a couple other guys in there. A local guy named Caleb Engler.

Charles Potts was in there. Charles Potts was one of the first publishers of Bukowski. I met some guys here: Travis Catsull, Dirk Michener, another guy, James Oswald. These people were part of *Haggard and Halloo* who worked at The Temple bookstore. It's this weird connection to Walla Walla, Washington. Charles Potts was this sage guy that they knew and, anyway, I met him and he gave me my first advice on small press. He said, "You're gonna burn out. Until you do, go crazy." That's what I did. I think that first two years there were probably eight or nine books. That's all I did. We made books. We just made books.

KS: Three years: eight or nine books. How did you get from the magazine to the books?

SP: It was quick. I realized real quick that a magazine was a lot of work. There's correspondence with various people, you had to corral shit, you had to read through crap that you didn't like, you'd sort of have to deal with your own self as a diplomat, and figure out what you were doing. Why? Why were you publishing this person? Why were you publishing this work? Is it 'cause you like them or you really like this work? How does this work talk to the other work before? That kind of stuff.

I had no clue as an editor what I wanted to do, which at the time I felt was okay, but I've learned since that is not okay. An editor should know what they want, and they shouldn't pussyfoot around that. They should really do exactly what they have in mind and there should be no exceptions. I found working with individuals on individual books to be far more rewarding for me. Maybe it was evading my own self as far as an editor, or my position in poetry. I don't think I had a well-formed idea of what was even out there much less what I wanted to contribute or what I wanted to foster. But I could believe in an individual and a body of work. I could deal with that a lot better.

KS: So, you stopped doing the magazine and went to books?

SP: No, I didn't stop with the magazine. I just simply toned it down and it took a backseat. I edited three issues of it and then I gave up editorship. Since then I passed the editorship around. Eight or nine years later, there's only been nine issues. But I haven't edited an issue since 2003. Thank God.

KS: What was the first book?

SP: The first book was called *Isle of Asphalt* (2004) by Travis Catsull, one of the *Haggard and Halloo* editors, and a local poet here in Austin who I don't talk to anymore. It's a very James Tate-like, American Surrealist chapbook, and I really liked it at the time. I made 150 copies and it took probably three years to sell them. I didn't know much about bookstores. I didn't know anybody so it took some time to make relationships with that, figure out who was doing what, and then as I started to cook with other books, which wasn't long, I realized that the world was much smaller than I thought it was. Back then in 2002 or so, you would think so many other people were doing this. They weren't. There weren't that many small press publishers of poetry. If they were doing it right, and doing it so local as not to be on some national scene.

KS: When did you get a website?

SP: Immediately. In 2002 the first website was up. It didn't take long. That's when I learned it was a smaller world than I thought. In my town there wasn't anybody. There were only one or two people, maybe. These circles did not rub together. Somehow, in Austin—you would think a town full of so much music, poster artists, and graphic artists, and conceptual artists, and generally hip people, "smart people," there'd be all this overlap, but there wasn't. The Skanky Possum/Effing years were a wonderful, strange time on an island in the middle of hipster city, but we were studying Blake, and we were looking at older work. We were being influenced more by the mimeograph revolution of small press culture that didn't really exist anymore, but that didn't stop us. The idea was "make the work; send it out." Don't try to sell it. I mean, selling the work is your first mistake. Dale Smith told me early on, "You really want to do this, you're gonna lose money. You need to really learn to love to lose money." And I did. I was happy to. Still happy to.

KS: **It seems to me that I started hearing about the Austin poetry community in 2003 or so. Suddenly, I started getting all this amazing shit in my mailbox from Austin, Texas. And there were readings that I was hearing about through the Poetics listserv. There was this spark around 2003 or so when it seemed like this was the place to be a poet.**

SP: Well, you know, none of us here thought it was the place to be. We thought it was exactly not the place to be a poet. But it was a wonderful place to be a poet because as far as poetry went there was nothing else happening. You got the University of Texas, you have the Michener Center, you do have the Texas writer society or whatever, you have this high class stuff, this walled off ivory tower poetry shit going on that none of us knew about, you have the spoken word cafe shit that none of us could deal with either. What we had here was a community, and we had people here. They were not renowned poets. I mean, we were making food, right? We were pot-lucking food, and then running presses. There was no scene here. There was nobody hanging out.

Once my press was established I got interns. I taught some people how to do some crude stitching, how to run a few machines, how to set some type, and we just jammed like that. We just made stuff. It was that easy. And it didn't seem like anybody was paying attention. Of course, the internet helped us 'cause we were able to start selling books through the internet, and that was great. That only helped us make more books and lose more money. And then I started doing letterpress, of course, and I could make more money doing jobwork which I could put into more books. Eventually I just turned my attention to the few poets I really loved, mainly my best friends: Dale Smith and Hoa Nguyen. Later, poets like Farid Matuk and Susan Briante came, as well as Friedrich Kerksieck, Micah Robbins, and David Hadbawnik. Farid came in 2005 and I think that's when I met him. He had been here, but he wasn't really here. I mean, he was there at the Michener Center. I remember meeting him and thinking, "Who is this cocky bastard? What kind of poetry is this?" And then he started hanging out. If you want to talk about somebody who just really picked up the street, like that poetry is a living thing in your mouth. It's not like a thing you wall yourself away and research, and then think hard about and write. He really picked up that poetry was a living thing, and that was an amazing thing. Micah I didn't know too well. He was down in San Marcos. But he started his press, Interbirth, early. David Hadbawnik came here kinda late from San Francisco. I was already aware of his work at Habenicht Press in San Francisco having published people. I had read at his series before. It just kept getting better and better. There still weren't a lot of books being made here. Dos Press was here, too. Chris Martin and Julia Drescher ran that but they were never really in Austin. Maybe they were. They were more in San Marcos, and in between here and Austin. But there were people doing some really neat stuff.

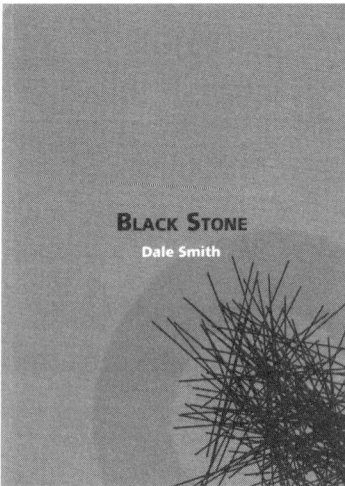

KS: Let's talk a little bit about design. How do you make a book?

SP: Let's first state the obvious amongst all of us people who care about this stuff. I love 'em, you know? I was looking at 'em long before I ever really started tearing 'em apart and looking at 'em. I liked 'em. I did what a lot of people did. I had no formal training. I pulled books off my shelves.

KS: What kind of books?

SP: Poetry books, or even Heritage Press books, you know. Even something like that: real clean printed stuff.

KS: Who were some good printers?

SP: Who are some good printers? I was interested in more of a punk rock style, so I was looking at stuff that was roughly printed. I was looking at Frontier Press stuff. I was looking at Skanky Possum stuff. I was very much interested in Spork Press out in Tucson. Of course, Ugly Duckling was making some really neat stuff. Portable Press at Yo-Yo Labs. Those were some of the first chapbooks I really, really loved. Looking at those books out of Brooklyn. I was looking at contemporary stuff. It wasn't until well after I started making books that I started to go back in time to see great printing. I'm still not as educated as I wish I were on the history of printing and bookmaking. I've read a lot, I've looked at a lot, but I picked and chose what I wanted to use. And I'm still very much learning, right?

I mean, a book should be readable. It should be clean. There's something really sweet about a book that comes not from the factory, all the integrity's still in there. You can take a piece of wood, a piece of linoleum, or a piece of rubber, you can cut the lines into that. That impression can still be as sweet, it can still be as clean, it can still be that crisp, and it does something to you. You say *wow*. It's like what a full bleed image does to you. Something happens.

KS: Who have you published?

SP: I'm gonna miss some books but this can be amended. Let's see. I'll go backwards. Tom Clark, Kent Johnson, Anne Boyer, Hoa Nguyen, Dale Smith, Tony Tost, Farid Matuk, Anna Eyre, Travis Catsull, David Meiklejohn, Gloria Frym, Amiri Baraka, Marcia Roberts, another Tom Clark, another Kent Johnson, another Dale Smith, another Hoa Nguyen. Fucking hell. Who the fuck else? We'll be publishing David Meltzer. I haven't talked to him in three years. I became a drug addict, went to rehab, and I got clean. Now on the other side, the urgency is not there as much to do publishing since, you know, you gotta stay alive and take care of yourself. It's coming back like a freight train. God help us all.

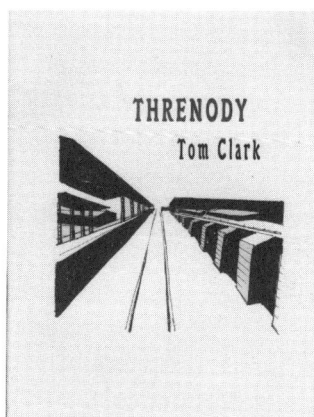

I love a moment. I mean, I don't like a program for publishing. I'm not putting out books right now but I wish I were. In a lot of ways I'm glad I'm not because there are other things I need to focus on in order to get to a place where I can make books and not die doing it. Printing's a whole other world. It's plain ink on paper, one of the oldest and simplest things, and such an enigma to me, and it's like a drug. It's my new drug.

Did I ever tell you about the time, maybe 2004, 2005, I went to San Francisco to release a book from another poet I've worked with several times? His name is Joseph Massey, a great poet up in Eureka, California. I was actually putting out a book of Joe's, and also celebrating another poet, Anna Eyre, who I'd actually gone to school with in New Mexico, who's a real poet. We were reading. The three of us were reading at Habenicht Press' reading series run by David Hadbawnik there in San Francisco. I drank a lot more in those days, and I want to get the details right, but to get 'em right would probably be an insult to the myth. Dale and Hoa were there, too, releasing a book of Dale's. They had read the night before, and the next night us younger people were gonna be reading in Hadbawnik's series. We had spent a few days with Roger Snell, a great, great printer and friend who went to New College with Dale and Hoa. Anyway, there were poets there with a lot of bad blood between themselves that I really, even to this day, don't know the backstory. There were a lot of intersecting stories here because, you know, San Francisco is weird like that. There are histories there amongst people. There are a lot of older generations mixed in with the younger generations at these series. There's people jockeying for, I don't know what, attention? People offend each other more easily. Look at someone funny by accident and they get weirded out—it's much more polite. You don't even have to look at 'em funny, you think about 'em funny and they feel your aura change.

Anyway, the reading was packed, absolutely packed. David cleared out everything for this reading, and, it was packed. We get there late. And we're young. We don't read much in front of this many people. Joseph Massey has severe anxiety issues. He also has three or four people there, one being David Hess: another poet here in Austin that's not a poet anymore as far as I know, and he might not even be in Austin. But he was one of the people that Skanky Possum published and fostered for several years. Well, he and Joseph Massey had some history between them, and from the second we walked in the door they were literally staring each other down. They were yelling at each other. It was what a lot of people predicted might happen there, which I, being very naïve to it all, had no idea about. And I really didn't care. Furthermore, I like it. I kind of like that. It involved a woman. Another poet.

KS: Sure.

SP: Sandra Simonds. I don't know her very well. I mean, I spent a nice afternoon with her that day, and the poet Andrew Mister who's a painter now and, I think, not doing poetry. Anyway, it felt like walking into an oven that had been on for two days, and the cupcakes in the oven were angry.

KS: Angry cupcakes?

SP: Angry San Francisco cupcakes all boiling over, and leaking into each other's cupcake space. If I may use the San Francisco trope—the *energy* was "off" as they say. It was "off." The vibes were bad, but the reading was fantastic.

KS: Who read?

SP: Anna Eyre read first, Joseph Massey read second, and I read third. I read—we should also mention, the Iraq war just started. George Bush was just elected. George Bush II. G.W., you know? My neighbor here in Austin. My press was located about two blocks from the governor's mansion.

Anyway, Joseph Massey reads. I hate to offend him, but he's a Cid Corman student and his poems are short, eloquent, succinct, nature-based poems. You know, you call 'em nature poems. Anyway, he would read his short, succinct, nature-esque poems, and in between each poem he would belch, fart, offend people in the room. It was quite amazing to see. It was good theater. I mean, Joe being a very well-read person and very knowledgeable about poets out there it wouldn't surprise me that this was all preordained by his studies in some other person's behavior.

The reading happened. I read. My poems consisted of one poem based on my interpretation of President Bush's State of the Union. It was a war society. War. The march was on. Everybody was thumping for war. We were in San Francisco, the place of peace, and the room was full of war. It was fuckin' hot in there. It was cold outside and it was hot in that fucking house. I'm happy to say that Joe Massey, the person that I had just published, who's book had sold out the day I released it, two days before—I should mention that I did a quantity of 300. I ended up doing a reprint of 400 and sold out. I never kept the book in print for very long. That guy has an ability to… he just has a lot of readers. I never understood.

After the reading I'm meeting all sorts of people I'd only corresponded with. I think I met Brent Cunningham that night in that room. Many other people I can't remember the names of—there were about three different fist fights that occurred at the same time and I don't remember who. I wasn't a part of either one, and then I became a part of one. It turned out I was fighting Joseph Massey: my friend, a dude I deeply loved, love, and was there to promote and celebrate. Yeah, we ended up kickin' the shit out of each other. We were broken up by, of all people, Roger Snell who's all of about 5'10" and 160 pounds, and Joe and I being a bit bigger than that. I thought we were boxing like a couple of athletes, but to hear it later from Roger, and a few other more sober people, we looked like a couple of old drunk ladies cuddling on the floor.

We were both bruised and bloodied. We knocked the hell out of each other. It felt like we were rolling on the floor for hours. I was saying shit like, "But I just published your book." And he said, "I love that book." "Why are you hitting me?" "Because you're hitting me!" "But I just wanted to help you." "I didn't need your help." "I thought you were gonna go after so and so." "I'm not here to fight." "Somebody threw a book at me. I thought it was you."

Anyway, the next day we had a wonderful day. First, I met Gloria Frym, one of my absolute heroes. And then of course, we went to Joanne Kyger's place out in Bolinas and spent a wonderful day out there. Me, and Dale, and Hoa, and Anna Eyre. I smoked pot with Joanne Kyger, which is a milestone in my life. For Hoa, too. We all just... it was wonderful. I've read a few times since then, but I haven't exactly published a lot of my own writing in the last eight years because I'm spending most of my time publishing others and I've neglected some of my own shit.

KS: Seems to be a common complication among publishers who are also poets.

SP: Yeah, I know. It's not unusual, is it? It's not unusual. I've written plenty. I've not ever slowed down on the writing. Something did happen, though. I got very distrustful of other publishers. I got very strange about leaving work in other people's hands, not that I didn't like what they did, or trust them, or something. Maybe I was personally afraid of my own work not being up to par with some of the work I had handled? That's totally plausible.

KS: Do you want to be read?

SP: That's a good question, man. That's a good question. I don't know. I think possibly, maybe, I do not want to be read. But I'm only saying that as a possibility. I don't know.

KS: Well, what do you want poetry to do?

SP: There's a feeling. There's a feeling I get sometimes reading books or being at a reading. Rarely at a reading but mostly reading a book, speaking some words; you get into another person's mouth. You get it. And it's not comfortable in your mouth, but you still get it and it's delightful. It's invigorating. It reminds you that you're not the only person with a mind, and a heart, and that there are other people struggling, or thinking, or paying attention to certain things. It's fucking wonderful. It's like an erection. It's like a buzz from a drug when it's good. It doesn't happen a lot. We spend a lot of time trying to figure out if we like a thing or not, without saying, "Should I like this?" I mean, am I supposed to like this? I was told this is really good, and this is all quote-unquote "required reading." There aren't many poets I know that are really comfortable with poetry postmodern and after. We think we know what we like but things go in and out of fashion and that fashion shit really poisons poetry, too. There's a pop culture within poetry, as sad as that is, that conflates the literature, and it confuses the literature. I'm thinking of things like Flarf. It confuses the literature, which is fine, and that perhaps is the aim, and it gets people thinking, but on a personal level you're thinking about yourself and your relationship to a thing, and all of a sudden you get confused. I mean, ten years later I'm not sure. What the hell?! I really don't even know. And I don't even appreciate what I think I'm supposed to appreciate.

I feel sometimes I'm more comfortable with humor now. I'm more comfortable with something less dramatic. There's a thing that happens, and I think publishers get to see this more than readers. You get to see this machinery, this thing that happens, this—you know what, I hate to say it, but the word "product," this commodification. There's some really good work and it's permanent. It's relevant right now so publish it right now. Don't wait. Don't clog it up in a machinery that's gonna take a long time. Deal with it right now and put it out right now. It's conversation. Why are we doing it in paper? Because paper's intimate, and there's a history here.

KS: Sounds like the mimeo revolution is alive and well!

SP: This is the idea that it's important work and it's work that can get you in trouble. This is work that's hot. It's hot work. It's not meant for email. This is intimate work. But here's the fucking rub: you can't get arrested for that shit anymore. Back then you could. You could very much get arrested for that stuff, and many people did. Ed Sanders. I think Baraka did. These are two of the guys that got arrested for publishing things; you know, lawsuits or charges against you. You can't offend anybody now. Revolution is not on our tongue. There's nothing revolutionary to speak of as far as a people. But in the literature, and in a writer's and a reader's relationship to words and their ideas that fight in that fucking moment, it's all still possible. It's all still very possible. The people that got me are the people that really believed in that. "You're gonna publish 400 books," Dale says to me, "You send 300 of those out for free." "But Dale, I can't afford it." "Well, let's get the money." "But we're not gonna make any money." "I told you in the beginning there's no money here. This ain't about money. Selling books, who cares? Do something else. Deal with bookstores. Print more if you have to. That's not what this is about. Put it in the hands of the people who you fucking respect, who you want to read this, and the people that perhaps are your enemies, your adversaries, or whatever, the people we're bumping up against with other ideas." Enemies and adversaries, that's a little dramatic, but there is relevance. There are things to fight for and it's worth doing what it takes to get in there. The mode you do it in: we choose paper in books, and I always will. I fuckin' hope I always will because there's that history there. You still want to feel that romantic feeling of "My God, I got a rare thing in my hand. I want to read this. I want to keep it forever untouched and unedited the way it is." It can't be deleted. It can be burned in fire. It can be destroyed in a flood.

[2010]

MY VOTE COUNTS

Dale Smith

Dale Smith, *My Vote Counts* (Effing Press, 2004)

Glossary

Notes on printing terms, printers,
publishers, producers, and printshops

*You have but to know an object by its proper
name for it to lose its dangerous magic.*
—Elias Canetti, *Auto-da-Fé* (tr. C.V. Wedgwood)

A.B. Dick – a company founded in 1883 in Chicago, best known for licensing key autographic printing patents from Thomas Edison and coining the word "mimeograph." These small duplicator presses were an integral part of the small press "mimeograph revolution" that flourished between the 1950s and the 1980s. They also produced some of the more popular one- and two-color offset presses used in small printshops.

accordion fold – an ancient Asian form of bookbinding for two or more parallel folds (typically the same size). Also called "zig-zag fold" and "fan fold," this is a common form for commercial brochures and artists books alike.

Adana – a tabletop platen letterpress suitable for printing small works, such as postcards and business cards. The Adana was popular in educational environments, but not suitable for large editions.

against the grain – folding or gluing at right angles against the grain of the paper. The cover of a book may warp, and pages may curl if the paper is folded against the grain. *Against the Grain: Interviews with Maverick American Publishers* is also the title of a collection of interviews with small press publishers of poetry edited by Robert Dana (University of Iowa, 1986). The present collection elaborates on the ideas that Dana explored in his interviews.

Albion Press – a type of iron handpress manufactured in London in the early 1800s.

Allen, Lewis – author of *Printing with the Handpress: Herewith a Definitive Manual*, and partner in the Allen Press with his wife Dorothy.

aperture – the openings of letters such as C, c, S, s, a, and e. Humanist faces such as Bembo and Centaur have large apertures, while Modern faces such as Bodoni and Realist faces such as Helvetica have small apertures. Very large apertures occur in archaic Greek inscriptions and fonts such as Lithos, which are derived from them.

artists books — a still-contested term, generally referring to book made by artists outside of trade publishing structures. Both practitioners and scholars have tried to define the artist book for decades. The spelling has also varied and one may find a variety of terms designating the genre— "the artist's book" or "the artists' book" or "the artists book" (the latter is adopted for the present edition). For a history on the discourse, see Stefan Klima's *Artists Books: A Critical Survey of the Literature* (Granary, 1998); for a thorough overview, see Johanna Drucker's *The Century of Artists' Books* (Granary, 1995/2004).

ascender — that part of the letter which rises above the x-height, as in b, d, and k.

Auerhahn Press — a small press founded in 1958 in San Francisco by Dave Haselwood (1931–2014), which made high-quality early books by the key poets of the San Francisco Renaissance. The first book was John Wieners' *The Hotel Wentley Poems*. When the commercial printer took the liberty of censoring the work, Haselwood bought a letterpress and taught himself how to print, restoring the poem to its original form. West Coast artists such as Bruce Conner and Wallace Berman contributed to Auherahn editions.

axis — in typography, the axis of a letter generally means the axis of the stroke, which in turn reveals the axis of the pen or other tool used to make the letter. If a letter has thick strokes and thin ones, find the thick strokes and extend them into lines. These lines reveal the axis (or axes; there may be several) of the letter.

Barker, Nicolas — prolific author and authoritative British historian on printing and books and former Head of Conservation at the British Library, where he served from 1976 until 1992.

baseline — the imaginary line upon which a line of type rests. The descenders of letters such as p, q, and y drop below the baseline.

Benveniste, Asa (1925–1990) — poet, letterpress printer, typographer, and founder of the legendary Trigram Press in London.

Benveniste, Pip (1921–2010) — painter, printmaker, photographer, filmmaker, rug designer, and collaborator with her husband Asa Benveniste and her son, Paul Vaughan, at the Trigram Press in London.

Besant, Annie (1847–1933) — a British socialist, theosophist, women's rights activist, writer, publisher, orator, educationist, and philanthropist.

binders' board — a paperboard often used in making the cover of a hardcover book that is usually covered with paper, cloth, animal hide, or a combination of these materials.

bitmap — a morphed or illegible digital image, often caused by low resolution on a computer, that results in a distorted, pixelated, or jagged geometric appearance.

Black Sparrow Press — Los Angeles-based small press, initially founded by John Martin in 1966 to publish the work of Charles Bukowski. Black Sparrow went on to publish hundreds of books over the years. Its authors included Lucia Berlin, Paul Bowles, Wanda Coleman, John Fante, Robert Kelley, Ed Sanders, Charles Reznikoff, and Diane Wakowski. Noel Young and Graham Mackintosh printed and designed many of the Black Sparrow books, and Martin's wife Barbara often produced art for the covers. When John Martin retired in 2002, he sold the Press to David Godine.

bleed — the continuation of an image off the edge of a sheet of paper. If an image is printed so that it reaches beyond the trim line, it will bleed when the page is trimmed. Images, rules, solids, background patterns, and occasionally type, may bleed.

blind stamp — a text or image that is stamped or printed without foil or ink producing a colorless impression. A blind stamp is embossed.

board shear – a large, hand-operated machine forged from iron used by bookbinders to cut book (or binders') board. Originating in the early nineteenth century, the technology has not changed much in the last century; many antique board shears are still in use today.

bond paper – a grade of writing or printing paper used where strength, durability, and permanence are essential.

bone folder – a handheld tool made out of a large animal's leg bone, alternatively bamboo, ivory, or plastic, that is used to create a sharp fold in a piece of paper. It is about the size of a butter knife and shaped similarly.

book arts – an inclusive term for all forms of the book as a form of art that includes zines, small press productions, artists books, fine press editions, private press editions, etc.

book paper – a general term used to define a class of commercial papers having common physical characteristics that, in general, are most suitable for the codex.

Bradley, Will (1868–1962) – illustrator, artist, and type designer central to the Art Nouveau movement in America.

Briggflatts – a long poem by Basil Bunting published by Fulcrum Press in 1966. Bunting read the poem for the first time in public at the Morden Tower (Newcastle-on-Tyne) reading series on December 22, 1965.

Bringhurst, Robert – poet, typographer, translator, and author and author of an authoritative guide to typography and book design, *The Elements of Typographic Style*, among other many other works.

Burke, Clifford – founder of Cranium Press in San Francisco. During the 1960s, Burke published many poets on the West Coast and taught printing to writers and activists so they could get their messages into the streets quickly and affordably. Burke is the author of *Printing It*, a handbook that furthered his mission to empower people through the art of publishing, as well as *Printing Poetry: A Workbook in Typographic Reification*. After leaving San Francisco for New Mexico, he started Desert Rose Press with his wife Virginia Mudd.

Butler, Frances — an influential American clothing and textile artist associated with the Pop art movement, also a book artist, educator, and co-founder of Poltroon Press with Alastair Johnston.

California job case — a wooden case for type containing all the main characters for text setting, introduced in San Francisco. In the previous convention, upper- and lowercase type were kept in separate cases, or trays. This is why capital letters are called uppercase and the minuscules are lowercase.The combined case became popular during the western expansion of the United States in the nineteenth century.

Callahan, Eileen — a founding member of Five Trees Press, which she left to pursue her own Hipparchia Press, and later (with husband Bob Callahan), established Turtle Island Press, which published seven volumes of Jaime de Angelo's work. Arthur Okamura served as art director. Zephyrus Image did much of the typesetting and Cranium did much of the printing. The Callahans established the Before Columbus Foundation in 1976, a nonprofit dedicated to the promotion and dissemination of contemporary American multicultural literature.

camera ready — a term used by offset printers to suggest that a document is ready to be printed. After the layout, or paste up, is complete, a stat camera is used to photograph the document, which is then transferred to an offset plate from the camera's negative.

Cape Editions — the publishing imprint for a series of short books released in England by Jonathan Cape between 1967 and 1971. Many titles in this series are translations into English. Authors include Václav Havel, Claude Lévi-Strauss, Bohumil Hrabal, Alfred Jarry, and Louis Zukofsky.

Cape Goliard — a book publishing imprint which is the result of the absorption, in 1967, of Goliard Press by Jonathan Cape through the efforts of Nathaniel Tarn and Tom Maschler.

Captain's Bookshelf, The — a bookstore in Asheville, North Carolina, founded in 1976.

Carter, Harry (1901–1982) — a type designer and acclaimed historian of typography, he served as the Archivist at Oxford University Press.

Centaur — a serif typeface designed by Bruce Rogers in 1914 for the Metropolitan Museum of Art and released by the Monotype Corporation in 1929.

Center for Book Arts, The — founded in 1974 in New York City, CBA fosters conversation and collaboration between artists, writers, and book artists. It was the first non-profit of its kind in America. Today, there are centers for book arts all over the country.

Caslon, William (1692/1693–1766) — a British typefounder whose designs revolutionized the field and are still in use today.

chapel (chappel) — a synonym for a printshop introduced by the printer William Caxton in the late fifteenth century.

codex — From the Latin caudex (meaning "tree trunk," "woodblock," or "book"), the codex once referred to early manuscript books, but today it refers to the book form most prevalent in the Western world.

coffin — the bed of a letterpress.

cold type — a photocomposition technology that emerged in the 1950s where a keyboard, rather than a metal type, was used to prepare a text for printing.

collate – in binding, the assembling of sheets or signatures in order.

composing stick – a handheld rectangular metal holder in which the compositor sets metal type in words and lines backwards.

Chandler & Price – a letterpress manufacturing company founded in Cleveland in 1881 by Harrison T. Chandler and William H. Price, best known for their hand-fed platen jobbing presses, which are referred to as "C&Ps" for short. They also manufactured paper cutters, book presses, and other printing equipment. After WWII, when offset printing became the industry standard, Chandler & Price's business suffered, and eventually ceased production in 1964.

chapbook – a short book; in modern parlance usually a single-author pamphlet of poetry. There are many different definitions and histories of the term, but most can agree that the chapbook consists of forty-eight pages or fewer, typically has a pamphlet stitch or stapled spine, and is small in format. The term probably derives from "chapmen" who would deliver small, affordable ("chepe") printed books and broadsides on horseback to small towns and villages before the advent of industrial printing, tree-pulp paper production, and the newspaper.

chase – a rectangular metal frame in which type and plates are locked up for letterpress printing.

chipboard – an inexpensive, textured, kraft brown paper that is ideal for letterpress printing.

Challenge KA 15 – a flatbed cylinder proof press.

Cross, Michael – a poet, educator, editor, scholar, printer, and publisher of Compline Press, Oakland, California.

Cushman, Don – editor of *Cloud Marauder*, which ran for six issues between 1968 and 1970, and published the poetry of William Stafford, George Hitchcock, James Tate, Anselm Hollo, and others.

Cutts, Simon — writer, printer, and publisher of Coracle (with Erica Van Horn), which specializes in artists books and poetry. After many decades in England, Coracle is currently based in Ireland.

color — in letterpress, the darkness of the type as set in mass, which is not the same as the weight of the face itself. The spacing of words and letters, the leading of lines, and the incidence of capitals, not to mention the color of the ink and the paper it is printed on, all affect the color of the type.

concertina — an accordion-fold book where all of the pages (panels) are connected; a sculptural book form that can be read in many different ways.

Conner, Bruce (1933–2008) — West Coast American artist who worked in assemblage, film, drawing, sculpture, painting, collage, and photography.

Courier — Howard "Bud" Kettler designed a monospaced slab serif typeface for IBM's typewriters. Digital versions are available on most computers. Because Courier is monospaced, many visual and concrete poets working with the typewriter embraced it, while for poets who composed their manuscripts in Courier on the typewriter, translating the monospaced font into a properly kerned font for traditional letterpress printing took some consideration. Some poets were not interested in that translation and insisted on publishing their manuscripts as facsimiles.

crack-n-peel — printers' stock for labels or bumper stickers that can be separated from its backing to expose adhesive.

crop — to eliminate portions of an image, usually on a photoengraver or plate, or desktop publishing software such as Photoshop or Illustrator.

dandy roll — a wire cylinder on papermaking machines that makes wove or laid effects on the texture, as well as the watermark itself. Used in the manufacture of better grades of business and book papers.

dead bank — where printed matter sits awaiting distribution. Also known as "dead matter" or "standing type."

descender — the part of the letter which extends below baseline, as in p, j, or q.

devil (printer's devil) — an apprentice printer. There are numerous amusing stories about the origin of this phrase.

Dewey, John (1859–1952) — American philosopher, psychologist, educational reformer, and author of *Experience and Education* (1938) among many other books. Dewey was a proponent of learning by doing.

Dine, Jim — a prominent sculptor, painter, printmaker, poet, and performance artist who has collaborated with many poets.

dingbat — an ornament cast in lead.

display type — type set larger than the text, used to attract attention. The title page of a book and the masthead of a newspaper are examples of display type. Some fonts are designed specifically to be used as display type; others are simply used for that purpose.

distribution — in letterpress composition, the act of returning type, rules, leads, slugs, furniture, and other materials to their proper places after use.

Donahue, Don (1942–2010) — an underground comic (or comix) book publisher, operating under the Apex Novelties imprint. Donahue revolutionized the genre by creating the countercultural publication Zap Comix featuring the work of Robert Crumb and Gilbert Shelton, as well as psychedelic art by Victor Moscoso and Rick Griffin.

DPI — abbreviation for "dots per inch." DPI is the usual measure of output resolutions in digital typography and in laser printing.

Dreamweaver — a web-development tool created by the Adobe Corporation in 1997.

drop cap — a large initial capital or versal mortised into the text.

dropped-out — type or art that is reversed from the background so that it appears as a negative or contrasting color to the foreground.

dummy — a prototype for an edition that includes printers' proofs. The purpose of a dummy is to show the publisher a book's dimensions, paper, weight, and other vital attributes before it is printed. Also known as a mock-up or "size copy."

dwell time — the amount of time that paper and type contact one another while printing on a hand- or platen press. Dwell time is adjusted during setup and is determined by pressure, paper, ink viscosity, etc. It is typically 0.25 to 1 second. Also applies to foil stamping.

e-book — a text designed to be read on a computer screen or digital tablet.

Eclipse — edited by Craig Dworkin, Eclipse is a free on-line archive focusing on digital facsimiles of the most radical small-press writing from the last quarter century. Eclipse also publishes carefully selected new works of book-length conceptual unity.

edition — the quantity of printed matter produced at a particular time for a particular book, broadside, etc., as in "How big was the first edition of your chapbook?" "My chapbook was produced in an edition of 120 copies." A "second edition" suggests that the text has been revised or expanded, not to be confused with a "reprint" or "second printing" which means that more copies of the original edition have been reproduced with minor or no variations.

elevated cap — a large initial capital or versal set on the same baseline as the first line of the text.

endsheets – in a hardcover book, the endsheets are typically a printed heavyweight paper that strengthens the binding by connecting the front and rear inside cover to the text block.

em – the square of the body of metal type; for example, in pica type it is twelve points wide by twelve points high.

en – half an em. To avoid misunderstanding when instructions are given orally, typographers often speak of ems as "muttons" and ens as "nuts."

Everson, William (1912–1994) – a poet associated with the San Francisco Renaissance and a letterpress printer; also known as Brother Antoninus. With architect and printer Kemper Nomland, actor Kermit Sheets, and editor/librarian William Eshelman, Everson established the Untide Press in a camp of conscientious objectors in Waldport, Oregon in 1943. The Untide is often considered the first press in the mimeo revolution. Everson went on to establish several other presses in his lifetime.

exposure unit – an important piece of prepress equipment that illuminates a film negative with the image in direct contact with a photosensitive surface (such as a photopolymer plate). The light hardens the polymer that is exposed, while the areas of the plate covered by film remain soft and can be washed away in warm water. Also known as a "contact copier" or "contact printer."

face – the printing surface of a piece of type, just above the shoulder.

fat take – a typesetting job with a lot of blank space, as in poetry or display work; also called "fat matter."

Figures, The – a small press founded in Berkeley by Geoffrey Young and Laura Chester in 1975, which has published more than one hundred books, many by younger writers associated with Language poetry. When the partnership with Chester ended, Young continued running the press in Great Barrington, Massachusetts until 2005.

filling in — a condition in letterpress, mimeo, or offset lithography where ink fills the area between the halftones dots or plugs up the type; also called "filling up."

fine press — a term similar to "private press" that may have emerged after Sandra Kirshenbaum started the journal *Fine Print* in 1975. Fine press printers are skilled typographers who distinguish themselves from the more conservative tradition of the private press. For example, a fine press printer may choose to print a previously unpublished book of poetry by an innovative author using asymmetrical typography, where a private press printer is more likely to choose to publish classical works of literature using symmetrical typography. The materials and production quality, as well as the cost of these limited editions may be comparable to those of the private press, and they may be similarly marketed to wealthy intuitions and collectors; however, the fine press self-identifies as more edgy.

Five Trees Press — Cameron Bunker, Kathleen Walkup, Jaime Robles, Eileen Callahan, and Cheryl Miller founded Five Trees Press in a rented storefront in San Francisco's Noe Valley in 1973. Five Trees specialized in publishing poetry by women at a time when a disproportionate number of presses were owned and operated by men.

fleuron — a horticultural dingbat; a typographic ornament ordinarily in the shape of an abstract leaf.

foil stamp — a relief printing technique where dry ink or foil are transferred to a surface at a high temperature. Also called a "hot stamp."

folio — in bibliography, a folio is a piece of paper folded in half to create a page in a book. A folio can also refer more generally to a sheet or leaf, especially in an antiquarian context.

font (fount) — a complete set of type characters of the same design and size, i.e., upper and lower case, numerals, punctuation marks, accents, ligatures, etc., not to be confused with "typeface." "Font" is a corrupt spelling of "fount," but the accepted spelling for media other than letterpress, such as the typewriter or computer. A type family often includes founts of roman, italic, semi-bold, condensed, sans-serif, and Greek. In relation to a phototype, it refers to the assortment of standard patterns forming the glyph palette, without regard to size, or the actual filmstrip on which these patterns are stored. In the world of digital type, the font is the glyph palette itself or the digital information encoding it.

fore-edge (foredge) – outside edge of a book opposite the spine.

forme (form) – in letterpress printing, the type and other matter locked in a chase and ready for printing.

format – the size, style, margins, printing requirements, etc. of any magazine, catalogue, or printed work.

Fredman, Stephen – literary critic and Professor of Twentieth-century American Poetry at the University of Notre Dame.

frisket – in letterpress printing, a frisket is a sheet of oiled paper that covers the space between the forme and the paper that will be printed on a handpress.

Fulcrum Press – publisher of carefully crafted books of poetry by authors such as Ezra Pound, Basil Bunting, Allen Ginsberg, Larry Eigner, and Ian Hamilton Finlay. Fulcrum Press was founded in 1965 by Stuart and Deirdre Montgomery in London. The Montgomerys closed the Press in 1974 and Stuart went on to become a successful psychiatrist specializing in depression.

furniture – in a letterpress lockup, the wood or metal blocks used to create the negative spaces in a forme, such as margins.

galley – a steel tray with one side open for holding and transporting metal type. A galley proof may be taken on a galley press and sent to an editor. After the editor makes corrections to the proof, it is returned to the compositor who adjusts the forme. In a more contemporary context, a galley or proof might refer to sheets printed digitally or offset, but the term originates from the letterpress lexicon.

Gill, Eric (1882–1940) – British type designer, sculptor, author, and printer associated with the Catholic Church and the Arts and Crafts Movement. Gill designed many prominent fonts, including Gill Sans, Perpetua, and Joanna.

Goudy, Frederic (1865–1947) – American type designer, artist, and printer who designed many popular fonts, including Kennerley, Goudy Old Style, and Copperplate Gothic.

Grabhorn Press – a private press in San Francisco operated by the brothers Edwin and Robert Grabhorn from the early 1920s until the mid-1960s. The Grabhorn building, which Jonathan Greene mentions in his interview, was the home of the press. Andrew Hoyem, formerly affiliated with Arion Press, acquired much of the Grabhorn Press' equipment.

Granjon, Robert (1513–1590) – French typographer and printer. In the interview with Alastair Johnston, he is referring to his translation of Hendrik D.L. Vervliet's *Cyrillic & Oriental Typography in Rome at the End of the Sixteenth Century: An Inquiry into the Later Work of Robert Granjon (1578–90)* published by Poltroon Press in 1981.

Griffiths, Bill (1948–2007) – poet, Hells Angel, Anglo-Saxon scholar, and publisher of Pirate Press; essential member of the British Poetry Revival.

grotesque – type without serifs, synonymous with "unserifed" and "sans-serif."

guillotine – a machine designed in the early nineteenth century used to cut large quantities of paper, usually with a single-edge blade. Today, these machines may be operated manually or mechanically.

gutter – the blank space or inner margin from the printed area to the binding.

Hall, Barry (1933–1995) – a British engraver who collaborated with Tom Raworth in the books printed by Goliard Press, a force in the British Poetry Revival.

Hamady, Walter (1940–2019) – founder of The Perishable Press Limited, an innovative letterpress printer, papermaker, publisher, book artist, and teacher at the University of Madison in Wisconsin. For many years, Hamady ran the press with his wife Mary Laird, whose interview is in this book. The Perishable Press Limited produced expensive, extravagant books that are in the fine press tradition, although many of the authors Hamady published wrote in the New American Poetry tradition associated with the mimeo revolution. Hamady's series of artists books, known as the Gabberjabbs, are perhaps his most sought after works.

handpress (hand-press) – the most traditional type of letterpress dating back to Gutenberg in the mid-fifteenth century. Originally constructed of wood, and later iron, it was modeled on the wine or cheese press. Sheets are fed into the press one at a time by hand, then pressure is exerted by a large screw, lowering the platen to press the paper into an inked forme, transferring the ink from the type to the paper, creating a printed sheet.

handset type – typographic matter composed letter by letter in a composing stick, also referred to as "hot metal" or "moveable type."

hanging quotes – a technique for typesetting where punctuation is placed in the margin to the immediate left or right of the text so as not to disrupt its spacing. Hanging quotes, or more generally "hanging punctuation," usually only appears in text blocks that are fully justified. This book has hanging quotes.

Hayden, MaryAnn – an artist from Berkeley who, with poet Jerry Ratch, founded Sombre Reptiles Press in 1978, publishing eighteen books of prose and poetry before closing in 1984. Authors include Darrell Gray, Alastair Johnston, Kathleen Fraser, Jerry Estrin, Robert Peters, and Michael Wolfe.

Heidelberg (letterpress) — a modern automated printing press that originated in 1914 capable of producing more than four thousand impressions an hour with remarkable precision. The Original Heidelberg Platen Press is a letterpress manufactured by the Heidelberger Druckmaschinen company in Germany. It is often referred to as a "windmill" because the of the shape and movement of its paper feed system. A clamshell-like mechanism performs the actual printing. While the windmill is excellent for small formats, the Heidelberg cylinder is suitable for larger formats. The company continues to be a leading manufacturer of offset presses.

Heliczer, Piero (1937–1993) — printer and publisher of Dead Language Press, and an innovative poet, actor, musician, filmmaker. Heliczer's Trigram Press book, *The Soap Opera*, contains illustrations by Wallace Berman, Jack Smith, Andy Warhol, and others.

hellbox — a receptacle for broken or worn type to be melted down.

Higgins, Dick (1938–1998) — a prolific artist, writer, and composer at the center of the art movement known as Fluxus. He founded Something Else Press in 1963 and published exceptional books by Bern Porter, Daniel Spoerri, John Cage, Emmett Williams, Alison Knowles, and other artists and writers associated with Fluxus.

hot metal type — in letterpress printing, hot metal type is created when molten metal is injected into a mold in the shape of a glyph. Once cooled and hardened, the type may be used for printing. The Monotype, Ludlow, and Linotype are all examples of hot metal typecasting machines that developed in the late nineteenth century. Once a major industry, in the twenty-first century there are very few people who know how to make hot metal type.

IBM Mag Card Composer — a key component in the IBM Magnetic Card Selectric Typewriter, the first word processor, introduced in 1969. These revolutionary electronics interfaced typing mechanisms and keyboards that could be used for editing, recording, and replaying typed material.

Immoral Proposition, The — a collaboration between the American poet Robert Creeley and the French artist René Laubies published by the Jargon Society in 1953.

imposition — the process of arranging pages of type in a chase so that they will be in the correct order after the printed sheet is folded into a signature.

imprint — the name of the printer or publisher of a book.

impression — in printing, the pressure of type, plate, or blanket when it meets the paper. A powerful impression will emboss the paper. Traditional printers scoff at a deep impression, although it is common in jobwork, such as greeting cards, business cards, and wedding invitations. A lighter impression, sometimes referred to as a "kiss," is more traditional.

InDesign — desktop publishing software for typesetting manufactured by the Adobe Corporation. Preceded by PageMaker and Quark, it is the first desktop publishing software that makes it quite simple to convert a book into an e-book.

inline — a letter in which the inner portions of the main strokes have been carved away, leaving the edges more or less intact. Inline faces lighten the color while preserving the shapes and proportions of the original face. Outline letters, on the other hand, are produced by drawing a line around the outsides of the letters and removing the entire original form. Outline letters, in consequence, are fatter than the originals and have less definition. Castellar, Smaragd, and Romulus Open, are examples of inline faces.

italic — a class of letterforms more cursive than roman but less cursive than script first developed in Italy during the sixteenth century.

Jargon Society, The — an American publisher of poetry and artists books founded in 1951 by Jonathan Williams and David Ruff. Williams continued to publish throughout his life, bringing out important early works by innovative artists and writers, some associated with Black Mountain College where Williams studied. Jargon Society books are impeccably designed, no two alike, and manufactured with integrity, and yet devoid of pretension.

jobwork — a form of commercial printing of ephemera such as stationary, posters, and cards for clients. Jobwork is not used to describe steady employment at a newspaper or publishing house.

justification — in composition, the spacing of lines of type in a uniform length and alignment to create "full justification" or a "ragged edge" to create uneven justification in the right or left margin in a block of prose. Justification can also be centered, as in many of Michael McClure's poems.

Kelsey — a tabletop letterpress suited for printing postcards and business cards that was often used in educational environments to teach people how to print. The Kelsey Company manufactured the Excelsior Press for about 100 years (1875–1975).

kern — part of a letter that extends into the space of another, beyond the body. In roman alphabets, the italic *f* kerns to the right and to the left.

kerning — the act of making fine adjustments to the space between letters to optimize legibility.

Kluge — An American graphic arts company that started producing platen presses in the 1920s.

Kornblum, Allan (1949–2014) — started a mimeograph magazine called *Toothpaste* in Iowa City in the 1970s, and later started using a letterpress to print books and chapbooks under the Toothpaste Press imprint. Kornblum relocated to Minneapolis in the 1980s and started Coffee House Press, now one of the largest small presses in the United States.

Kromekote — a glossy coated cover stock.

Kyle, Hedi — a conservator, innovative bookbinder, teacher, and book artist. Originally from Poland, she resides in upstate New York.

laid paper — paper having parallel lines watermarked at equal distances, giving a ribbed effect.

Lange, Gerald — founder of the Bieler Press in 1975 and author of *Printing Digital Type on the Hand-operated Flatbed Cylinder Press.*

laser printer — an electrostatic digital printing machine that creates a text or image by repeatedly passing a laser beam to and fro over a negatively charged cylinder or "drum." The drum then collects electrically charged toner and transfers it to paper, which is heated to essentially bake the powdered ink to the sheet. It is a common form of domestic and office printing and can also be used for short-run commercial printing.

leads — thin strips of metal placed between lines of type to separate them vertically.

leading — the distance between two parallel lines of text; rhymes with "heading."

letterpress — printing from type-high material, distinct from intaglio and lithography. It is the technology that introduced literacy to much of the world.

ligature — two or more letters tied into a single character. The sequence f-f-i, for example, forms a ligature in many text faces.

Ruth Lingen — a master printer who has worked with many of the greatest contemporary artists and writers to produce artists books and prints in her studio in New York City.

linotype — a typesetting machine invented by Ottmar Mergenthaler in 1893 that casts complete lines of metal type for printing by letterpress.

Little Caesar — a literary journal edited by Dennis Cooper with an anarchist, punk rock edge, published in Los Angeles between 1976 and 1980. Cooper is also the publisher of Little Caesar Press, who brought books by Joe Brainard, Amy Gerstler, Eileen Myles, Gerard Malanga, as well as Cooper himself into print.

livre d'artiste — French for "book art." The livre d'artiste often brings the work of a writer and visual artist together in limited editions that utilize precious materials and the skills of master craftsmen an are usually published by a private press and marketed to affluent collectors.

Ludlow Typograph — a hot metal typecasting machine that cast large type that could be melted down after use. Unlike the Linotype, the Ludlow used matrices, or "mats," that could be set by hand rather than by keyboard.

Mackintosh, Graham (1935–2015) — an ingenious book designer, letterpress and offset printer. Working closely with Robert Duncan and Jack Spicer, Mackintosh was publisher of White Rabbit Press; he also worked for the Black Sparrow Press, Oyez, Four Seasons Foundation, Capricorn, and Capra Press, among others. Job printers are not always credited for their work, so it is hard to say how many books he printed and designed, but he was prolific. Mackintosh worked for a number of years in Los Angeles, then moved to Santa Barbara where he lived for thirty-five years. He spent the last years of his life in San Francisco.

make-up — the art of breaking galleys of composition into pages.

makeready — in letterpress printing, the building up of the press forme so that heavy and light areas print with the correct impression; a form of troubleshooting that involves inking the press, locking up the forme, and finding remedies for correcting imperfections in printing.

marbled paper — a decorative sheet invented in Japan in 800 CE. Marbling is the act of transferring floating pigments in a gum solution and transferring the colors to a sheet of paper.

Maschler, Tom — a British writer and editor at Jonathan Cape known for publishing Gabriel García Márquez, Ian McEwan, and Bruce Chatwin.

matrix — a mould in which type is cast in linecasting machines. In stereotyping, the paper mould made from a type form.

Mattingly, George — editor and publisher of Blue Wind Press and the poetry periodical *Search for Tomorrow*. Blue Wind was established in Iowa City and later moved to Berkeley, publishing books by Keith Abbott, Ted Berrigan, Lorenzo Thomas, Anselm Hollo, and Darrell Gray.

Mayer, Hansjörg — a German poet, printer, and perhaps Europe's foremost publisher of artists books. Raised in Stuttgard in a family of printers, he trained as a typesetter and studied graphic design and philosophy. Founded in 1964, Edition Hansjörg Mayer produced some of the earliest portfolios of concrete poetry and went on to published the work of artists such as Dieter Roth, Tom Phillips, Emmett Williams, Claes Oldenberg, Dorothy Iannone, and Jan Voss.

McBride, John — a Bay Area book designer who, with Paul Vangelisti, started the Red Hill Press in 1969. They published nearly 80 books together, as well as the literary periodical *Invisible City* (1971–1982).

McElroy, Penny — an artist and teacher whose drawings, paintings, artists books, and ceramics have been widely exhibited.

Merker, Kim (1932–2013) — one of the greatest handpress printers of the twentieth century. He left his home in New York in the mid-50s to study poetry at the University of Iowa, where he met Harry Duncan, who taught him to print. Merker established the Stone Wall Press in 1957, publishing some of the great modernist poets, as well as younger writers. In the late sixties, he founded the Windhover Press in conjunction with the university, and in 1986 he formalized his publishing program when he established the Center for the Book.

Merrymount Press — founded by Daniel Berkeley Updike in Boston in 1893, known for producing books of superior quality. Updike also wrote extensively about the history of typography.

mimeo revolution (mimeograph revolution) — an international small press movement that took place between 1945 and 1980. Although it was named after the mimeograph machine (see below) many of the books and journals that were part of the mimeo revolution incorporated other printing techniques. For a historical overview, see *A Secret Location on the Lower East Side: Adventures in Writing 1960–1980*, edited by Steven Clay and Rodney Phillips (The New York Public Library & Granary Books, 1998).

mimeograph — a small, low-cost, duplicating machine invented by Thomas Edison in 1880. Ink was forced through a stencil onto a sheet of paper, creating a print. The mimeograph was easy to use and ideal for printing short runs, which is why they were popular in churches, offices, and schools. The mimeograph allowed people with little or no training in printing to become publishers. Photocopiers gradually replaced the mimeograph between 1960 and 1980.

minuscule — a lowercase letter.

Monotype — Founded in Philadelphia in 1887, the Lanston Monotype Machine Company patented a machine that casts metal type for letterpress printing. The Monotype machine is comprised of a keyboard and a caster, each with its own operator. Monotype flourished, commissioning typographers to design hundreds of new fonts, and set up a factory in England. In the 1960s, the company made a transition from hot to cold type, and later, from cold type to digital type.

Montgomery, Stuart — poet, psychiatrist, and publisher of Fulcrum Press with his wife Deirdre.

Morden Tower Reading Series — Tom and Connie Pickard began hosting poetry readings in an ancient turret-room on Newcastle's city walls in 1964, and the series remains one of Britain's most celebrated. Poets and writers of multiple generations have shared their work at Morden Tower, including Basil Bunting, Ted Hughes, Seamus Heaney, Allen Ginsberg, Alice Notley, and Bobbie Louise Hawkins.

Morison, Stanley (1889–1967) — influential British typographer, author, and authority on the history of printing.

Morris, William (1834–1896) — influential British textile designer, novelist, poet, activist, and book artist at the center of the Arts and Crafts movement, who founded the Kelmscott Press, which many regard as the beginning of the private press tradition.

Myers, Michael (1948–1982) — an American artist known for his remarkable linoleum cuts and drawings. Myers grew up in Wisconsin and studied book arts with Walter Hamady at the University of Wisconsin in Madison. He moved to the Bay Area, where he met printer Holbrook Teter at Cranium Press, and began collaborating on books, broadsides, artists books, and ephemera under the Zephyrus Image imprint. They also produce a lot of jobwork for many notable publishers. Myers died in a tragic car crash in Healdsburg, California on July 3, 1982.

Nash, John Henry (1871–1947) — a talented printer who spent most of his life in San Francisco. He worked for a number of businesses, including the Twentieth Century Press, Tomoye Press, and Elder & Company. In 1938 he established the John Henry Nash Fine Arts Press at the University of Oregon.

New American Poetry 1945–1960, The — an influential poetry anthology published in 1960 by Grove Press edited by Donald Allen that highlighted distinct trends among then-younger American poets, organized in categories, such as Black Mountain, Beat, New York School, and the San Francisco Renaissance.

New Directions — one of the most significant independent presses of the twentieth century; based in New York City and founded in 1936 by James Laughlin on the advice of Ezra Pound to "do something useful."

O Books — founded by Leslie Scalapino (1944–2010) in the Bay Area in 1986. O Books published attractive trade edition books of poetry, essays, and plays by poets including Fanny Howe, Norma Cole, Tom Raworth, Ted Berrigan, Laura Moriarty, and Scalapino herself.

Oak Knoll — a bookstore in New Castle, Delaware established by Bob Fleck in 1976 that specializes in rare and antiquarian books, as well as books about books. In 1978, Fleck started Oak Knoll Press, a leading publisher of books about books.

Ochs, Larry — avant-garde saxophonist; married to Lyn Hejinian.

offset — lithographic printing that is made from a photo negative contact exposed to a metal plate; the image is offset onto a rubber blanket and then transferred to paper. Today, most high-volume printing is offset: packaging, newspapers, posters, books, etc.

OpenType fonts — scalable digital fonts, developed by the Microsoft Corporation, that succeeded the TrueType font. Presently, this is the most common form of type on most computers.

Oulipo — a literary club of primarily French authors and mathematicians who wrote using constraint-based writing techniques, spearheaded in 1960 by Raymond Queneau and François Le Lionnais.

overlay — in letterpress makeready, a piece of paper placed in the packing to make that part of the forme print more heavily.

packing – hard sheets of paper of varying thicknesses and dimensions that a letterpress printer inserts under the tympan to achieve the correct impression from the forme of type; part of the makeready process.

PageMaker – An early and revolutionary form of desktop publishing software introduced in 1985 by Aldus for Apple Macintosh. In the mid-90s, QuarkXPress became a major competitor, and ultimately dominated the market, leading to the demise of PageMaker in 2001.

paratexts – refers to all printed matter in a book that is not part of the text proper, such as page numbers, title pages, glossaries, and pressmarks. Paratexts can change in different editions, while the text remains stable.

paste up – a preparatory step for offset printing. Before the advent of desktop publishing software on the computer, a paste up artist would make a camera-ready paste up using cold type (or hot-type repros) and images which would be arranged, then pasted down. A stat camera would then be used to create a film negative to create a plate which would then be used to print on an offset lithography press.

Perishable Press – see Hamady, Walter.

Perpetua – a transitional serif typeface designed by Eric Gill in the early 1920s for the British Monotype Corporation.

photopolymer plate (polymer plate) – a light-activated, water-soluble resin used for letterpress printing, usually produced in a platemaker. As digital typography improved in the late twentieth century and analog type foundries became scarce, photopolymer plates became more popular, introducing a new approach to letterpress printing that bridges analogue and digital technologies.

Photoshop – an early raster graphics editor produced by Adobe (1988) that remains the industry standard.

pica — printers' unit of measurement. A pica is divided into twelve points and is approximately equal to one-sixth of an inch. A pica rule resembles a ruler and includes points, picas, inches, and centimeters.

Pickard, Tom — celebrated British poet and co-founder of the Morden Tower Reading Series.

pig — a predominately lead bar melted gradually in a Linotype machine to create a line of metal type.

platemaker — a machine that makes photopolymer plates.

platen press — a type of letterpress named after the heavy flat plate, or "platen," which is pressed against the forme; also called a "clamshell" or "treadle press," it may be operated with a treadle or driven by a motor, and most are fed by hand.

pochoir — the name for a hand-colored illustration process occasionally used for contemporary editions de luxe, popular in eighteenth century France and revived in the 1920s and '30s.

Poco Proof Press — Poco presses have reciprocating beds and stationary carriages. Patented by Walter G. Potter in Chicago in 1910, examination of the nameplates indicate that they were first manufactured by A.F. Wanner (1910–14), then Hacker Manufacturing (1914–1931). In 1931 Challenge acquires the Poco and Potter brands from Hacker. The 1935 ATF Catalog shows Challenge-Poco presses.

point — the basic typographical unit (a twelfth of a pica, about 1/72nd of an inch).

Potter Proof Press — Potter presses have reciprocating beds and stationary carriages. Some later models have paper grippers and ink rollers. Manufactured by A. F. Wanner until 1914 when the company was renamed the Horace Hacker Co. In 1931 Challenge Machinery acquired the Poco and Potter brands.

prepress — in publishing, the term refers to activities that occur after the text is complete and before printing begins. Prepress pertains to typesetting, design, and layout.

Price, Robin — American printer known for her high-craft approach to book arts. Price established her first press in 1984 in Los Angeles.

print on demand (POD) — the printing of books and documents using digital printers, as opposed to more traditional methods (offset or letterpress). POD allows for printing books one at a time or in small quantities, allowing smaller presses to avoid warehousing their inventory or making a substantial investment in a single title. Although the unit cost is typically higher than offset printing, for editions of fewer than five hundred copies, POD is a viable alternative.

Printed Matter — a non-profit organization founded in 1976 that sells artists books in New York City.

private press — small publishers and printers that put emphasis on extravagant materials, high-craft publications marketed to wealthy patrons may be considered private presses. They have their roots in the turn-of-the century Arts and Crafts Movement in England—specifically in the Kelmscott Press (founded by William Morris)—which sought to restore integrity and craftsmanship to products that were being produced increasingly by machines during the Industrial Revolution. The Kelmscott Press produced expensive, extravagant books in limited editions. Joseph Blumenthal's *The Printed Book in America* (David Godine and Dartmouth University, 1977) offers a satisfying overview of the private press tradition in America.

proof — an impression taken on a proof press for a proofreader.

proof press — a small- and medium-sized press (usually hand-operated) for making proofs, also referred to as a flatbed cylinder proof press. After proof presses became commercially obsolete, they began to be re-purposed by small press publishers and book artists to make small editions; some are now used for specialty small-run printing.

quad – spacing material less than type high used to fill out lines in type composition for letterpress printing.

QuarkXPress – referred to as "Quark" for short, an early form of desktop publishing software (1987) designed for Windows. It was released two years after Adobe introduced Aldus PageMaker for Apple's Macintosh computer. Once the standard for desktop publishing, Quark has been superseded by Adobe InDesign.

quoin – a device for locking up formes; a quoin is usually spring-loaded and expands or contracts with the turn of a quoin key.

Randle, John – editor of the printers' journal *Matrix* and founder of the Whittington Press.

repro – a proof taken from metal type used for offset printing. In the transitional period, between 1950 to 1980, before phototype became widespread, it was common to have books set by Linotype and one copy printed from which negatives were made for offset reproduction.

Rogers, Bruce (1870–1957) – an American typographer, printer, and type designer, Rogers is best known for designing Centaur in 1914 and his classical approach to book design.

rounce – the crank of an iron handpress.

rule – strips of type-high metal cast in different point sizes and lengths to print plain or ornamental lines.

Rummonds, Richard-Gabriel Price – an expert handpress printer and author of *Printing on the Iron Handpress* as well as *Nineteenth-Century Printing Practices and the Iron Handpress*.

run – the number of impressions taken of a forme at one time. Also used to indicate the quantity of books or other printed matter in an edition.

Ruscha, Ed – an American artist associated with the pop and conceptual art movements who has worked in painting, printmaking, drawing, photography, film, writing, and the artists book, specifically the genre known as the "democratic multiple," which sought to bring affordable works of art in book form to the masses in the 1960s.

Salient Seedling Press – founded by Katherine Kuehn in 1978. The Salient Seedling Press has published many books in the fine press tradition as well as artists books. Kuehn studied with Walter Hamady at the University of Wisconsin in Madison, and later became his assistant at the Perishable Press Limited in Mt. Horeb. Kuehn has also worked as a master printer for Pace Editions.

Schneemann, Carolee (1939–2019) – American painter, performance artist, experimental filmmaker, and writer. Her work explored the body, sexuality, feminism, and gender. She made several works in the form of artists books, sometimes utilizing unbound structures (cards, etc.).

Scobey, Pati – a graduate of the printmaking MFA at the University of Wisconsin-Madison, living and working in Concord, Michigan.

score – to impress or indent a line in a sheet of paper to make folding crisper; this may be performed on a press using a rule, on a score board, or with a bone folder, using a rule or a jig.

Semina – a revolutionary underground poetry periodical published between 1955 and 1964 in various locations in California by the artist Wallace Berman (1926–1976).

serif – the short cross-lines at the ends of the main strokes in roman typefaces.

show-through – the condition where printing on one side of paper can be seen from the other side when the latter is viewed by reflected light.

signature – in book, magazine, and catalogue work, the name given to a large printed sheet after it has been folded to form a gathering of several pages.

silkscreen – a printing technique where a fine mesh (silk or more often nylon) is used to transfer ink onto a substrate except in areas made impermeable to the ink by a blocking stencil, one color at a time. A silkscreen maybe used to create images in books, posters, hats, T-shirts, textiles, banners, etc.

sizing – that property of paper that relates to its resistance to the penetration of liquids, particularly water or vapors.

slipcase – a box with one open side designed to house one or more books that is often produced by a bookbinder.

slug – a cast lead block, either Linotype or a stereocasting, used for logos, rubber stamps, or other items that require frequent use. Also a thick piece of leading.

small press – a publisher whose interest is in books rather than profits; or a term identifying a kind of independent publishing peripheral to commercial trade publishing. A small press is rarely affiliated with the communications industry or multinational corporations. A small press may also be referred to as an independent press or a micro press; if it publishes in the manner of a periodical, it may be referred to as a zine. Many small presses are literary, but there are plenty that focus on non-fiction and visual art as well. Small press culture is extremely diverse. There are no restrictions on genre, printing technique, methods of distribution, etc. The book you are holding was produced by a small press.

Smith, Rod — poet and publisher of the small press Edge Books as well as *Aerial Magazine*; manager of Bridge Street Books in Washington, D.C. and host of countless poetry readings.

Stephenson Blake — a British type foundry established in 1818 by William Garnett, John Stephenson, and James Blake. The company ceased production of metal type in the 1990s and became an engineering company. Stephenson Blake was the last metal type foundry in England.

stereotype — a printing technique popularized in the early 1800s that presented several advantages to traditional letterpress. After type is set, a papier-mâché or plaster mould is taken from the forme of type which is then used to cast a stereoplate (or "stereo" for short).

stock — paper or other material to be printed.

strike-through — the penetration of ink through the paper.

Stymie — a slab serif font designed by Morris Fuller Benton in 1931 which has been used primarily in advertising. Many variations of Stymie have been developed over the years by other typographers, for digital and analog use.

Tarn, Nathaniel — a French-American poet, essayist, anthropologist, and translator who emigrated to the United States in 1970. From 1967 to 1969 he worked as an editor for Jonathan Cape and served as founding director of the Cape Goliard Press in London. He taught for many years at Rutgers University and has lived outside of Santa Fe since the mid-1980s.

Telephone — Poet Maureen Owen printed and published *Telephone* magazine and Telephone Books from 1969 to 1984. Anne Waldman, Larry Fagin, and Tom Veitch taught her how to use the mimeograph at St. Mark's Church in New York City. The magazine featured attractive cover art by Joe Brainard, Donna Dennis, John Giorno, George Schneeman, and others. Telephone Books published editions by Jim

Brodey, Sandy Berrigan, Susan Howe, Sotère Torregian, Fanny Howe, and others.

Tombouctou — a small press founded by Michael Wolfe in Bolinas, California, which published books by Jim Carroll, Bobbie Creeley, Gailyn Saroyan, Leslie Scalapino, and others from the mid-1970s until the early '80s.

Teter, Holbrook (1948–1999) — established Zephyrus Image in San Francisco with Michael Myers (1948–1982). Teter was a polyglot, fluent in five languages, and served as a relief worker and teacher in Pakistan, France, Russia, and throughout Central America. He also worked as a counselor with refugees, trauma survivors, and as an advocate for prison reform.

text — the body matter of a book or page as distinguished from the headings, pagination or any other traces of a particular edition or version.

Thames & Hudson — a publishing company founded in 1949 by Walter and Eva Neurath. Their passion and mission was to create a "museum without walls" and to make accessible to a large reading public the world of art and the research of top scholars.

tipped in — referring to separately printed illustrations that are glued or pasted into a book.

Trigram Press — founded in 1965 by Asa and Pip Benveniste in London. Trigram is celebrated for its high-quality books, printed letterpress and silkscreen with the assistance of Pip's son Paul Vaughn, brilliant typography, and the innovative roster of poets and artists they published, which included George Barker, Tom Raworth, Jack Hirschman, Robert Creeley, Piero Heliczer, Andy Warhol, Jack Smith, J.H. Prynne, David Meltzer, Jim Dine, Jeff Nuttall, Anselm Hollo, and Lee Harwood.

Tschichold, Jan (1902–1974) — typographer, author, book designer, and calligrapher that changed twentieth century design at least twice; first by developing and promoting a new brand of modernism, and later by promoting classical design practices. He improved the design of Penguin Books when he left Germany for England and designed the typeface Sabon, which is used throughout the book you are holding.

tympan – the waxed paper that covers the platen or cylinder of a letterpress.

typeface – the printing surface of any type or character of metal type. Also, a group or family to which any particular type design belongs.

type gauge – a printer's tool calibrated in picas used to measure the various sizes of fonts.

type high – the standard height for metal type (0.918″ in the U.S.).

typewriter – a mechanical or electromechanical machine used to compose characters. Commercial typewriters were common in offices by the late 1800s and remained in use until the 1970s when word processors, and eventually computers, became more commercially viable.

uncial – a term of disputed origin for the majuscule (capital letter) form of writing used as a book hand for the Christian church from the fourth to sixth centuries, after which it declined, being superseded by the half-uncial. Distinctive features are rounded forms of a, d, e, m, and u; also the minuscule forms of h, l, and q. The shapes of unicals are held to have been influenced by Byzantine art.

Updike, Daniel Berkeley (1860–1941) – type historian, author, and founder of the Merrymount Press.

Vandercook & Sons – an American manufacturer of proof presses founded in 1909 by Robert Vandercook. The Vandercook was the most popular and well-designed twentieth century proof press because it was easier to use and more precise than its competitors (the SP models stand for "simple precision"). When the letterpress was no longer commercially viable, the company was sold in 1968. Although they are no longer manufactured, the Vandercook is still very desirable.

Varityper — the proprietary name of a kind of typewriter that has interchangeable typefaces (such as the IBM Selectric) and a kind of type-composing machine with similar operation.

Vervliet, Hendrik D. L. (1923–2020) — a Belgian scholar of the history of typography and writing systems. Vervliet served as a professor at the University of Amsterdam and librarian at the University of Antwerp.

versal — a large initial capital, elevated or dropped; also called a "lettrine."

Warde, Beatrice (1900–1969) — an expert on typography who was employed as the marketing manager of the British Monotype Corporation at a time when very few women were so influential in the world of printing and design. She is perhaps best known for her polemic essay, "The Crystal Goblet."

Washington Hand Press — a rugged iron handpress popular among mid-nineteenth century newspaper printers.

watermark — in papermaking, the name or design produced by the raised patter of the dandy roll during manufacture.

Watten, Barrett [Barry] — established This Press and *This* magazine in Iowa City in the early 1970s with Robert Grenier, which published many of the poets associated with Language writing. Watten is also a poet, professor, and literary critic.

wayzgoose — a celebration sponsored by a master printer for employees or assistants on or about Saint Bartholomew's Day (August 24). It marked the traditional end of summer and the start of the season of working by candlelight. Later, the word came to refer to an annual outing and dinner for the staff of a printing works or the printers on a newspaper. Also spelled "wayz-goose," "waygoose" or "wayzegoose."

Werkman, H.N. (1882–1945) — an experimental Dutch printer, typographer, and artist known for his "hot printing" technique through which he created variegated multiples—prints that were not meant to be reproductions, but original works of art using type-high matter not traditionally used on a letterpress. Werkman was shot by the Gestapo and died during the final days of World War II.

West Coast Print Center — a print shop in South Berkeley subsidized by the National Endowment for the Arts that produced low-cost offset books for the poetry and arts community from the late 1970s through the early '80s. Their clients included Tombouctou Books, Blue Wind Press, *Gay Sunshine*, *Vile Magazine*, The Figures, Oyez!, Red Hill Press, Kayak, San Dollar, Yanagi, and many others.

widow — a solitary word at the end of a paragraph, to be avoided in typesetting. Not to be confused with an orphan, a paragraph-opening line that appears at the bottom of a page or column. An easy way to remember the distinction: "an orphan has no past; a widow has no future."

Williams, Jonathan (1929–2008) — American poet, photographer, and founder of The Jargon Society, a publishing house known for its high-quality production, creative designs, and a luminary list of authors and artists, including many associated with Black Mountain College.

Women's Studio Workshop — a center for the arts founded in 1974 by Ann Kalmbach, Tatana Kellner, Anita Wetzel, and Barbara Leoff Burge in upstate New York with an emphasis on supporting women with professional opportunities to create. At the time of this publication, Women's Studio Workshop maintains facilities for etching, letterpress, papermaking, book arts, silkscreen, 3D work, ceramics, and photography.

Word (MSWord) — popular word-processing software released to the public in 1983 by the Microsoft Corporation.

work-up — in letterpress, a space, lead or other spacing material that works itself in the surface during printing due to poor lockup.

Xerox — an American manufacture of various printing machines founded in 1906 in Rochester, New York. Xerography (meaning "dry writing") was developed after World War II and was the first printer to use a dry powder called toner. Xerox continues to manufacture photocopiers, large-format printers, digital presses, scanners, and other office equipment for commercial and domestic use.

x-height — the distance between the baseline and the midline of an alphabet, which is normally the approximate height of the unextended lowercase letters—a, c, e, m, n, o, r, s, u, v, w, x, z—and of the torso of b, d, h, k, p, q, y.

Clark, Thomas A. — a Scottish poet and publisher of Moschatel Press, established in 1973 with artist Laurie Clark. Moschatel has published books by Ian Hamilton Finlay, Cid Corman, Jonathan Williams, Simon Cutts, and others.

Zdanevich, Ilia (1894–1975) — a writer, artist, and publisher associated with Russian Futurism and Dada. Born in Georgia, Zdanevich (also known as Iliazd) studied in Petersburg but returned to Tbilisi during World War I, where he joined the avant-garde group 41° which included Aleksei Kruchenykh and Igor Terentiev, as well as his brother, the artist Kiril Zdanevich. He moved to Paris in 1921, where he wrote several innovative novels and became a pioneer in the field of avant-garde typography and graphic design, and produced luxurious livre d'artiste editions with such artists as Pablo Picasso, Max Ernst, and Joan Miró.

Zephyrus Image — a collaborative adventure in publishing between Michael Myers and Holbrook Teter in Northern California during the 1970s. The works of Zephyrus Image—subversive, ephemeral, hilarious, political, literary, irreverent, performative, visual, structurally and typographically innovative—are unlike those of any other press. Zephyrus Image defied mainstream distribution techniques, and often gave their work away for free. For their first collaboration they printed a linocut of a hippie Jesus with a Ford logo and displayed it among the rubble and trash at a dump in the Bay Area. They worked closely with the poets and printers Tom Raworth and Edward Dorn, and published the work of Joanne Kyger, Stan Brakhage, Lucia Berlin, and Fielding Dawson, as well as their own collaborative efforts.

Zero Press — a small press founded in Paris in 1948 by Asa Benveniste and Thermistocles Hoetis. Zero Press' first publication was *Zero Magazine,* featuring the work of Lionel Ziprin. In the second issue, they published Paul Bowles, James Baldwin, and others.

zincs (zincos) — the product of zincography, a planographic printing process developed around 1800 as an affordable alternative to Bavarian limestone. The result is a type-high block, usually a halftone image, for the purpose of printing on letterpress. Commonly used in newspapers, they were made of copper or lead in the nineteenth century, then zinc in the early part of the twentieth century, then magnesium, and have largely been replaced by polymer. Magnesium zincos tend to oxidize unless coated with ink or oil.

This book was designed and typeset by Ugly Duckling Presse using Jan Tschichold's Sabon and Jeremy Mickel's Fort. The text was printed and bound by McNaughton & Gunn in Saline, Michigan. The cover was printed in Brooklyn, New York by Prestige Printing (offset) and Ugly Duckling Presse (letterpress) on Mohawk Via cover. Nine hundred copies of the first edition are distributed to the trade; one hundred copies are set aside as a special edition, with each copy containing ephemera from every publisher featured in the book.